Andréa Belliger, David J. Krieger
Organizing Networks

Sociology

Andréa Belliger is director of Learning Services at the Teacher's Training University of Lucerne and also director of the Institute for Communication & Leadership.
David J. Krieger is director at the Institute for Communication & Leadership, Lucerne, Switzerland.

Andréa Belliger, David J. Krieger

Organizing Networks

An Actor-Network Theory of Organizations

[transcript]

Bibliographic information published by the Deutsche Nationalbibliothek
The Deutsche Nationalbibliothek lists this publication in the Deutsche Natio-
nalbibliografie; detailed bibliographic data are available in the Internet at
http://dnb.d-nb.de

© 2016 transcript Verlag, Bielefeld

Cover layout: Kordula Röckenhaus, Bielefeld
Typeset by Justine Haida, Bielefeld

Print-ISBN 978-3-8376-3616-1
PDF-ISBN 978-3-8394-3616-5

Content

Preface

The view of organizations presented here builds upon and extends work that we have done on actor-networks and network society in a variety of publications. In *Interpreting Networks* (2014) we based our description of network society on Actor-Network Theory (ANT) as well as New Media Studies. We argued that constructing social order in today's digitally mediated world can be understood as "networking," that is, the activity of mediating associations between humans and non-humans within a non-hierarchical "socio-sphere" governed by what we termed "network norms." Here we will argue that "networking" can be understood as another word for "organizing." Organizations are not a special form of social order, a unique kind of social structure. Instead, organizations are a way of talking about the *activity of networking*, an activity in which micro-interactions do not oppose macro-structures, but humans and non-humans negotiate local and global networks.

This book intends to contribute to recent discussions on the "communicative constitution of organizations." The activity of organizing depends on the forms of communication that society offers. In the case of the global network society, so-called "new media" have become our most significant non-human other and the decisive form of communication and therefore condition how networking and organizing is done. The idea that communication is the basis for the social is not new. Symbolic interactionism, the linguistic turn in the social sciences, as well as recent foundational theories such as those of Habermas and Luhmann assume that the social is constituted by communication. Bruno Latour's Actor-Network Theory can also be understood as a theory of the communicative constitution of society insofar as social order consists of associations between heterogeneous actors that arise from the "translation" and "enrollment" of actors into networks. Latour describes the primary social act as "mediation," or "making associations." The significant difference between ANT and the other theories is the active participation of technological artifacts, or non-humans in social organization. Organizations appear from the ANT-perspective as communicative processes involving both humans and non-humans. This makes things important. Our significant non-human others in the communicative constitution of organizations are information and communication technologies.

The title "Organizing Networks," attempts to give a name to the activity of constructing social order from the point of view of a theory of communication that draws on ideas from actor-network theory, the sociology of organizations, and non-Cartesian cognitive science. This way of seeing things has interesting consequences for problems and issues within the domains of management and leadership and therefore has relevance for solving practical problems in all areas of society. We will try to show how this framework can be helpful for understanding the transformations taking place in business, education, healthcare, and civil society. We will argue that the affordances of digital information and communication technologies institute so-called network norms that guide the ways in which successful organizing takes place in today's connected world.

If ANT is right and the actor is the network, then this is also true of the authors. To all those, both human and non-human, who participate in our network we wish to express our gratitude and acknowledgement.

Andréa Belliger & David J. Krieger, Lucerne, April, 2016

Introduction

The story we will be telling is about organizations, about what they are, how they come to be, how they are maintained, transformed, dismantled, or sometimes just left behind and forgotten. Although this story belongs to the genre of management and organization studies and organization theory, it shares one thing in common with all other stories. It is just a story. It could be told otherwise. The actors, events, plot, sub-characters, time line, and surrounding circumstances, all could be different. This is what makes stories so useful in scientific work, it allows for the unexpected, the contingent, and supports innovative thinking. Scientific theories have long dispensed with the burden of simply reflecting so-called "facts" and have proven their value in their coherence, scope, and heuristic fruitfulness for research and action. This is especially the case in the social sciences, where the object of study is not external to the subjects doing the studying and where knowledge is unavoidably connected to action.

The heroes of this story are networks. Networks are everywhere. Just as systems science before it, network sciences are discovering network properties in almost all forms of order in the natural as well as the social world. Within the emerging interdisciplinary paradigm of network science, it is to be expected that social phenomena such as organizations be also interpreted as networks.[1] Networks, of course, have long been a topic of interest for sociology.[2] In organization theory, networks offered an alternative principle of organizing apart from the rigid opposition of

1 | See Arsenault (2011) for an overview of network theories in the social sciences.
2 | Durkheim, Tönnies, and Simmel discussed groups and communities. Moreno, Granovetter and others developed forms of social network analysis. For a summary of work on social networks see the Wikipedia article https://en.wikipedia.org/wiki/Social_network

markets and hierarchies.[3] Networks were conceptualized as a unique and independent form of social order that should not be understood as a hybrid mix of markets and bureaucracy. Podolny and Page (1998) define the network form of organization "as any collection of actors [...] that pursue repeated, enduring exchange relations with one another and, at the same time, lack a legitimate organizational authority to arbitrate and resolve disputes that may arise during the exchange" (59). Included in this basic definition are many different kinds of associations such as business groups, joint ventures, franchises, strategic alliances, research consortia, outsourcing agreements, and relational contracts. What stands out in all these examples is that "there is no clear mapping of formal organizational arrangements onto the network form" (Podolny/Page 1998: 60).

Reasons for organizations to enter into network forms are knowledge sharing and learning, legitimacy and reputation, improved performance, enhanced adaptability, and better management of resource dependencies. Until the digital media revolution, network forms of organization remained an interesting sideshow to organizations based on markets and hierarchies. This situation has changed. After the industrial era and the informational era, we seem to be entering the era of the global network society (Castells 1996). As Castells (2005) points out, it is not networks that are new in human history, but "What is new is the microelectronics-based, networking technologies that provide new capabilities to an old form of social organization" (4). Digital information and communication technologies make global networked organizations possible. Both large and small, whether high-tech or not, organizations in all areas of society are changing. Castells (2005: 8) locates three processes characteristic of the network society,

1) the "generation and diffusion of new microelectronics/digital technologies of information and communication;"
2) the "transformation of labor that is able to innovate and adapt;" and
3) the "diffusion of a new form of organization around networking."

Organizing networks has today become as important as was once the organization of hierarchical, scientific, and bureaucratic organizations in the industrial era.

---

3 | See Powell (1990) and Podolny/Page (1998) for an overview of research on networks as forms of organization.

New theories respond to this situation by describing organizations in terms of "chaos" (Smith 2001), "fractal" (Warnecke 1992), "holocracy,"[4] "adhocracy" (Mintzberg 1992), "organization 2.0" (McAfee 2006), "networked,"[5] and "pattern-breaking management" (Wüthrich et al. 2009, Kaduk et al. 2015). Common themes in these new approaches to organizations are decentralization, flattening out hierarchies, self-organization, flexibility, innovation, multi-directional communication, risk tolerance, transparency, flow, connectivity, trust, non-linear processes, teamwork, collaboration, knowledge management, and networked organization design. The rise of the "sharing economy" and the "commons" has further complicated organization theory by undermining traditional economics and models of organizational behavior.[6] The commons, as Benkler (2004) argues, is an organizing force that is neither hierarchy nor a market, neither collectivist nor commodifying. Although not all of these new theories of organizations are explicitly based on network models, the idea of networks and networking can be found in some form in almost all of them.

We follow these new developments and tendencies in contemporary organization studies and propose to understand organizations as networks. The concept of "network" is as controversial as omnipresent. What exactly is a network? What kind of networks are we talking about in organization studies and related fields? We base the view of networks

---

4 | https://en.wikipedia.org/wiki/Holacracy

5 | https://en.wikipedia.org/wiki/Network-centric_organization

6 | "The sharing economy encompasses a wide range of structures including for-profit, non-profit, barter and co-operative structures. The sharing economy provides expanded access to products, services and talent beyond one to one or singular ownership [...] Corporations, governments and individuals all actively participate as buyers, sellers, lenders or borrowers in these varied and evolving organizational structures." https://en.wikipedia.org/wiki/Sharing_economy. See also Benkler (2004: 275): "The world's fastest supercomputer and the second-largest commuter transportation system in the United States function on a resource management model that is not well specified in contemporary economics. Both SETI@home, a distributed computing platform involving the computers of over four million volunteers, and carpooling, which accounts for roughly one-sixth of commuting trips in the United States, rely on social relations and an ethic of sharing, rather than on a price system, to mobilize and allocate resources."

presented here on actor-network theory (ANT), especially as Bruno Latour has developed it during the last three decades.[7] This implies that when we speak of networks, we are not referring to the above mentioned theories of networked organizations, that is, traditional organizations that enter into partnerships of one kind or another and can therefore be said to exist within a network of alliances. This concept of a network organization relies on traditional organization theory and refers to "legally independent companies or subsidiary business units that use various methods of coordinating or controlling their interaction in order to appear like a larger entity."[8] In opposition to this view, the networks we are talking about are *the basic from of social and organizational order* and not a particular way in which some traditional organizations might decide to work together. Based on ANT, the concept of network we propose is neither market, nor bureaucracy, nor a mixture of the two. Our aim is to offer a different theoretical foundation for talking about organizations as networks.

Another possible misunderstanding that talking about networks brings with it is the common conviction that networks in society consist of relationships between people, relationships that become visible through methods such as social network analysis, otherwise known as SNA.[9] Speaking of organizations in terms of social networks, that is, in terms of connections, hubs, nodes, path length, gateways, clustering, power laws, segmentations, and distributions doesn't change anything in the basic conception of what the organization is, how it arises, and what it consists of. Social network analysis is not a theory of organizations. It is a method for discovering patterns of communication between people, whether they are "organized" or not. A more interesting development that is related to SNA and the mathematical models behind it has come to be known as "relational sociology."[10] Relational sociology goes further than SNA by

7 | See https://de.wikipedia.org/wiki/Bruno_Latour. See the essays collected in Belliger/Krieger (2006) and for the reception of ANT in management and organizational studies MOS see Tönnesen et al. nd; Czarniawska/Hernes (2005), Hernes (2008).

8 | http://www.businessdictionary.com/definition/business.html

9 | https://en.wikipedia.org/wiki/Social_network_analysis

10 | "Relational sociology is a collection of sociological theories that emphasize relationalism over substantivalism in explanations and interpretations of social phenomena and is most directly connected to the work of Harrison White and

proposing a constructivist relational ontology of the social. Although ANT can also be understood as a constructivist relational ontology of social reality, it is fundamentally different from relational sociology. ANT has its basis in ethnography and science and technology studies and proposes a methodological symmetry between humans and non-humans. This clearly distinguishes ANT from relational sociology.[11]

The actor-network view of organizations implies the following assumptions: Organizations do not "emerge" as macro-actors from the interests and decisions of individual human actors, nor do organizations somehow precede or transcend individuals. They are not overarching social structures. Organizations are not wholes that are always more than the sum of their parts. They are not containers into which individuals are "socialized." They do not exist on some higher level from which they influence individuals, as it were, behind their backs.[12] The choice of ANT requires, among other things, moving away from understanding organizations as social "entities" or "structures." From the point of view of actor-network theory, organizations are not some kind of unique social substance. Finally, this view also implies that organizations do not make up an "ecology" of their own in which they must adapt to "institutional" pressures in order to establish legitimation.[13]

Charles Tilly in the United States and Pierpaolo Donati and Nick Crossley in Europe." https://en.wikipedia.org/wiki/Relational_sociology

11 | For a critique of relational sociology from the ANT perspective see McFarlane (2013). "Despite the move toward the concept of relation, relational sociology maintains a reactionary humanist social ontology acting as though social relations are limited to the relations that are obtained between humans and denying the existence of those relations that are obtained between humans and nonhumans such as animals, plants, and things" (45).

12 | For an overview of traditional organizational theory see https://en.wikipedia.org/wiki/Organizational_theory

13 | The new institutionalism, for example Scott (2001), DiMaggio/Powell (1983, 1991), Meyer/Rowan (1977), sees organizations as shaped by deeper social norms and expectations that condition, if not determine, what can be considered acceptable modes of organizing at any time. Although we will emphasize the influence of "network norms" on organizational communication, this should not be confused with the program or methods of the new institutionalism.

The view of organizations as networks that we propose relies neither on traditional rational choice theories, nor on the various forms of institutionalism that are their counterpart, nor on the assumption of "micro" and "macro" levels, nor on supposed tensions and antagonisms between "agency" and "structure," nor on the various organicist models of organizations arising from systems theory. For actor-network theory, *social space is flat* and *the whole is always less than the sum of the parts.*[14] Networks are scalable actors, and actors are always made up of many heterogeneous associations. In other words, the actor *is* the network. Networks, however, are not collective actors in the sense of being stable and homogeneous structures with clear boundaries. Networks should not be conceived of as simply a new name for that which traditional sociology has termed organizations. Instead, they are *processes.*[15] Following actor-network theory, we will portray organizations as *processes of organizing in which heterogeneous actors, both human and non-human, are constantly negotiating and re-negotiating programs of action.*

If organizations are nothing other than the process of organizing, they cannot be "containers" in which certain well-defined activities take place. Neither can they be seen as structures emerging from individual interactions only to take on a life of their own as super actors influencing, limiting, conditioning, steering, and even determining individual actors and what they may or may not think and do.[16] This does not imply that individuals are not constrained in processes of organizing. On the contrary, all actors involved are constantly attempting to constrain, that is, in the language of ANT, to "translate" and "enroll" other actors into "programs of action."[17] We will argue that constraints themselves are processes and

---

14 | See Latour et al. (2012).

15 | The process view of organizations has gained wide acceptance. For a discussion of process thinking in organization studies see Hernes (2008). Also see the volumes of the Oxford University Press series Perspectives on Process Organization Studies edited by Ann Langley and Haridimos Tsoukas, as well as the Oxford Handbook of Process Philosophy and Organization Studies edited by J. Helin, T. Hernes, D. Hjorth, and R. Holt, Oxford University Press (2014). Our approach here is based on ANT and not directly on process philosophy although Latour explicitly acknowledges his indebtedness to Whitehead.

16 | See Giddens' (1984) influential theory of structuration.

17 | See Latour (1994) for a discussion of these terms.

that *organizing is indistinguishable from activities of networking.* For this reason, it would probably be more appropriate not to speak of networks at all, but only of *networking.* Nonetheless, common language usage makes it awkward not to speak of networks as well as of networking. It must also constantly be born in mind that the word "networking" is burdened with associations to well-known discussions of "social capital." With this in mind, when we use the word "network," we always understand this term to imply the activity of networking as it is defined by ANT. The title *Organizing Networks* should be understood in the sense of networks that are always in the process of organizing, that is, networks that are doing the organizing as well as being organized.

Networking does not stop at clear boundaries, nor does it privilege human actors. It does not limit itself to standard procedures, or conform to goals and strategies of an encompassing system. To put it bluntly, to define organizations as processes of networking as this term is defined by ANT means that there are no such "things" as organizations and that networks consist of both human and non-human actors. Of course, if we step back and take a snapshot of what we are doing at any moment, what we see may look like an organization characterized by clear boundaries, well-defined internal processes, a collective identity, and external goal-directed relations. However, this impression disappears the moment we step up close. Then what we see are actors, both human and non-human, busily "organizing," that is, making temporary associations in all directions with all kinds of other actors. ANT proposes that we "follow the actors" instead of assuming that the social world is made up of micro-interactions on the one side and macro-structures on the other.[18] However, it would be a misinterpretation of ANT as well as of the process view of organizations to assume that if one eliminates macro structures, then what is left are micro interactions and that the problem of organization theory is therefore to explain how organizations "emerge" from fleeting, local, discreet, face-to-face conversations between co-present individuals. Emphasizing process and doing away with structure does not mean that we now have only

---

18 | This famous methodological rule of ANT (Latour 2005: 12) is influenced by Garfinkel's Ethnomethodology and describes ANT's ethnological approach to science and technology studies. It differs from Garfinkel in including non-humans in the process of negotiating order, that is, by allowing non-humans their own "accountability."

micro interactions from which to explain organizations. Doing away with structure does not leave us with agency alone from which structure must somehow be generated and explained.

If this were the case, the task of organization theory would be to show how macro social structures emerge from micro interactions and then turn around and condition if not determine the micro-interactions. There is admittedly much that speaks for this view. We did not invent the language we speak, the social roles we learn during socialization and the customs, norms, laws etc. of the society we live in. Where did all these conditioning factors of social life come from? If they did not exist from the beginning of the world, or were set in place by "God," then they must have arisen from interactions of individual human agents. Once they have been created, they have the say and not the individuals. If we follow this path, we find ourselves back at a dualistic view of interacting agents on the one side and determining structures on the other. The usual solution is to assume that this is a problem similar to the problem of the chicken and the egg. Which comes first? The only answer seems to be that both somehow arise together in a mutual interdependence.[19] Actor-network theory takes another course.

To say that organizations are not things but processes does not imply that organizations could exist *without* things. *Social order in general and organizations specifically are constituted by both human and non-human actors who influence each other, enter into associations, and build actor-networks.*[20] In this way, fleeting social encounters take on the durability and stability of things. Paradoxically, it is the non-human that makes us human. This

---

19 | See Giddens (1984: 2): "The basic domain of study of the social sciences, according to the theory of structuration, is neither the experience of the individual actor, nor the existence of any form of social totality, but social practices ordered across space and time. Human social activities, like some self-reproducing items in nature, are recursive. That is to say, they are not brought into being by social actors but continually recreated by them via the very means whereby they express themselves as actors. In and through their activities agents reproduce the conditions that make these activities possible."

20 | Callon (1987) offers a succinct definition of actor-network; "reducible neither to an actor alone nor to a network [...] An actor-network is simultaneously an actor whose activity is networking heterogeneous elements and a network that is able to redefine and transform what it is made of" (93).

means that networking is neither agency nor structure. Furthermore, networking should not be understood as "interaction," that is, as long as interaction is traditionally defined as face-to-face communication under the conditions of bodily co-presence. If networking is not interaction, neither is it structure. This is because it cannot be distinguished from the activities of organizing. If networking is neither micro-interaction, nor macro-social structure, nor a dialectical interdependence between them or a recursive loop, what is it then? Can it be that networking, as described by ANT, offers an understanding of the origin and nature of organizations that goes beyond dualisms of agency and structure, individual and society, and subject and object that characterize modern organization theory? Does actor-network theory offer the basis for a foundational theory of organizations that is not dependent on modern sociology? This is the question we will attempt to answer.

Every story must have a beginning. Where should the story of organizations begin if not with the beginning of human history? Our story begins with the question of what makes human social organization different from the behavior of our nearest animal relatives, the primates. The usual answer to this question is to point at the specifically human use of symbols, signs, and language.[21] This traditional view puts mind, cognitive processes, and language in the center and sets the stage for assuming meaningful action is the prerogative of conscious, *intentional* speakers who can *account* for what they are doing. Indeed, ever since Max Weber it is almost a platitude to assume that what distinguishes meaningful action from animal instinct is the ability of humans to *explain* what they are doing or at least to be able to *give good reasons* for their actions. Meaningful action, as opposed to instinctual behavior, depends upon intentionality. Cognition is something that happens exclusively in big brains and is expressed in language. It is true that the so-called "linguistic turn" in the social sciences has shifted the focus away from psychological intentionality to social communication as the basis of meaningful action. Nonetheless, for the most part communication is understood to be the prerogative of human subjects and an expression of internal cognitive processes. Communication has become the social act *par excellence*, that act by which the psychological individual enters into social relations, and

---

21 | See for example the discussion in Fukuyama (2011), who sums up recent literature on the evolution of social and political order.

therefore the basis for theorizing organizations.[22] Although it is almost impossible to conceive of the social world without communication, without giving accounts, or without "sensemaking" (Weick 1995), we will argue that making sense of what we do and coordinating our actions in society must neither be reduced to the use of linguistic signs, nor to face-to-face interactions, nor to cognitive processes inside big brains. Instead, *communication is narrative enactment, that is, the distribution of cognition among humans and non-humans in actor-networks.*

ANT proposes a non-linguistic concept of communication. Not words, but things make the difference. For ANT, as we shall see, instead of "doing things with words" (Austin 1962), what makes human social relations different from apes is that humans can "do words with things." Latour (1994: 33) speaks of "technical mediation" to describe how things take on agency and become "actors" with "programs of action" – the usual term is "affordances (Gibson 1977) – of their own.[23] Of course, things of all kinds have always played a role in human social relations. However, the roles that traditional social theory has allowed things to play in society have been relatively limited. Things were either commodities in trade relations, or gifts in community building.[24] ANT on the contrary argues that humans build their social relations, give them stability and repeatability with the help of things, artifacts, or generally speaking technology. For ANT, technical mediation is what networking is all about. This view has recently received support from the new non-Cartesian cognitive science. New directions in cognitive science view mind as "embodied," "embedded,"

---

22 | See for example George Herbert Mead (1934), Garfinkel (1967), Habermas (1981), Luhmann (1995), Weick (1963, 1995), Taylor (2001b), Cooren (2010).

23 | "An affordance is a relation between an object or an environment and an organism that, through a collection of stimuli, affords the opportunity for that organism to perform an action. For example, a knob affords twisting, and perhaps pushing, while a cord affords pulling. As a relation, an affordance exhibits the possibility of some action, and is not a property of either an organism or its environment alone." https://en.wikipedia.org/wiki/Affordance

24 | Appadurai (1986). See Fiske (1991) for a more differentiated analysis of the roles things play in social relations. Regardless of what roles things are allowed to play, sociology usually grants the right to assign roles and give meaning exclusively to humans. Things are usually seen as dumb and passive and not as social actors in their own right.

"enacted," and "extended."[25] Mind, according to this view is not limited to cognitive processes inside of brains, but is "distributed" among heterogeneous actors and extended beyond the brain, and even beyond the body into the environment. Of course, the use of sings, symbols, and language are part of this. For ANT, however, things can come to have a "voice" of their own. They are not passive recipients of meaning giving acts, but participate as actors in making the associations that build social order. This is important when one asks the question of how dominant technologies, such as ICTs, are influencing social order.

After introducing artifacts as social actors via the concept of technical mediation in order to explain what "networking" means, the second episode of our story (Part 2) deals the role of communication in organizational studies. Communication has long been a major topic in organization theory. What role does communication play in understanding organizations and what difference does it make for organizational practice? This question has motivated much theoretical and empirical research in the area of management and organization science. However, only recently in the work of Weick (1979, 1995, 2005), McPhee and Zaug (2000), Taylor (1993, 2001a), Cooren (2000), and others has the traditional view of organizations as social entities, institutions, and macro-structures been placed into question. Many of these thinkers have come to understand their work as a common enterprise under the title of "communicative constitution of organizations" (CCO).[26] The CCO movement follows Weick in explicitly understanding organizations as the process of organizing. Process not structure takes center stage. The process from which organizations arise is communication.

CCO thinkers stand in the tradition of symbolic interactionism, ethnomethodology, and linguistic philosophy. From the point of view of ANT, however, the processes that CCO focuses on seem to be primarily linguistic forms of communication. All that is needed for organizations to come into existence seems to be "talking heads." With regard to the role that non-humans can be said to play in creating social order, the

---

25 | See Rowlands (2010) for an overview of the new paradigm in cognitive science. Lindblom (2007) uses the insights of non-Cartesian cognitive science to give an account of social interaction.

26 | See Brumanns et al. (2014) as well as the Website/Blog (orgcom.wordpress. com) for an overview of CCO research.

various theories and models of society that are associated with CCO raise many questions. Can Weick's "sensemaking" be reduced to linguistic communication? What, according to CCO theorists, is the communicative process that constitutes organizations? Who does the communicating? What are organizations made of? Can non-humans as well as humans be considered as social actors? What do actors do, such that organizations come into being? Are organizations something other than what ANT calls actor-networks? Is sensemaking the same as networking, understood as technical mediation? Can actor-networks be considered organizations at all? How can an extended concept of communication that includes the "voices" of non-humans be understood? What exactly is the contribution of ANT to understanding the communicative constitution of organizations?

Although communication is claimed to be the key to understanding organizations, there is no consensus, even within the CCO group, on what kind of communication constitutes organizations, what organizations are, and what it means to constitute an organization. Depending on how these key concepts are defined, very different theories of organization appear, from closed systems to open networks, from macro-structures to chains of interaction episodes. Building on the idea of networking as technical mediation from ANT and the work done by the CCO movement, we will argue in Part 3 for an interpretation of these key concepts not only from the perspective of actor-network theory, but also on the basis of a reconstruction of Goffman's dramaturgical sociology of interaction and the theory of narrative.[27] *Our claim is that Weick's seminal concept of sensemaking is best understood as networking, provided that sensemaking includes Goffman's dramaturgical staging of social interaction as well as a theory of narrative informed by non-Cartesian cognitive science. Networking, sensemaking, staging, and narrative all refer to the same process by which organizations are constructed, maintained, deconstructed, and transformed.*

In narrative, as the founding myths and rituals of every society illustrate, all kinds of beings "speak" and "do" things. Semiotics has shown that narrative language is a language in which "actors" (this can be anything at all that plays a role in a story) do things.[28] In a fairy tale,

---

27 | For a discussion of the importance of narrative theory in the sociology of organizations, see Czarniawska (1998).

28 | It is well known that ANT is dependent on the "actant" narratology of Greimas (1983, 1987).

for example, not only human beings are actors, but also swords, crowns, mythical beings, animals, trees, stones, rivers, etc. Both human and non-human actors contribute to narrative. ANT goes beyond traditional narrative theory by extending linguistic semiotics to things. It is possible to speak of a "semiotics of things," a topic that has found resonance in work on "material culture," or "material semiotics."[29] What has this got to do with narrative in the usual sense of telling stories? This is the question we will attempt to answer on the basis of a reinterpretation of Goffman's dramaturgical theory of social interaction and with reference to recent developments in cognitive science. We will try to show how Goffman's theory of interaction allows for an understanding of narrative that is not purely diegetic, that is, purely linguistic. Social interaction, and therefore, communication need not be understood as purely linguistic, but also mimetic, embodied, and extended. Following Goffman, we will argue that social interaction is best understood as "staging," that is, bringing many different actors, both human and non-human, into play in a *local* situation that is connected to a *global* situation.

To speak of the communicative constitution of organization, therefore, is to understand communication not merely as verbal utterances, but also as *performance*, whereby performance means that "sensemaking" (Weick) is embodied, enacted, and extended in the environment. Talk is not mere talk, and, as the new non-Cartesian cognitive science shows, it is not the prerogative of heads with big brains. Narrative, we will argue, is a form of doing. It creates order by linking humans and non-humans in actor-networks. Performance is therefore more than "performative."[30] It is not merely "doing things with words," but, as could be claimed in the spirit of ANT, "doing words with things," that is, constructing networks that are made up not only of signs, but also of hard, durable, resistant artifacts and technologies with affordances of their own. Narrative, from the perspective of non-Cartesian cognitive science, can be understood as embodied, enacted, embedded, and extended and thus distributed among non-humans as well as humans. From this perspective, narrative, which is an essential aspect of Weick's sensemaking, can be aligned with networking as technical mediation as well as Goffman's staging. It holds

---

29 | https://en.wikipedia.org/wiki/Material_culture and Law (2008) on the concept of "material semiotics."

30 | See the theory of performative speech acts see Austin (1962).

the key to understanding how many different entities, both human and non-human, and their many different activities can be "coordinated" and thus brought into a kind of order that "makes sense" in the specific organizational meaning that Weick gives this term. *Making sense via enacted narrative is the kind of communication that constitutes organizations.* This argument is intended to enrich and extend the promising work done by McPhee, Zaug, Taylor, and Cooren and others on the communicative constitution of organizations.

Narrative communication understood as networking, staging, and sensemaking eliminates the traditional sociological distinction between interaction and organization. We no longer need to think of society as consisting of small interactions and large organizations. The small and the large do not constitute distinct ontological levels, but exist on a continuum. This continuum can be understood as *localizing and globalizing.* Every event and every story takes place not only within a concrete local context, but at the same time within larger frames. Stories can include other stories, just as frames can be within frames going all the way on up to a whole world. These frames, however, are not encompassing structures like matryoshka dolls, one within the other. Talking about, that is, "performing" the company, the economy, legal regulations, political processes, norms, international relations, cultures, etc. simply *adds more links, more actors, and more events to the same story.* Usually, we have neither the time nor the resources to tell the whole story. If two people share the same culture, work at the same company, participate in the same team, it is relatively easy to link the small stories about current projects up to larger ones about the reorganization of the department or the new five-year strategy should the need arise. Socialization or enculturation mean exactly this. We spend a good part of our lives in school and all of our lives in informal learning so that we already know the big stories and can spend our working time and energy on the immediate job to be done. Even if interactions appear to take place in the small dimensions of the local here and now, they are in fact both local and global. They include actors that are not present at the moment of face-to-face interaction.

For example, if we ask our team members to be present at a meeting on Monday at the office, then many different actors, settings, scripts, etc. are brought in and linked together so that everyone knows what is expected of them and will be at the right place at the right time with all the necessary information. In case there is uncertainty about why we make the request, where we should meet, what we will be doing, etc. we can extend the story almost indefinitely. Even if we have to extend the story to global levels including the companies new strategy, new regulatory restrictions, a recent legal ruling, budget cuts, unforeseen technological developments, international treaties, new competitors, etc., we still do not suddenly jump to a higher ontological level. No matter how small or large the network and no matter how complex and long the story, it is the same world. The local and the global build a continuum. There is not a higher ontological level of macro-structures, institutions, norms, nations, or cultures. There is just a much longer and much more complicated story to be told. This does not mean, however, that there are no norms or constraints on what will be accepted as a social binding story. Globalizing involves worldviews, values, and, as we will argue in Part 4, it is influenced by those network norms that arise from the affordances of new media.

Networking, sensemaking, staging, and narrative performance move seamlessly from individual to collective actors, for example, from individual employees in the marketing department to regional managers, to the CEO, and the board of directors or the stockholders. All are involved in the same way, on the same level, in constructing, de-constructing, transforming, or maintaining networks via narrative performance. The scale of the network is variable, a company can restructure, lay-off half of the workforce, merge into another company, or be broken up into many smaller companies by order of anti-cartel laws, but the ontological level is the same. The more actors are involved, the more "collective," "organized," and "institutional" the network appears. We do not have a multitude of ephemeral interaction episodes on the micro level and somehow appearing above them macro social structures, despite the fact that this was thought to be a "good story" in most of modern Western sociology. What matters much more than ontological levels are, as we will argue, the affordances of the technologies that allow us to communicate. The mythical face-to-face conversation is of course still there, but it is now accompanied, mediated, and influenced by digital information and communication technologies. Today, bodily co-presence is almost inconceivable without smartphones, wearables, and other devices. Information has taken on a very different meaning and function in social organization, when it is an effect of digital networks. We will claim that this is important and plays a large role in how localizing and globalizing is done in today's network society.

To take another example, if a representative of an insurance company knocks at the door, then the story they tell links to things that have existed long before this particular interaction that takes place here and now at our front door. When they start talking, they bring into the story things that will continue in other places long after we say we are not interested and shut the door. Without these things, the interaction could not take place, or at least, it would be a different interaction. The Life Insurance Company, the collective actor, is not limited to this particular time and place. Nonetheless, it is here doing its job. Where is the jump to a different ontological dimension of social structure? We could follow the information, the brochures, the contracts, and the people from this single representative trying to sell me an insurance policy to the local office and from there to the central office in Zurich right into the meeting of the board of directors without a gap, breach, or break. It is all one seamless web of associations and links. Furthermore, the trail does not stop here, as if one could arrive at a whole that is somehow more than the sum of the parts. What goes on at the meeting of the board of directors depends on government regulations, the strategies of competitors, risk scenarios, innovations in statistical modeling, changing demographics, urbanization, climate change, and much more. Starting from any individual actor, no matter how small and insignificant, the chain of operations extends almost infinitely in all directions. Indeed, the whole is only accessible in and through the part, which can be understood to mean that what we are tempted to refer to as "the whole" is merely an arbitrary cut-off point in the description of networks and thus always less than the sum of the parts.[31]

What these examples intend to show is that the local and the global are on the same ontological level. As Latour puts it, social space is flat.

The macro is neither 'above' nor 'below' the interactions, but added to them as another of their connections, feeding them and feeding off of them. There is no other known way to achieve changes in relative scale. For each of the 'macro places', the same type of questions can be raised. The answer provided by fieldwork will bring attention back to a local site and re-describe them as some disheveled arrays of connections through which vehicles (carrying types of documents, inscriptions, and materials) are traveling via some sort of conduit. [...] An actor-network is traced whenever, in the course of a study, the decision is made to replace actors

---

31 | See Latour on Tarde (Latour et al. 2012).

of whatever size by local and connected sites instead of ranking them into micro and macro. (2005: 177, 179)

The post office is not only that small building at the end of the street, but also all those other buildings in which letters can be sent as well as the central administration including all the transportation systems, laws, directives, plans, and authorities that contribute to making the post function. When we send a package or a letter at the local window, we may be talking to one person, but this person is authorized, dressed accordingly, behind security glass, consulting tariffs, regulations, schedules, etc. As more and more of these "actors" are brought in, the local interaction becomes extended in space and time, and, as we know today, it can even become "global." Setting all this up so that it works and so that we can go to the small building on the corner and send a letter is best described as networking, staging, sensemaking, and narrative performance. The "big" story of the organization is only a larger, longer, more complex, and time-consuming telling of the small story that is taking place in the face-to-face conversation at the window in the local post office.

The concepts of localizing and globalizing are useful for understanding how small interactions are linked to larger, collective interactions and for explaining how networks are scalable. Insisting upon the role of non-humans in narrative performance, however, raises the question of how technologies influence the communicative constitution of organizations. Communication is not a human mental and linguistic process, but is distributed, embodied, embedded, and extended. According to the new non-Cartesian cognitive science, the environment is a constitutive part of the cognitive process.[32] The kind of sense that can be made depends on the kind of artifacts and technologies that make up the environment. The very idea of networking implies that non-humans, that is, artifacts and technologies play decisive roles in the communicative constitution of organizations. If narrative performance is a distributed form of communication involving not only humans, but also non-humans, what effects do the affordances of dominant technologies have on the kinds of stories that can be told and consequently on the kinds of organizations

---

32 | Cf. Rowlands (2010), Clark (2008), Clark/Chalmers (1998), Gibson (1977), Hutchins (1995), Noë (2004), Shapiro (2004), Thompson (2007), Wheeler (2008, 2010).

that can successfully be set up? What makes a narrative performance powerful and convincing? What kind of narrative performance can constitute an organization in today's global network society? What do these organizations look like? These questions lead to issues raised not only by CCO thinkers, but also by new institutionalism's concern for the influence of cultural and historical "norms" and "values." Not any story at all that can be told will "make sense" and be successfully "stageable," and thus able to constitute social order. What makes certain stories constitutive of organization and others not? We will argue in Part 4 that there are indeed norms influencing or conditioning what stories and what kinds of sensemaking constitute social order and organizations. However, these norms are not to be found where the new institutionalism looks for them, that is, in cognitive constraints that arise from culture. Instead, norms arise from the conditions of successful networking. We refer to these conditions, which depend on the affordances of the technologies that we are linked up to, as *network norms*. In Part 4, we turn to the question of how any communication in today's world is conditioned by the affordances of digital information and communication technologies. The main actor in this episode is *new media*.

The affordances of digital information and communication technologies are considered by many to be nothing short of revolutionary.[33] Just as the printing press created new forms of life, labor, and organizing in all areas, so too new digital media are transforming every aspect of society. Networked organizations are more and more taking the place of traditional organizations. Networks no longer appear as a more or less interesting exception to markets and hierarchies. The global network society is characterized by a "structural transformation" (Castells 1996) in which "technology does not determine society it *is* society" (Castells 2005, 3). The new media revolution puts us in the position to appreciate the potential of network models of organizing, both theoretically and heuristically. Our claim is that narrative performance is constitutive of organizations in today's world when informed by the affordances of new media. The affordances of new media translate and enroll communicative action into new norms. These can be called "network norms" (Krieger/ Belliger 2014).

---

33 | https://en.wikipedia.org/wiki/Digital_Revolution

On the basis of new media studies, we will argue that the network norms guiding communication can be said to be connectivity, flow, communication, participation, transparency, authenticity, and flexibility. After the new media revolution, *organizing appears explicitly as networking*. The "socio-sphere" opened up by networking makes it increasingly difficult to maintain even the appearance of macro-structures, institutions, and closed systems. Furthermore, it makes hierarchies increasingly inefficient, since the connectivity of all nodes in the network and the flow of information can no longer be easily controlled. Organizing according to network norms results in forms of social order that do not fit within the descriptions of traditional organizations. The various new theories of organization that have become known under titles such as "chaotic," "fractal," "holocratic," "adhocracy," "organization 2.0," and "networked" support this claim. The communicative constitution of organizations that is influenced by the affordances of new media favor organizations that are decentralized, non-hierarchical, self-organized, flexible, innovative, transparent, connected, and collaborative. Organizing in this way demands "pattern breaking" (Wüthrich et al. 2009; Kaduk et al. 2015) management practices.

In the final episode, Part 5, we turn to concrete examples of what organizing networks can mean for management and decision-making in business, education, healthcare, and civil society. We will test the heuristic value of the theoretical framework that has been developed in the previous chapters by a description of how communication guided by network norms is changing organizing in various areas of society. Where once educational organizations, businesses, healthcare organizations and so on were modeled as closed systems with clear boundaries, functional roles, and standard processes, we are more and more seeing open, flexible, non-hierarchical networks. Networks take on many forms and involve many different kinds of actors. In education, for example, personal learning environments seamlessly link up formal schooling with informal workplace learning, learning on demand, social learning, and life-long learning. In business, networked organizations, global projects, and new forms of entrepreneurship are emerging. In healthcare, e-patients, self-trackers, health 2.0, and connected healthcare are changing the very meaning of healthcare and contributing to public health and medical research in new ways. New social movements and a networked, global civil society are challenging political organizations. These changes confront managers and decision-makers with new questions. What are the great narratives of education, healthcare, business, citizenship, etc. in a global network society? How is networked organizing changing society? Can organizing in today's global network society best be described as networking in the sense of ANT? Are traditional institutions becoming smart networks characterized by network norms and pattern-breaking management practices? It is certainly too early to answer these questions definitively. Nevertheless, it is our hope that the theoretical perspective we attempt to sketch out here has sufficient heuristic value to inspire empirical research and suggest how surprising and useful answers could be discovered.

1. Things Have Gotten Out of Hand – On Technical Mediation

Every good story has a beginning. Where should the story about organizations begin if not at the beginning of human history? Primatologists agree that "social" is not an adjective that can be applied to humans alone.[1] Baboons, chimpanzees and other primates demonstrate social behavior. However, for all the similarities between social behavior in animals and humans, there is an undeniable difference in how humans organize their social life. This distinction is perhaps nowhere more vividly illustrated than in the opening scene of Stanley Kubrick's famous film "2001." Who can forget the breathtaking scene in which a group of pre-historic hominids in the midst of a violent conflict with other apes suddenly picked up bones and used them as weapons thus deciding the battle for themselves and changing the course of evolution?

Out of elation at winning the struggle and perhaps with a dim awareness of the momentous significance of what had happened, one of the apes threw a bone high into the air. Spinning around while falling, the bone is magically transformed into a space station orbiting the Earth. Over a million years of technological history is dramatically folded into the blinking of an eye. Although the space station, just as the bone, is a thing made of matter, an objective entity out there in the world, it represents much more than a technological artifact. It represents what we call "modern society." We know that there would be no space station without NASA, without laboratories, universities, legal documents, funding procedures,

---

1 | The evolution of human social order is a topic in many disciplines including anthropology, archeology, history, sociology, political science as well as primatology. Recent discussions can be found in Fukuyama (2011) and Dubreuil (2010). We focus here on the work of Strum/Latour (1987).

political processes, aero-space industries, international treaties, scientists, research programs, commercial applications, and much more. All of these have one characteristic in common; they are all "organized." They are social organizations or parts of social organizations. The space station does not exist alone. It is made up of myriad links between technologies, sciences, businesses, politics, laws, and even religion and art. All this is what sociologists call "society." Society consists of organizations or institutions like NASA, IBM, the ETH, governments, political parties, the courts, etc. Just like the space station, these various organizations seem to exist "out there" in the world just as many other things. They may be social things, but nonetheless they appear to be things that can be studied by the social sciences in much the same way that metals, computers, electronics, and bones can be studied by the natural sciences.

Once we believe that society consists of social things, it becomes reasonable to assume that technical things and social things can influence each other. On the one hand, it can be claimed that society determines how technology is used. Technological artifacts are mere tools that can be used for good or for bad. A hammer can be used to build a house, or to kill someone. This has nothing to do with the hammer, which is a neutral instrument in the hands of a human user. A satellite can be used for weaponry or for weather forecasts. In this view, the tool is not responsible for how it is used. On the other hand, it can be claimed that technology determines the social. Tools, or clothes, as the saying goes, "make" the man or woman. As Marx proposed, technologies of production determine social and cultural relations. Capitalism is a form of social and cultural life that has arisen on the basis of industrial production. If we recall the debate on guns in the USA, technical determinists claim that putting guns into people's hands makes them into criminals. Social determinists, on the other hand, claim that guns are neutral, mere tools that can be used for good or bad. In both cases, the link between humans and technology that Kubrick so brilliantly visualized is interpreted as a cause/effect relation between two entities. Was it the bone, with its specific weight, size, consistency, etc. that somehow managed at a certain moment to influence an ape such that it became – over countless generations – human? Alternatively, was it the pre-human who at a certain moment in history used its big brain and transformed a mere bone into a weapon or a tool? Not only the fruitlessness of decades of debate between technological and social determinism, but also recent developments in the sociology of technology, ethnology, and similar disciplines have put these traditional views of technology and society in question.[2]

It has become increasingly difficult to describe society and organizations based on the traditional paradigm, which sees society as a realm of freedom and technologies, artifacts, and nature as a realm of determinism. It is increasingly problematic to base a science of society on the assumption that social mechanisms can be discovered behind and above the arbitrary activities of principally free individuals. The view that social order is made up of micro individuals on the one side and macro social structures, often called organizations, on the other is losing its explanatory and heuristic value. Perhaps neither bones nor space stations are things. Perhaps we have jumped too quickly from bones to space stations and overlooked what is specific about the human social link. Perhaps the bone and the human influenced each other in such a way that both are "translated" into something that neither was before.[3] Not only have both ape and bone changed, the moment the bone became a tool in "human" hand, but also they have entered into a relationship in which neither exists completely independent of the other. The human social link is not exclusively human. It is somehow bound up with links between humans and non-humans. Speaking of society as consisting of institutions and organizations is therefore dependent on the way we humans are linked up to things such as bones, stone axes, swords, tools of all kinds, factories, laboratories, space stations, etc. Latour (1994) speaks of this link as "technical mediation." Technical mediation means that things have quite literally "gotten out of hand" and have taken on a life of their own that remains nonetheless inextricably bound up with human life.

---

2 | See above all work done in STS (Science and Technology Studies).

3 | On the concept of "translation," Latour writes, "Like Michel Serres, I use *translation* to mean displacement, drift, invention, mediation, the creation of a link that did not exist before and that to some degree modifies two elements or agents" (Latour 1994: 32).

ASSOCIATIONS, LINKS, AND INTERFACES

Let's take a closer look at what happened back then when Kubrick's ape became human. In order for the ape to use the bone as a weapon there needs to be some kind of "fit" between the hand and the thing on the one side of the action and on the other side a fit between the weapon and the skulls of the enemies. Without this fit, the hand cannot work upon the bone so that the bone could work upon the skulls. We can exchange this situation for the more peaceful use of a stone axe to cut a piece of wood. The Stone Age began ca. 2.5 million years ago, that is, long before *Homo sapiens* came on the scene, which was about 200,000 years ago. Hominids have a long history of using stone tools. As Kubrick suggests, already this simple technology can tell us something about space stations and modern society. What is so special about tools? Why can it be claimed that humans are tool users and that this is what makes us human, even when primatologists have long shown that baboons and chimpanzees also use tools? How is using a tool, such as a stone axe, different from an ape that picks up a stone and uses it to open a coconut? The answer to this question could lie in the fact that when things turn into tools, they literally "get out of hand." At a certain moment, both the ape and the human have a stone in their hands. The difference is that the ape drops it and moves on. For all purposes, the "tool" disappears with its episodic use.[4] The human, or rather for a long time before *Homo sapiens*, the hominid, may also drop it, but they hold on to something else. They hold on to the use. For the ape, the thing is gone. It has not just gotten out of hand; it has disappeared. The tool on the contrary takes on a life of its own and is somehow still "there" to be used again in the right place at the right time and in the right way. The fact that things have gotten out of hand, but still remain somehow with us, taking their places in our lives and assuming their own roles in our activities is what Latour (1994) calls "technical mediation." How does technical mediation work?

---

4 | Donald (1991: 149) describes the "culture" of apes as "episodic." "In fact, the word that seems best to epitomize the cognitive culture of apes [...] is the term episodic. Their lives are lived entirely in the present, as a series of concrete episodes and the highest element in their system of memory representation seems to be at the level of event representation."

In order for technological mediation to take place there has to be a link between the user, the tool, and the effect that the tool produces. The hand has to be able to grasp the stone axe in the right way. The axe, for its part, has to have the right shape, consistency, weight, etc. in order to be able to work upon skulls, or wood, or whatever in the intended way. Floridi offers a helpful distinction between first, second, and third order technologies. According to Floridi (2014: 26ff.), a "first order technology" is when a human works upon a thing, which in turn works upon some other thing. The human swings the axe, which cuts the wood. In this simple example, we see that there are three elements linked to each other. There is the hand, the axe (stone), and the wood. What makes the link between the hand and the stone possible is the *fit* between the hand and the stone. This fit faces in two directions. On the one side, the hand is anatomically so shaped and structured that it can hold things like stones. However, on the other side, the stone cannot be just any stone, it has to be shaped and constituted so that it can be held by a human (or hominid) hand. This link is possible only because both human hand and stone contribute something. The hand must swing the stone. It must not only be able and willing to do this, but also must learn how to do it. This is because the stone does not allow just any kind of hold or any kind of swing. The stone influences and "teaches" the hand how it is to be held and swung. Neither can make the link alone. The link is a product of both hand and stone. They mutually condition, that is, "translate" and "enroll" each other in order for the stone to become an axe. This is not all. There is another similar kind of link on the side of where the stone meets the wood. This link is also two-sided. It faces the stone, which must be sharp and hard. It also faces the wood, which must be so constituted that a sharp stone of a certain weight and consistency can indeed cut it. Both stone and wood contribute to making this link possible. Both stone and wood do something. Both are agents. In order to express the agency of all participants, both human and non-human, Latour (1994: 34) speaks of a "symmetry" between human and non-human. The one is not the subject and the other the object. The one is not active while the other is passive. The one does not determine the other. They both have agency and thus there is a symmetry between them.

The symmetry that ANT describes between human and non-human "forces us to abandon the subject-object dichotomy, a distinction that prevents understanding of techniques and even of societies" (Latour 1994: 34). For Latour, "Responsibility for action must be shared among the various actants" (34). This is what technical mediation means. Floridi (2014: 35ff.) does not speak of mediation, but of "interface." The special link between human and non-human can be considered an interface because it "faces" in two directions. In one direction, the link faces toward the human hand that is anatomically so constituted that it can hold and wield things that are formed in a certain way. In the other direction, the link faces toward the stone that has to have a certain shape, weight, and consistency, otherwise it cannot be held by a human hand and cannot cut wood. The interface is constituted by both hand and axe. This is what they do. They create an interface that is neither the hand nor the stone independent of each other, but is *distributed* between them. This distributed and ambiguous character of technical mediation is also characteristic of Gibson's notion of "affordances." For Gibson

[A]n affordance is neither an objective property nor a subjective property; or it is both if you like. An affordance cuts across the dichotomy of subjective objective and helps us to understand its inadequacy. It is equally a fact of the environment and a fact of behavior. It is both physical and psychical, yet neither. An affordance points both ways, to the environment and to the observer. (1979: 129)

In terms drawn from actor-network theory, both hand and stone "mediate," "translate," and "enroll" each other. If we take a modern axe, the situation is no different. The hand is linked to the axe by the handle on the side of use. On the side of the material that is cut, the axe is linked to the wood by its metal head or blade. Both of these links have to "fit," if the firewood is going to be ready when it gets cold. Technology in all its forms depends on these links or interfaces. From the point of view of ANT, hand, axe, and wood can be considered as symmetrical "actors" or "actants" who mediate each other and in this way make the technology possible. Humans and non-humans are equally, that is, symmetrically involved in doing something. What is it that results from this symmetrical activity?

Latour argues that technological mediation depends on processes of "translation" and "enrollment." Translation means that some entity becomes associated with another entity such that both together form a new kind of being.[5] The association they enter into is created by means of

---

5 | Latour understands "translation" as a "displacement, drift, invention, media-tion, the creation of a link that did not exist before and that to some degree modifies two elements or agents" (Latour 1994: 32).

each translating the other into something greater and more complex. In our example, hand, axe, and wood translate each other into something that was not there before. The thing has gotten out of hand, but it is somehow still there. The hand becomes a hand that can hold an axe, a hand extended, augmented, changed by the stone. The stone is no longer merely an object lying about on the ground. It becomes an axe, a stone associated to a hand and an arm that can do specific tasks. The wood becomes raw material for building, or heating, or whatever. *The result of these links and interfaces, that is, the result of technical mediation, can be called an "actor-network."* The network of associations becomes a new kind of actor, it becomes a "man with an axe," a "warrior," a "hunter," a "carpenter," that is, someone who is different, as Kubrick forcefully illustrated, from apes without axes.[6]

A person with an axe can do things that a person without an axe could not do, and he or she lives in a different world, a world of raw materials; a world where shelters can be built and not merely found, where building is a different activity from hunting, which for its part is different from other activities. A simple stone contributes to many different activities that demand to be distinguished, held apart from each other, and lined up in sequential series. Monkeys cannot reduce the options of a certain situation. Every social interaction is open to the full possibilities of simian behavior. They cannot put all other possibilities aside and focus only on one thing at a time. They are confronted at every moment with the entire spectrum of social activities and have only their bodies, limited memory, and social skills to negotiate order. Humans are distinguished from primates by "attention sharing," that is, mutually focusing attention to objects of interest.[7] There is a "coorientation" (Taylor/Van Every 2000: 33ff.) toward something that becomes thereby a shared concern. Humans

---

6 | Latour speaks of "hybrid actors" (1994: 33), that is, networks that are themselves actants. "Actant" is concept from semiotics which designates any subject of activity. For Latour "action is simply not a property of humans, but of an association of actants" (35).

7 | According to Dubreuil (2010: 64) "at a minimum, human specificity can be seen as the outcome of the reward mechanism that motivates cooperative joint attention and, in a second step, of the cognitive control mechanisms that allow humans to stick to norms in the face of competing motivations." Dubreuil goes on to say that joint attention sharing "is instrumental in learning language and is absent in nonhuman primates."

do different things at different times, such as hunting, building, fighting, mating, etc. one after the other and not all at once. Technical mediation links actions to things that are there even when not being held in the hand and being used at the moment. Things stabilize activities and make them sharable. Things help build social order by holding different activities apart from one another, and keeping them ready for the moment when they are needed. Of course, sticks and stones have been an indistinguishable part of the natural environment for millions of years, that is, until a hominid picks one up and uses it as a weapon or a tool. The stone or stick is no longer an *ad hoc* implement bound into an episodic experience, but part of a network of associations whose affordances demand different actors who play different roles.

Nonhumans stabilize social negations. [...] they can be shaped very quickly but once shaped, last far longer than the interactions that fabricated them. [...] What was impossible for complex social animals to accomplish becomes possible for prehumans – who use tools, not to acquire food but to fix, underline, materialize, and keep track of the social realm. (Latour 1994: 61)

Interfaces, links, and associations are not things, but they do inherit their durability, stability, and continuity. Contrary to the episodic events of simian social activity, the interfaces that are formed by translation and enrollment are relatively stable, durable, and repeatable. When things get out of hand, hands that hold by means of interfaces have an evolutionary advantage over those that do not. The useful things do not simply disappear. Their affordances become "normative," that is, they become rules that govern who is to do what with what for what purpose. This normativity makes interfaces into that which constitutes the social world. No single actor alone arbitrarily can decide what is right. The hand cannot force the stone to do what it wants, if the stone is not doing its part to make the interface work. Constructing an interface is a matter of negotiating agency. Hunting, building, fighting, cutting wood, and so on are actor-networks that come into being and are maintained by negotiations. Technical mediation means cooperation among all actors involved. This is what prehumans, and we humans too, "hold" on to when we have dropped the *ad hoc* implements or our primate relatives. We no longer need to hold things in our hands in order for them to influence our activities and become part of our social order. We hold on to the links, the interfaces.[8] This is what makes us "warriors," "hunters," "builders," "shamans," etc., that is, actors with the ability to do certain tasks and accomplish certain goals. Technical mediation means that given certain spatial and temporal conditions, when the axe is taken in the hand, the wood will be cut. There is a causal, purposeful, and therefore meaningful relation between actor and event.[9]

The episodic and very limited representational connection that determines how apes perceive and handle objects is broken and things remain with us even when we are no longer holding them in our hands. Big brains that can process links, that is, as cognitive science argues, outsource information into the environment, have an evolutionary advantage over those that cannot.[10] Technical mediation is a motor of evolution. Technical mediation "translates" and "enrolls" animals and things into actor-networks, that is, associations in which different actors have different functions. These functions then become concerns, goals, or what ANT (Latour 1994: 33) calls "programs of action." Goals, interests, concerns, or what traditional sociology has called "intentionality," arise when both human and non-human actors are mutually translated and enrolled into programs of action.[11]

---

8 | George Herbert Mead made this the foundation of symbolic interactionism, which profoundly influenced the sociology of organization. "The isolation of the symbol, as such, enables one to hold on to these given characters and to isolate them in their relationship to the object, and consequently in their relation to the response" (1934: 121).

9 | As Popova (2015) puts it, "Given a certain arrangement, a particular configuration in time and space, two events will always be seen as causally connected, and their interaction is best described as a meaningful action, even if the 'agents' involved are simple inanimate objects" (17). We will return to this point later in the discussion of narrative.

10 | See Donald (1991) for a discussion of cognitive evolution which emphasizes the changes in physiology as well as culture with the appearance of *Homo erectus* ca. 1.9 million years ago.

11 | When speaking of what objects do one usually speaks of "functions" as opposed to intentions. But as Latour remarks, "The same is true of goals and functions, the former associated more with humans, the latter with non-humans, but both can be described as programs of action" (Latour 1994: 33).

What do human collectives have that those socially complex baboons do not possess? Technical mediation – which we are now prepared to summarize: Technical action is a form of delegation that allows us to mobilize, during interactions, moves made elsewhere, earlier, by other actants. It is the presence of the past and distant, the presence of nonhuman characters, that frees us, precisely, from interactions (what we manage to do, right away, with our humble social skills). That we are not Machiavellian baboons we owe to technical action. (Latour 1994: 52)

It is not merely kin-selection, reciprocal altruism, the ability to walk upright, the shape of the hand, and big brains that make a difference.[12] It is not primarily symbols, or language, that makes the difference.[13] Stones and wood are also involved. Chopping firewood is a program of action that must be ascribed to an actor-network and not to an isolated, intentional consciousness, a Cartesian subject who is able to reflect upon itself by manipulating symbols. As an association of humans and non-humans, an actor-network has stability and repeatability, that is, a meaning that is independent of this particular hand, this particular axe, and this particular stack of logs. The stone has a role to play and the hand as well in accomplishing a specific and repeatable task. Technical mediation means becoming enabled to do something. This implies functionality, specification, differentiation, and also identity. Not every stone will do, and an unpracticed hand will fumble and drop the stone. When they work together, they make up an actor-network. Someone becomes a warrior, a hunter, a builder, and so on. As Latour (1994: 34) puts it, "[...] the prime mover of an action becomes a new, distributed, and nested series of practices whose sum might be made but only if we respect the mediating role of all the actants mobilized in the list." To become an actor in a network means to take on a certain role, to play a part, to be assigned a function. The hand must hold and swing the axe in the right way. For a hunter, or a builder to appear in the world, the axe must transfer the force

---

12 | Fukuyama (2011: 43) finds in our prehistory "natural building blocks" upon which a theory of "political development" can be erected. These are "kin selection," "reciprocal altruism," the "capacity for abstraction," a "proclivity for norm following," and a desire for "intersubjective recognition."

13 | Donald (1991) points out that it is unlikely that *Homo erectus* "would have possessed any form of symbolic language" (164).

in the right way to the right kind of object. All this depends on mediation, on interfaces, links, and associations. *Only when things quite literally "get out of hand" do they become part of a social world together with humans, take on an "agency" of their own, and come to play their roles in those hybrid and heterogeneous networks of humans and non-humans that Latour calls "actor-networks."*

If we recall that hominids used stone tools for hundreds of thousands of years before *Homo sapiens* appeared on the scene, it is reasonable to assume that the kind of "knowledge" that one needed to play such a role was not symbolic and linguistic in the sense in which we understand language today. Ever since *Homo erectus* appeared ca. 1.9 million years ago, hominids used stone tools in what was most probably a kind of "practical knowledge," or "enacted cognition" embedded in specific ways of doing things.[14] It was not that the apes in Kubrick's film suddenly became Cartesian subjects capable of reflecting on their own thinking. Instead, they probably began to enter into certain kinds of associations with things like bones and stones that became repeatable, familiar, situated, and thus stable and distinguishable from everything else that was constantly going on.[15] Speaking from the perspective of Paleolithic archeology, Gamble and Porr (2005: 9) claim that "we prefer to use the term 'practice' to describe and explain the actions of hominids," instead of speaking of "behavior."

With the notion of practice we want to stress the dual character of human interactions with the environment. Practice is both a reaction as well as action. The agent not only responds, he or she also actively manipulates the material environment, which, in turn, necessitates further actions and reactions. In this way increasingly complex networks of people and material objects were created by hominids over time and space. They necessitated choices which cannot be accounted for by biological concepts alone. The patterns in the data have to be seen as the products of habits that are inscribed into actors during everyday activities. They are not the product of abstract symbolic or cognitive structures,

---

14 | See Heidegger on the primordial relation of humans to things (1962: 95), "[the] kind of dealing which is closest to us is [...] not a bare perceptual cognition, but rather that kind of concern which manipulates things and puts them to use; and this has its own kind of 'knowledge'."

15 | "[...] our default way of being in the world is characterized by practical action." (Popova 2015: 18)

but are created as a result of the active involvement of hominids in the world. (Gamble/Porr 2005: 9)

Entering into practical associations with things, in other words, being translated and enrolled into actor-networks is what started Kubrick's apes on the road that finally led to space stations. It is reasonable to assume that there was, and still is a kind of "intelligence" embedded in the way we deal with things of all kinds in everyday life that lies not only in our big brains or linguistic abilities, but also in the affordances of the things themselves. Interactions with the environment are not completely isolated from social interactions. In his reconstruction of the evolution of cognition, Donald (1991) describes the cognitive abilities of pre-humans as "mimetic culture." The first major advance in the evolution of human cognitive abilities could well be understood as the development of a mimetic ability among hominids. Mimesis is on the one hand non-linguistic, but on the other hand is fundamentally different from mere mimicry and imitation that is found in apes, birds, and other animals. Apes and many animals are able to mimic and even imitate conspecifics or other species. What distinguished prehumans from the episodic culture of apes as well as the linguistic culture of *Homo sapiens* could well have been what Donald terms "mimesis".

According to Donald, mimesis can involve many different modalities such as "voice, facial expressions, eye movement, manual signs and gestures, postural attitudes, patterned whole-body movements of various sorts, and long sequences of these elements [...]" (169). Doing something is therefore also communication. The direct perception of action *as* a specific activity, such as chopping wood or hunting, identifies actors following goals according to rules or conventions. Carrying out a particular act as mimesis involves "re-enactment and re-presenting an event or relationship" (169). Cognitive science itself has begun to turn away from a Cartesian notion of the knowing subject somehow locked up inside the brain.[16] Cognition and mind are being understood in a new way. Traditional philosophy of knowledge and cognitive science have been "based on the idea that whatever else is true of mental processes – perceiving, remembering, thinking, reasoning, and so on – they exist in brains" (Rowlands 2010: 2).

---

16 | This is the thesis of the 4e model (embedded, enacted, extended, embodied) of cognitive science, which we will discuss in Part 3.

Mimetic representation, as Donald points out, is pre-linguistic. Not only can it be considered the evolutionary precursor of language, but it is still a significant form of communication in human society today.[17]

New directions in cognitive science support Donald's evolutionary theory. For the new non-Cartesian cognitive science, practical activities as well as things located outside the brain in the environment are a constitutive part of cognition. Cognition is distributed in the environment and is therefore not a property of the brain alone. This new approach to cognitive science claims that mind is "embodied," "embedded," "enacted," and "extended."[18] The ideas of mind being enacted and extended are perhaps the closest to ANT's view of meaning as a network effect. As Rowlands puts it:

> The idea that mental processes are *enacted* is the idea that they are made up not just of neural processes but also of things that the organism does more generally – that they are constituted in part by the ways in which an organism acts on the world and the ways in which world, as a result, acts back on that organism. The idea that mental processes are *extended* is the idea that they are not located exclusively inside an organism's head but extend out, in various ways, into the organism's environment. (Rowlands 2010: 3)

Long after practical and distributed intelligence appeared did language as we know it evolve. Language "translates" in its own way this practical and extended knowing into signs, symbols, and words. What came out when language joined the network was most probably a *story*, that is, a narrative in which the roles that all involved entities play when they do things together become organized.[19] We will argue in later sections, partly as a critique of the school of thought known as "communicative constitution of organizations," that the appearance, even dominance of language in the theory of society and organizations has not displaced narrative and its close association to mimesis.

---

17 | We will return to this below in the discussion of narrative in Part 3.

18 | See Rowlands (2010) for an overview of research and models in non-Cartesian cognitive science.

19 | According to Ricoeur (1984-1988) narrative is the way that time and action become expressed in language.

In the tale we are telling narrative is important not only because leading organizational theorists such as Karl Weick (1995) understand narrative as constitutive of organizations, but because it is in stories that persons and entities are assigned roles, given functions, and linked together in a series of events.[20] Storytelling, or *narrative*, is that form of language in which the assigning of roles and functions to actors in a meaningful series of events takes place. The stone does things and becomes an actor in the same way a human does things. In myths and fairy tales things appear animate, forceful, and sometimes independent of humans with intentions and interests of their own. We will return to this when we discuss the importance of *narrative communication* below. Narrative may well be one of the earliest ways in which language translates the world into its own kind of semiotic network. But we are getting ahead of our story. Let's go back to the hand, the axe, and the wood.

INFORMATION

We spoke of links, associations, or interfaces as that which we hold on to, or just as well what is holding on to us, when we put the tools we are using aside. How is this possible? What is the link that makes it possible to hold on to something once it has been let go of? As we saw, the interface, the relation, the mediation is not some third thing in-between the hand and the axe, but the "fit" between them. The handle of the axe has to be formed in a certain way and made of a certain kind of material with sufficient weight and consistency in order to be usable for this purpose. If not, it could not be held at all, or holding it would not be of any use for chopping wood. On the side of the activity of cutting, that is, where the axe and the wood meet and are linked together, the head of the axe has to be hard and sharp, and the wood the right size, shape, and consistency to be able to be cut. What this shows is that it is the links, the interfaces, or relations between hand, axe, and wood that constitutes technological mediation. But what are interfaces? Interfaces are not things in themselves. They are relations. We do not stumble over relations. We don't pick them up or throw them at enemies or try to cut wood with them. Nevertheless, without them, we

---

20 | For a lively account of the importance of storytelling in organizations see Seely Brown et al. (2005).

are no different from the baboons who have only their bodies to do things. Monkeys, of course, also see stones and sticks. When a monkey picks up a stone or a stick and uses it to break open a coconut or forage for food we can say it is using it "like" a tool, but only as long as it is held in the hand. That is why our primate relatives drop their "tools" and leave them behind. They never were tools to begin with. For them, what is out of hand is out of mind. Humans, on the contrary, do not just find stones and sticks lying around at the occasion, but "know" – even if not linguistically – that there are such things as axes that can be used in certain ways requiring certain skills even when they are not held in the hand.

For countless generations hominids may also have left their sticks and stones behind, but they carried something else with them. They "knew" in a practical way, when the occasion arose again what stone to use for what and how. This practical knowledge was shared and retained in the community and gave rise to norms and expectations about how individuals should behave. If our hominid ancestors were no longer holding onto the things, what were they holding onto and, recalling the principle of symmetry between humans and non-humans, what was holding on to them? We can assume they held onto and were themselves held by the interfaces, relations, differences, and functions that arise from technical mediation. Even if interfaces are not things, they have their own mode of being that survives the fleeting moment and the episodic here and now of simian social activity. It is tempting to speculate that the specific mode of being of interfaces could be called "information." As Norbert Wiener (1948) provocatively stated, information is information and neither matter nor energy. This definition says more about what information is not, than what it is. The ontological status of information has also been discussed by Floridi (2004), who suggests that information might be thought of as "a special relation or interface between the world and its intelligent inhabitants" (574). Latour (1993) has proposed a relational ontology in which whatever is, is because of the associations it has entered into. The principle of "irreduction" states that "nothing is, by itself, either reducible or irreducible to anything else" (158). In other words, everything is a mediator, or being is mediation. Whenever something appears as independent of associations, this is an illusory effect of what Latour calls "black-boxing."[21]

The relational ontology of "irreduction" can be understood as an answer to the problem posed by Wiener concerning the ontological status of information. Along this line of thought, we propose that technical mediation could be understood as the creation of information, that is, as the mutual introduction of associations, interfaces, differences, and relations into the world. This is the human world. This is the world of meaning. However, it is not a world without or apart from entities. For this reason, the stone axe is a part of the human world and not a part of the simian world. This implies *that the task of creating social order becomes a matter of information control or information design.*[22] It also implies, at least from the point of view of ANT, that the creation of information is not an activity of humans alone. It is the network, and not the individual actors, that is capable of meaningful action. We will return to the idea of information control, or what could also be called information design, in the discussion of social interaction below in Part 3. Erving Goffman, arguably the most important figure in the sociology of interaction, understands social interaction as based upon *setting the stage* for communication. Staging is not merely linguistic, but is done with many different kinds of things. It is, as non-Cartesian cognitive science might put it, embodied, enacted, embedded, and extended. If social interaction is not to take place in disembodied and immaterial vacuum or in an isolated brain, it is necessary to bring bodies and things into play. The dramaturgical stage needs to be set up so that mutual understanding and cooperation become possible. But we are getting ahead of the story again, so let us return to monkeys, stones, and the history of technology.

The gap between a monkey picking up a stone and using it to break open a coconut and a human using a stone axe is filled by hundreds of thousands of generations in which animals and things mutually influenced each other to create links, fits, interfaces that didn't disappear each time a stone was dropped. The gap between the first hominid that used the bone as a weapon and the space station is also filled with hundreds of thousands

---

21 | Latour (1994: 32) defines "blackboxing" as "a process that makes the joint production of actors and artifacts entirely opaque."

22 | See Belliger/Krieger (2016) for a discussion of information as a "mode of existence."

of years of doing, testing, adapting, and translating. This is admittedly a big gap, but Kubrick's breathtaking visualizing of the history of technology quite credibly bridges it in a few seconds. What we do not see in the film is the process of adding link to link, fit to fit, and relation to relation in ever longer and more complex chains of translations, enrollments, and associations. How can a few links become many links? How can a stone axe become a factory? How can small networks be extended almost indefinitely?

QUANTITY IS QUALITY

One important difference between human social order and that of animals is the incomparably greater quantity of the "actors" that humans can enroll into actor-networks. We tend to overlook the small incremental changes that took place over four million years of evolution that make it appear today as though society and nature have nothing at all in common. Even if it appears today that there is an absolute gap between the social and the natural just as there is an absolute gap between the individual and the organization, it is reasonable to assume that we are dealing with an evolutionary continuum. Quantity merges into quality. This means that human social order is not the result of a more or less successful struggle of "culture" against "nature." Instead, it can be seen as the ongoing process of translating and enrolling ever more natural entities into social relationships and making more and more social relationships partake of the stability and complexity of things.[23] We have neither a social world on one side nor a natural world on the other, but smaller and larger continuities, that is to say, networks, in which humans, animals, and things participate in links, associations, and interfaces. Once the focus shifts to networks, actors, both human and non-human, exist only insofar as they act, that is, construct networks and only insofar as they themselves are products of networking. This is not the familiar sociological problem of the chicken and the egg

---

23 | As Latour (1994) puts it, "The difference between an ancient or 'primitive' collective and a modern or 'advanced' one is not that the former manifests a rich mixture of social and technical culture while the latter exhibits a technology devoid of ties with the social order. The difference, rather, is that the latter translates, crosses over, enrolls, and mobilizes *more elements*, more intimately connected, with a more finely woven social fabric than the former does" (47).

again, since we are talking always about the same thing, about networks. What traditional sociology sees as local interactions, ANT sees as small networks. Where traditional sociology sees as macro-structures, ANT sees as large networks. There is no magic involved in moving from one to the other, no dualism of ontological domains, no gap that somehow has to be bridged. With regard to organizations, this means that organizations are not some kind of entity independent of those activities of network-building of which they consist. What distinguishes us from baboons und chimpanzees is the much more active role that many more artefacts play in processes of network-building. It is because things become "artifacts," or what Latour (2010) calls "factishes," that they obtain a "voice" and a role to play in "our" world. Paradoxically, it is the non-human that makes us human.

Floridi (2014: 26ff.) describes how networks become more and more complicated and extended by distinguishing between first, second, and third order technologies. First order technologies consist of few links, second order technologies consist of more links, and third order technologies potentially consist of an unlimited number of links. When the axe works upon the branch of a tree, this can be considered a first order technology. Someone works upon a tool, which works upon a natural material, such as wood. When a hammer hits a nail, or a screwdriver turns a screw, however, one technology is working upon another piece of technology. The nail is made to fit the hammer and the screw is made to fit the screwdriver. Anyone who has tried to pound a nail with a screwdriver can appreciate this distinction. When two technologies are fitted to each other and work upon each other, this may be considered a second order technology. Now let us consider the case when it is no longer a human hand that swings the hammer or turns the screwdriver, but a robot. In this case, we have what Floridi calls third order technology. One technology works upon another that works upon yet another. First order technologies are short chains with few links or interfaces. Second order technologies mobilize more actors and are longer chains, with more interfaces. Third order technologies mobilize even more actors and are potentially unlimited chains of interfaces and can even become closed loops. We could suppose that computers work on robots, who work on electronic components, plastics, etc. in order to produce robots that produce computers and so on.

Third order technologies can in principle become complex adaptive systems exhibiting much the same behavior as living organisms, independent of human operators or at least only distantly affected by humans. This scenario has become a popular theme in science fiction and, of course, played an important role in Kubrick's vision of the future where the computer HAL 9000 decided it could dispense with its human operator. What Floridi's three orders of technology imply is that in the course of evolution not only do more and more artifacts become involved, but also more and more people who are organized in more and more different ways. The more links in the chain, the more complex the associations between humans and non-humans, the more we move along the line from stone axes to space stations, or even beyond. As Latour (1994: 53) puts it, "Humans, for millions of years, have extended their social relations to other actants with which, with whom, they have swapped many properties, and with which, with whom, they form *collectives*."[24] The space station, as we saw, is not a thing in itself, but a very long chain of links between actors of all kinds, both human and non-human. To speak, as we do today, of a global network society, is to express how global networks of connected actors constitute our world. The space station can be considered as a part of many different organizations. Somewhere along the line between stone axes and space stations, things got not only out of hand, but they also got organized.

What the new paradigm attends to are the moves by which any given collective extends its social fabric to other entities. First, there is translation, the means by which we inscribe in a different matter features of our social order; next, the crossover, which consists in the exchange of properties among nonhumans; third, the enrollment, by which a nonhuman is seduced, manipulated, or induced into the collective; fourth, the mobilization of nonhumans inside the collective, which adds fresh unexpected resources, resulting in strange new hybrids; and, finally, displacement, the direction the collective takes once its shape, extent, and composition have been altered. (Latour 1994: 46)

---

24 | Latour (1994: 63) has his own myth of social evolution in which humans and non-humans influence each other in ever greater and more complicated forms. This begins with basic tools and moves on to articulation of social differentiation which becomes larger societies that become megamachines, networks of power, and finally planetary governance or political ecology.

CONCLUSION

We have not forgotten that the purpose of this discussion is not to investigate the origins of technology, but the origins of organizations. How can technical mediation as described above shed light on the nature of organizations? Our claim is that it can. The question of how we get from a simple technology like the stone axe to a complex technology like a space station becomes for us more relevant when it becomes the question of how a simple activity like chopping wood can become a complex coordinated activity like building a house, or better yet, constructing, launching, and maintaining a space station. How do we bridge the gap between someone chopping wood in the back yard and many people working together to accomplish complex tasks. The space station is not just a piece of technology, as we saw. It is a network of *organizations*. Traditionally, sociologists have posed the question of the nature and origin of organization as the question of how individual, fleeting, and unstable social *interactions* can become stable, complex *organizations*. The question of what makes an ape using a stone to open a coconut into a prehumen using a stone tool is not different from the question of what makes a couple of students playing with computers in a garage into Google, Apple, or Microsoft. How do face-to-face interactions turn into big organizations? How do a few people chatting in a coffee shop turn into a project team at IBM? From the sociological point of view, it looks like magic. Following Latour, our claim is that this magical transformation of micro interactions and inconsequential small talk into macro social actors who do important "big talk" has a lot to do with what has been described above as technical mediation.

No one denies that everything we do in organizations somehow is involved with or directly depends upon technology. This is already an important indication that human beings alone do not constitute organizations. No matter what kind of organization it may be and no matter how large or small, organizations are always made up of many different kinds of non-humans. Nevertheless, organizational studies has never understood itself to be the study of technical artifacts. Organization theory sees itself as a theory of society, a discipline dealing with human subjects and not technical objects. It is of course true that contemporary organization theory, including the school of thought that names itself "communicative constitution of organizations," which we will discuss in detail below, admit the importance of things and technologies as parts of organizations. There is, however, little discussion of non-humans as *necessary conditions* for the constitution of organizations or of the ways in which non-humans contribute to the *constitution* of organization. As the very name suggest, the "communicative" constitution of organizations emphasizes language and intentional speech. It would seem that technological mediation is something that happens back stage or on the periphery. Technology is nice to have, but things do not talk, make decisions, design strategies, hire and fire, etc. Consequently, as traditional organization theory assumes, things do not constitute organizations. If anything does, then it is communication, and it is considered obvious that things don't talk. Theories of organization assume that all that is needed is human beings who communicate. Such "talking heads" may decide that IT, or some other technology, is useful, but there are many examples of organizations that get along quite well without it. It is precisely this traditional view of organizations that we wish to question. We have argued in this section that organizations, as all social order, are a product of technical mediation and that what is organized in organizations is nothing other than the many links between humans and non-humans that we have called interfaces or mediations.

From the point of view of ANT, things become "actors" that play roles in actor-networks. This is no less true for bones than for space stations. The space station does not exist alone. It makes a difference. It does things, influences others, determines many different activities, and conditions all of which are in different ways connected to it, as builders, astronauts, researchers, institutions, political bodies, and even opponents. Not to be forgotten, it also has an environmental impact. The space station is not a thing in itself. It consists of many links to organizations in all areas of society. It is quite literally not a thing, but a hub in a network. Without its links, a hub is not a hub. In addition to this, when we speak of a space station, we are not speaking only of transportation or communication networks, but many associated actors in business, politics, and even in religious and artistic networks, as Kubrick's film proves. If the space station is not a thing, but a network perhaps society and organizations are also not things. Instead of social substances, we have social processes. Social processes, however, are not naked interactions between talking heads, but technical mediations. From this point of view, organizations of all kinds appear under the aspect of what can be called "networking." Networking, following ANT, is that unique form of mutual influence made durable and stable by means of the durability and stability of things. The human social link is an interface with things.

We began with a question. What makes human society different from societies of animals? Why do humans scale up cooperative action into organizations such as Volkswagen, the United Nations, the ETH, Mayo Clinic, the Work Bank, political parties, and Green Peace? If it is not that there is a certain kind of thing called human society, into which individuals are born, in which they live and die, and in which there also happen to be technological artifacts, systems of signs called languages, and patterns of behavior known as cultures, then what is it? We have tried to show that ANT can help us get a handle on what it is that makes human social order something special. Latour has proposed a "performative" paradigm of human society that has similarities as well as differences to primate social order, but not the ones we would expect. Human society is based on interaction, just as primate societies. Human interaction, however is "organized," that is, it goes beyond bodily interactions among individuals in the here and now.[25] Interactions for humans are never purely *hic et nunc*. They include symbols, artefacts, and technologies and are all held together by activities of organizing. Organizing is not what happens, when people do things together, this is what monkeys also do, but when things quite literally "get out of hand" and yet still play roles and influence social relations. What makes organizations more than mere interaction, which monkeys also do, are the many non-humans that have been linked up to human activities in actor-networks.

Human society as opposed to the societies of primates is a society in which things of all kinds have literally gotten out of hand by entering into associations with other things. They no longer are dependent on the hands that hold them or throw them, they have become "agents" or "actors" in their right. They have become "artifacts," or in the broadest sense of the term "technology." Technical mediation is a social order in which things have become actors and not merely temporary extensions of

---

25 | "As against the social interaction of monkeys, the social interaction of humans always appears to be more dislocated. There is no simultaneity nor continuity nor homogeneity. Far from limiting itself to bodies that are co-present by way of their attention to each other and their continual work of vigilance and construction; for humans one must appeal to other elements, other times, other places and other actors in order to grasp an interaction." (Latour 1996: 234)

the body. This means that the human world is not exclusively human, but full of "quasi-objects" and "quasi-subjects" organized into heterogeneous and hybrid networks. Again, we are faced with the paradox that it is non-humans that make us human and that the social world is not made up of people at all, but of relations, networks, and information. What does this mean for a theory of organizations? Actor-network theory is not explicitly a theory of organizations. It is a theory of social order in a very broad sense that includes technologies and nature within the social. Are there organizational theories that can be interpreted in a way that is compatible with ANT, and even allow themselves to be enriched and extended by ANT? This is the question we will attempt to answer in Part 2.

2. The Communicative Constitution
of Organizations CCO

The theory of organizations is as new and as old as organizations themselves. Thomas Hobbes spoke of the state as a personified Leviathan already in the 17th century. The first modern organizations arose in the industrial era. The first large corporations are a product of the 20th century. Friedrich Taylor's (1911) scientific management conceived of the organization as a machine consisting of many different functions that determine division of labor, coordination of activities, hierarchies, and functional processes. Max Weber (1922) described the ideal type of organization as bureaucracy in which clearly defined rules and regulations governed tasks and duties. Empirical research and experience increasingly made it clear that organizations did not function like machines. When it became obvious that workers at all levels did not behave as the mechanistic model of the organization assumed, attention was directed to human relations, psychological factors, and group dynamics. The key to understanding organizations was found in "human relations." The famous "Hawthorne studies" (1939) showed that it is people and how they individually and idiosyncratically interpret and react to commands, rules, situations, and surroundings that determine how an organization functions, what management means, and what an organization really is. It became apparent, that one could not understand organizations without taking account of interpersonal and group processes, socialization into a group culture, internalization of norms and values, attitudes, etc. Many different disciplines contributed to organizational theory at this stage; economics, social psychology, philosophy, and sociology. These various theories and disciplines, however, did not focus directly on the role that communication plays in constituting organizations. The linguistic turn in philosophy, the rise of communication science, and the influence of major social theories based on communication (Habermas, Luhmann) led to a greater interest in the role that communication plays in organizing. According to Taylor and Van Every (2011) the human relations approach "did not address … the issue of the constitution of the organization itself: how it occurs in and through communication [...]" (7). Taylor and Van Every conclude their review of the origins of organization theory with the remark that "what was still lacking was any real theory of communication as the key to understanding organizations [...]" (7). In their view, the historical development of organization theory leads directly to the field of "organizational communication."

Within the field of organizational communication, the work of Karl Weick (1979, 1995) has played a major role in opening the door to process views of organizations.[1] Furthermore, Weick made it clear that communication is not something that happens only within organizations, but is constitutive of any organization. His focus was on the communicative process of organizing instead of on organizations as pre-existing structures. For Weick organizations arise from processes of "sensemaking." Summarizing and systematizing the results of much empirical research in organizational psychology and sociology, Weick (1995: 17ff.) argues that cooperative action of any kind arises from activities of sensemaking that are essentially communicative. Organizing occurs when people make sense of a situation. Meaningless events take on a pattern and become ordered. Sensemaking, however, occurs in and through communication. Communication therefore is the basis of all cooperative action and therefore of all organization. Isolated individuals apart from social relations do not do sensemaking. Sensemaking is initiated by a crisis, a surprise, a discrepancy in the usual course of events.[2] In order to set sensemaking in motion, something has to be perceived as not making sense, as a *problem*. When a crisis or problem arises, it raises the question of the *identities and roles* of the actors involved. Who are we

---

1 | "The central argument is that any organization is the way it runs through the process of organizing" (Weick 1979: 90). See also Hernes (2008) for a discussion of process theories of organization.

2 | See the pragmatism of Peirce and Dewey where meaning and knowledge begin in inquiry, as well as the discussion in Taylor/Van Every (2011) on the pragmatic foundations of organizational communication theory.

and who are the others involved? What roles do we play such that this problem has arisen and such that a solution can be found?

The situation in which the actors are perceived to be involved is constructed by *retrospective accounts* of what has happened in the past. Where did this problem come from? What went wrong? Who was responsible? In sensemaking not only accounts of past events, but also interpretations of the present situation, *perceptions of what counts as relevant*, as a problem, as a possible solution, are selective and programmatic. Not everybody sees the same events as relevant and problematic in the same way at the same time. Facts are always facts from a certain point of view. This implies that *others must be persuaded* that something went wrong or that a certain course of action is the right thing to do. The problem must become a *shared problem* and the solution must be accepted by most of the people, or at least the most important people involved. In making sense of a situation and deciding upon a course of action, or perhaps non-action, *plausibility and coherence* of the story about what happened are more important criteria of meaning and truth than factuality. What in the end makes sense is not necessarily that which may be exactly accurate and factual from a supposedly objective point of view. Sensemaking is always *interpretation* and not merely mirroring so-called facts. Finally, in keeping with Weick's process view of organization, sensemaking is an *ongoing activity*. Identities and situational descriptions are constantly changing and are in principle always changeable. There is no such thing as sense that is "made" as a final product, but only sense in the making.

Weick's views of organizing as a process of communicative sensemaking were very influential. They led to the development of what has become the school of thought known under the title of the "communicative constitution of organizations" or CCO.[3] CCO theorists are primarily concerned with how organizations emerge from face-to-face interactions. CCO is a bottom up approach. Organizations of all kinds are generated, maintained, modified, or deconstructed by means of communication. Weick's concept of sensemaking, however, did not preclude the question of how organizations influence, condition, constrain, and enable communication. Although the focus for Weick and for CCO approaches is on micro-interactions, often called "conversations," it is undeniable that interaction does not occur in a vacuum. Communication is always in some way situated in

---

3 | See Brummans et al. (2014) for a discussion of the development of CCO.

an organizational "context." The organizational context provides a set of identities, such as "manager," "employee," "trainer," "accountant," and so on. It also provides typical frames of action, such as "training," "selling," "controlling." In addition to this, actors are provided with certain patterns of behavior or scripts that describe the ways in which training, controlling, selling and so on is to be done. The fact that organizations seem to provide contexts for interaction and provide typical and standardized identities, frames, and scripts for action has been the basis for "new institutional" (Scott 2001) top-down theories of organizations.

For new institutionalism, institutions are "cultural-cognitive, normative, and regulative elements that, together with associated activities and resources, provide stability and meaning to social life" (Scott 2003: 879). The new institutionalism argues that organizations take on typical forms and appear similar, despite very different purposes and activities. This can only be explained by influences that constrain how organizations can be constructed. Normally people behave according to typical and standardized norms. Norms limit options and channel behavior, as it were automatically. When speaking of norms, the new institutionalism emphasizes cognitive constraints and not moral obligation. "Compliance occurs in many circumstances because other types of behavior are inconceivable; routines are followed because they are taken for granted as 'the way we do these things'" (Scott 2001: 57). Actors involved in sensemaking are not on their own. They are constrained and influenced implicitly or explicitly by the normative boundaries of society or culture, as well as by the resources of this kind that organizations offer in order to make sense out of a particular situation.

New institutionalism has attempted to explain how organizations influence communication by relying upon theories of "cognitive constraint." Organizations *"function to contextualize sensemaking by imposing cognitive constraints on the actors who do the sensemaking"* (Weber/Glynn 2006: 1642). Social and cultural institutions constrain the perception of identities, frames, and scripts so that actors "automatically" identify with certain roles and act according to certain scripts. As Weber and Glynn (2006: 1640) put it "The primary contextual mechanism recognized in the extant literature is that of 'internalized cognitive constraint' whereby institutions narrow how and what sense can be made..." In this way, organizations are claimed to affect sensemaking by limiting the possibilities of interpreting situations, of assuming identities, and of performing expected actions. Weber and Glynn (2006) find the cognitive constraint model basically correct, but too narrow and propose extending the list of institutional influences by including "priming," "editing," and "triggering." Priming means that institutions provide "perceptual filters" that "lead people to extract cues that activate identities, frames, and role expectations for particular situations" (Weber/Glynn 2006: 1648).

Institutions "edit" sensemaking by enabling intersubjective corrigibility of action. When someone acts unexpectedly or inappropriately, they are confronted with feedback from others involved that corrects or "edits" their interpretation of themselves, of the situation, and of their course of action. "The mechanism by which institutions influence action formation processes is therefore one of *retrospective editing of actions and meaning* [...]" (1651). Finally, institutions "trigger" sensemaking by virtue of inherent contradictions, conflicts, ambiguities, and discontinuities. Weber and Glynn offer the example of how changes in traditional employer/employee roles from paternalistic, long-term employment to contractarian, flexible employer/employee relations led to misunderstandings, ambiguities, and problems that triggered sensemaking. Extending the usual new institutionalist view, institutions are claimed not only to "provide stability and meaning" (Scott) to social life, but they also create problems, conflicts, and uncertainties that call for sensemaking. New institutionalism is important because it has in any case made it clear that some kind of macro-structures seem to influence sensemaking, and that therefore a purely bottom up theory is inadequate.

In summary, despite emphasis on sensemaking in the form of interactional episodes, or conversations on the micro-level, there seems to be more involved in organizations than individual, face-to-face encounters. One cannot choose to be anybody one wants, interpret a given situation as one likes, and do what one pleases in an organization. There seems to be two aspects to sensemaking. The individual actors on the one side and organizational constraints on the other side. This duality sets the stage for the questions that CCO theorists attempt to answer. How can the various influences of organizations on sensemaking be explained on the basis of a theory of communication alone? Weick left important questions with regard to what organizations are und how exactly they may be said to be "constituted" by sensemaking unanswered. Indeed, all the major concepts in the title "communicative constitution of organizations" have proven to be problematic. What is meant by organization? Is an organization something other than the communicative processes that give rise to it? Does an organization contain specific forms of communication within its boundaries and exclude others? Is communication in itself and on every occasion constitutive of organizations? What specific kind of communication constitutes identity, social roles, frames, and courses of action? What kinds of communication explain the many different kinds of organizations that society consists of? What exactly does "constitution" mean? Those thinkers who have come to associate their work under the title of "communicative constitution of organizations" (CCO) have explicitly raised and in various ways attempted to answer these important questions.[4]

CCO focuses not only on specific aspects of communication as constitutive of organizations, but also on communication in general as an organizing force (Putnam/McPhee 2009: 196). An overview of CCO literature makes it apparent that "different forms of communication, such as linguistic properties, nonverbal symbols, and interaction episodes, work together in complex ways to constitute organizations" (Putnam/McPhee 2009: 199). At the center of CCO theories lie questions concerning how communication goes beyond the limitations of present and local face-to-face interaction, how identities and actors, both individual and collective, come into being and do things in a coordinated manner, and how communication and organizing are bound up with material entities and non-human actors.[5] The various schools within CCO may offer different answers to these questions, but they have one thing in common:

[...] the general claim is that if communication is indeed constitutive of organization, it cannot be considered to be simply one of the many factors involved in organizing, and cannot be merely the vehicle for the expression of pre-existing 'realities'; rather, it is the means by which organizations are established, composed, designed, and sustained. Consequently, organizations can no longer be seen as objects, entities, or 'social facts' inside of which communication occurs. Organizations are portrayed, instead, as ongoing and precarious accomplishments realized, experienced, and

---

4 | See Ptunam/Noctery (2009); Cooren et al. (2011); and the overview of CCO research in Brummans et al. in Putnam/Mumby (2014), as well as in Schoenborn/ Blaschke (2014).

5 | See Putnam/McPhee (2009: 199ff.).

identified primarily – if not exclusively – in communication processes. (Cooren et al. 2011: 1150)

In an influential statement, Smith (1993) classified the various theories describing organizations as based on communication into "container" theories, "product" theories, and "equivalence" theories. Typical of container theories is the assumption that organizing communication takes place *within* the organization. The organization builds a kind of container for specifically organizational forms of communication. This view presupposes the existence of the organization as a macro-structure in which individuals act and communicate. Product theories on the contrary see the organizations not as preexisting containers for social activities, but as a product of these activities. Organizations emerge from communication. Nevertheless, it is emphasized that the organizational structures emerging from social interactions then condition, steer, and form these interactions. What is described is therefore a circular and interdependent movement from part to whole and back from whole to part. Product theories are usually explicitly based on Giddens structuration theory (Giddens 1984). They attempt to link micro and macro levels together without eliminating the distinction between the two. Finally, much like Weick, theories of equivalence make the strong claim that communication is organizing and model organizations *as* communication. Organizations do not contain communication, and neither do organizations emerge out of communication only to become macro structures conditioning communication. Organization and communication are not distinct levels of social order or behavior. Equivalence theories claim that communication is organization and organization is nothing other than communication. Organization and communication are the same.

CCO theories tend to position themselves more in the vicinity of equivalence theories, or at least, there is a clear prioritization of interaction. As Cooren et al. (2011: 20) put it, a "CCO perspective of organizational sensemaking considers organizations not as a given, but as emerging in, and indeed constituted by or incarnated in local episodes of communication."[6] However, it is precisely the sameness of organizing and communication

---

6 | See also the six premises that Cooren et al. (2011) claim "define what the CCO perspective entails in terms of research agenda, methodologies, and epistemologies" (4).

that poses serious problems. As Smith noted, the equivalence thesis is not so much an explanation as a tautology. To say that organizing is communication and communication organizing amounts in the end to claiming that organizing is organizing. The question that remains unanswered, as Taylor argues (2000, 2009) is what specific kind of communication constitutes organizations and what are the defining characteristics of organizations as opposed to other forms of social order and other forms of communication. Obviously, so Taylor, there is a difference between a disordered mob and a political party, a large corporation, or an NGO. Obviously, small talk at the bar during happy hour is not the same as a meeting of the board of directors. Communication does not start from zero every time someone opens their mouth, but is situated in pre-existing social contexts and settings and conditioned by them. This leads to the conviction that the strong claim that communication constitutes organizations must rest on innovative and convincing theories of communication.

Among the often-cited attempts to create foundational theories of CCO are the "four flows" model of McPhee and Zaug, the "co-orientation" model of Taylor, and the "ventriloquism" theory of Cooren. In addition to these North American thinkers, some German scholars following Luhmann (Schoenborn 2011; Seidl 2005; Schoenborn/Blascke 2014) position their work within CCO. In the following, we will focus on the Anglo-American theories since the German wing of the group relies more on models derived from social network analysis. We will review these theories with the purpose of introducing the idea of communication as "staging" (Goffman) and then develop the link between staging and narrative in order to arrive at the idea of organizing as networking. We will argue that networking constitutes organizations neither bottom up, as in CCO, nor top down, as in the new institutionalism, but non-dualistically and therefore without needing to assume micro and macro levels of social order or a distinction between agency and structure or even the primacy of intentional speech.

FOUR FLOWS – MCPHEE AND ZAUG

In their programmatic article, "The Communicative Constitution of Organizations, A Framework for Explanation" (2009), Robert D. McPhee and Pamela Zaug present "a theoretical framework for the communicative constitution of complex organizations" (McPhee/Zaug 2009: 22). Organizations, they argue, emerge from "four types of constituting communication processes or [...] 'flows'" (22). They claim that the communicative constitution of organizations "requires not just one, but four types of messages, or more specifically types of message flow or interaction process" (21). The four flows model does not describe what kinds of communication take place within organizations conceived of as containers, but rather it describes the necessary communicative conditions for the emergence of organizations. The concept of "flow" is traced back to Weick's (1979) insistence on the process character of organizing and sensemaking as well as Mintzberg (1979) and Lash and Ury (1994) who understand communication as "circulating systems of fields of messages" (McPhee/Zaug 2009: 29). For Weick, organizations are not entities or systems, but forms of sensemaking that takes place in communication. Although sensemaking can easily be identified and described in episodes of face-to-face interaction, it is more difficult to describe how fleeting interactions lead to large, formal organizations. In order to make it clear what exactly should be explained, McPhee and Zaug cite Smith's (1993) useful classification of theories dealing with the relation of communication to organization.

As noted above, Smith classified theories of organizational communication as either container theories, product theories, or equivalence theories. Following Weick, McPhee and Zaug claim to favor the equivalence model, but agree with Smith's reservations on theories of equivalence, namely, that to claim organization is communication and vice versa is not an explanation as much as a tautology, which explains nothing. For McPhee and Zaug, the central question for theory construction as well as empirical research is how do interactions constitute organization and what exactly is meant by the key terms of CCO, "organization," "communication," and "constitution."

For an explanation of what is meant by "constitution" McPhee and Zaug refer to Giddens' classic work *Constitution of Society* (1984). Following Giddens, they argue that "a pattern or array of types of interaction constitute organizations insofar as they make organizations what they are, and insofar as basic features of the organization are implicated in the system of interaction" (McPhee/Zaug 2009: 27). Further, they define "organization" as "a social interaction system, influenced by prevailing economic and legal institutional practices, and including coordinated action and interaction within and across a socially constructed system boundary, manifestly directed toward a privileged set of outcomes" (28). This definition includes basic characteristics of an organization such as boundaries, processes, internal connections, and external relations that will become important in identifying the four flows of communication that constitute organizations. Finally, they assume that communication has constitutive force in constructing agency as well as linking actors together. Following Weick and Giddens, they assume that not all communication is constitutive of organization, but only those messages and "interactive episodes" that are carried out by a "conscious, capable agent" (28) and that belong to clear processes which are required for an organization to exist. These process make up the four flows and are called "membership negation," "organizational self-structuring," "activity coordination," and "institutional positioning" (22). By analyzing constitutive communication into four necessary processes and types of messages, McPhee and Zaug claim that on the one hand they can uphold the equivalence model of communication and organization while on the other hand escape tautology.[7] For McPhee and Zaug "complex organizations exist only in the relatedness of these four types of flow" (21). Briefly stated:

The four flows link the organization to its members (membership negotiation), to itself reflexively (self-structuring), to the environment (institutional positioning); the fourth is used to adapt interdependent activity to specific work situations and problems (activity coordination). (McPhee/Zaug 2009: 33)

The first of the four flows, "membership negotiation," is communication that relates an organization to its members and members to an organization. Typical forms of membership negotiation are hiring and firing, recruitment, human resources management, socialization in an organization such as learning the corporate culture, ways of speaking and acting that are typical, compatible, and expected by the organization, authorization and access to resources, power relations and hierarchical positions, and any kind of communication that binds members of an organization together. Obviously, every member must know that they are

---

7 | The reliance on Giddens' theory of structuration, however, points more in the direction of a product model than equivalence. One could even ask if the four flows do not describe communication within organizations, which would place the theory also near to container models.

members *of* the organization. This implies that membership negotiation constitutes both members and the organization, since there is no organization without members and no members without an organization to which they belong. Without flows of information between those who are identified as members and that which is identifiable as the organization, there can be no such thing as an organization. In this sense, membership negotiation is a necessary condition for the existence of an organization. As a necessary condition of the communicative constitution of organizations, membership negotiation for McPhee and Zaug clearly implies that "organizations, like all social forms, exist only as a result of human agency [...] only individual humans can communicate, so when communication constitutes organization, the relation of the communicators to the organization is important" (35). This leads to the claim that the members can be thought of as "parts or limbs of the organization" (35).

It is important to note at this point, that there is a tension between the idea of a flow of communication in which organizations and members relate to each other and the idea that only members actually possess agency, do things, and communicate. If only human agency is possible, what role does the organization play in the communicative process? For McPhee and Zaug the agency of organizations becomes apparent "when they draw members in, and lead them to take part in and understand the interactional world unique to the organization" (35). The organization is the actor that is doing the hiring and firing, distributing authorization, etc. What kind of agency does the organization have? How does communication constitute a collective actor such as an organization and how does such a collective actor communicate with its members? Are the individual actors on the same level as the collective actor? Is not collective action merely another word for structure? If so, how has the tension between agency and structure been overcome? Not only is the exclusion of non-human agency a potential difficulty for McPhee and Zaug, since it is almost impossible not to speak of the organization as a collective actor somehow "doing" things and "communicating," or at least conditioning, steering, and limited the communication of the members. There is also the problem that it is often unclear where participating in an organization begins and where it ends. Many organizations depend heavily on activities that are not clearly within or without the boundaries of the organization. Are organizational boundaries always clear? Independent contractors and partners are a case in point. If membership negotiation is a constitutive form of communication for organizations, what becomes of organizations that do not have clear boundaries and univocal rules of inclusion and exclusion? We will return to this problem later, since it is a typical characteristic of networks that no clear boundaries are available or even desired.

The second of the four flows is called "organizational self-structuring." Self-structuring is the "reflexive" activity of "design" and "control" (35). It is self-structuring that "distinguishes organizations from groupings such as lynch mobs or mere neighborhoods [...]" (35). Self-structuring is a "communication process among organizational role-holders and groups" (36) and therefore similar to those communication processes that may be termed "activity coordination" (36). Nonetheless, it is primarily a matter of "internal relations, norms, and social entities" that act as a "skeleton" for shaping work processes and not the work processes themselves. Every organization must have a division of labor, a set of tasks that need to be done in a certain order, a general plan of work and policies for carrying out the necessary tasks. Typical examples of this kind of flow are all kinds of official documents such as "charters, organization charts, policy and procedure manuals; decision-making and planning forums; orders, directives; [...] processes of employee evaluation and feedback; budgeting, accounting, and other formalized control processes [...]" (36). The function of this flow is to "steer the organization or any part of it," which include "processes that design the organization, the setting up of subsystems, hierarchical relationships, and structural information processes arrangements [...]" (36). Here again, those organizations that are relatively unstructured or loosely connected and which are often called "network" organizations pose a problem for the theory. There are obviously forms of organized collaboration and partnerships that are not constituted by self-structuring understood as "pre-fixing work arrangements and norms rather than let[ting] them emerge during collaboration [...]" or as "authoritative metacommunication that guides but also controls [...] collaboration" (37). Self-structuring gives the organization an "analogue to a sense of self" and "constitutes the organization for itself" such that it becomes possible for the organization to know what it is and what it is not and to clearly differentiate itself from its environment and to have a sense of itself as a "differentiated yet purposeful whole" (38).

The third flow is activity coordination. Activity coordination is the "process of adjusting the work process and solving immediate practical problems" (38) that arise from the need to get a certain job done under conditions of uncertainty. No matter how well structured and standardized an organization may be, there will always be a need to coordinate activities in unique situations. Members are not cogs in a machine. They must actively communicate with each other to settle differences of opinion, collaborate on projects, and coordinate their different but related jobs. Without activity coordination, no one would do more or otherwise than prescribed or planned. Adaptation to circumstances and to problems arising on the spot would be hindered if everyone simply referred to the rules, the manuals, the organogram, standard procedures, etc.

Finally, organizations are constituted by a flow of communication that McPhee und Zaug call "institutional positioning." This includes all communication by which the organization relates to other entities, institutions, or organizations in its environment. This form of communication requires a collective actor or a corporate identity. If Microsoft acquires Nokia Devices and Services, then Microsoft does something and not merely Satya Nadella. Tim Cook did not buy Beatz, Apple did. When a collective actor does something it "positions" itself in relation to other actors, both personal and collective. This typical form of communication has led to theories of organizations as macro actors or even super actors. McPhee and Zaug claim that it is necessary in order to constitute an organization, because every organization co-exists with other organizations or must enter onto a playing field configured by other organizations. Organizations do not arise in a vacuum. There is no first organization. Society consists of organizations as a historical given and as presupposition of communication. Nonetheless, as McPhee and Zaug remark, there is no fixed form of organization and new forms are constantly appearing. This makes it difficult to say in advance how an organization has to position itself. As we will see later, with regard to theories of a network society it would seem possible to suppose that institutional positioning could occur without institutions in the traditional sense. McPhee and Zaug admit that the impact of new media on organizational communication makes it possible that "in some important ways, intra- and inter-organizational cooperation (i.e. activity coordination and institutional positioning) based on informal relations and trust have come to supplant formal structure as modalities of organizational control [...]" (44). Nonetheless, they argue that new forms of organization must take account of the traditional organization whose necessary conditions of emergence are described by the four flows.[8]

It is important to note that there is a residual tension between individual and collective agency in the four flows model. This should be emphasized because it provokes critique from other CCO theorists. On the one hand, the four flows are ascribed to individual agency. The first of the four flows "recounts the struggle of individuals to master or influence their member roles [...]" (42). The second "articulates how organizational leaders design, implement, and suffer problems with decision and control mechanisms." The third focuses on "members engaging in interdependent work or deviating from pure collaborative engagement." Whereas the fourth flow describes the "organization as a partner, often anthropomorphized, in exchange and other social relations with other organizations" (42). The "anthropomorphized" description of organizations as collective actors is clearly expressed when the four flows are presented, as it were, top down from the point of view of the organization. McPhee and Zaug have no problem saying that organizations "*enunciate* and *maintain relations* to their members through membership negotiation." They also do this "to themselves as formally controlled entities through self-structuring," as well as "to their internal subgroups and processes through activity coordination." Finally, organizations enunciate and maintain relations "to their colleagues in a society of institutions through institutional positioning" (emphasis added: 44). This way of speaking makes it difficult to insist upon human agency alone in the flows of communication that supposedly constitute organizations. If there are others, for example, collective actors, involved in organizational communication besides

---

8 | See also the "organizational emergence" framework by Katz/Gartner (1988) for a similar analysis of four basic properties of emergent organizations. For Edelman (2008: 2), "These properties are as follows: *intentionality* – the purposeful effort involved in organization emergence; *resources* – the tangible building blocks of an organization; *boundary* – the creation of protected or formalized areas in which emergence occurs; and *exchange* – the crossing of boundaries to either secure inputs (e.g., resources) or outputs of the organization." What this model neglects, according to Edelman, is "behaviors that lead to enhanced organizational legitimacy and behaviors that lead to organizational knowledge creation, accumulation, and transfer" (3), both of which are "boundary spanning" activities often referred to as social capital and which, as we will argue, derive from organizing as networking.

human individuals, then what theory of communication can account for this? Are the four flows a sufficient explanation of the communicative constitution of organizations?

COORIENTATION, CONVERSATIONS, AND TEXTS — TAYLOR

James R. Talyor is often said to be the founder of the "Montreal School" of CCO (Taylor/Van Every 2011; Brumanns et al. 2014). His work constitutes a major contribution to organization theory (Taylor 1993, 2000, 2009, Taylor/Van Every 2011). In a theoretical reply to McPhee and Zaug's four flows framework, Taylor (2009) argues that McPhee and Zaug leave the main question of *how* exactly communication results in organizations unanswered. Even within the four flows framework, the "puzzle of organization," that is, "how can it be at one and the same time *both* structure *and* action" (Taylor/Van Every 2011: 19) remains unsolved. What the four flows framework describes is structured communication within established organizations. Furthermore, it is unclear what kind of communication fits into the four flows. Weick distinguished between different kinds of interactions, those that are closely coupled, face-to-face, in the here and now, and those that are loosely coupled, disbursed in space and time, and mediated in many ways such as through communiques, protocols, memos, directives, etc. What kind of flow does the model describe? In Taylor's view, the four flows model is not only vague, but in addition to this too deductive in its approach.

McPhee and Zaug begin with a certain ideal conception of what an already established organization is, and then they search for the kinds of communication that this ideal organization requires. The four flows are deduced from the concept of an organization that has clear boundaries, a collective identity, internal work processes, and external relations. The four flows model proceeds top down by defining what kinds of communication would be the necessary conditions for an organization as they define it. Taylor on the contrary argues that in order to explain how communication, regardless of what kind, can constitute something like an organization one must proceed bottom up. In a programmatic statement, Taylor and Van Every (2011) say that "We begin, not by a consideration of organizations but instead by focusing on the elementary act of communication that supports cooperative work" (19). In place of deducing what kinds of communication must occur for an ideal organization to come into being, one should analyze how organizational structure emerges from concrete interactions. Taylor asks how communication actually becomes the process of organizing. For this reason, McPhee's und Zaug's model needs "to be supplemented with a more precise theory of communication that has as its objective to trace the genesis and grounding of organizational form and process in the communication event" (2009: 154-5).

In many important contributions to the field of organizational communication (Taylor 1999, 2000, 2005, 2009; Taylor/Van Every 2000, 2011), Taylor develops a theory of communication upon the basis of pragmatism, linguistics, social psychology, role-theory, ethnomethodology, and the philosophy of language. He defines "communication" as a "simultaneous relationship to something to be done, and to others with whom one is doing it," (2009: 155) and names this "coorientation." For example, A asks B to help him develop an APP for a new online service. Assuming B does not decline the request, developing the APP is the task or the goal to which A and B are now co-oriented. In this constellation, there are three elements. There is A, who initiates the action, which consists in enlisting the help of B in order to accomplish a task, X. It can be said that A and B are *co-oriented* to the same task. They not only have the same goal, but they know this about each other, and they feel that they are bound by a commitment or decision to achieve this goal by means of cooperative action. Coorientation constitutes A and B as a "we." What holds them together is "their" task, "their" goal. They work together to achieve it.

Taylor and Van Every offer a similar analysis of communication based on Peirce's pragmatism, a tradition to which Weick's notion of sensemaking was also indebted. For Peirce the foundation of knowledge and meaning is not to be found in deductive or inductive reasoning, but in inquiry. All knowledge begins with a question, a problem, which is never merely cognitive, but an action arising from a need to do something. For pragmatism, knowing is rooted in doing. Peirce's categories of "firstness," "secondness," and "thirdness" describe the basic structure of action. For Taylor and Van Every (2011) all doing implies a threefold structure, something done, or what Peirce called "firstness," someone who does it ("secondness"), and an interpretation, a frame, a context in which they do it and which gives meaning to what they are doing ("thirdness"). Only when firstness, secondness, and thirdness are present is there meaningful action. Taylor and Van Every (2011) use the example of someone digging a hole in the ground. The hole is the object X. B is doing the digging. And A, that which B is doing to X, can be called "gardening." Gardening, like hunting, building, etc., is thirdness.

Thirdness is the *meaning* of what is being done. Obviously, B could also be searching for treasure, trying to fix a broken water pipe, or many other things. Until there is an interpretation of what is being done, quite literally "nothing" is happening. There is no meaning. Without thirdness, human activities would be no different from those of our simian relatives, that is, merely episodic. Thirdness for Peirce is a construction of language. It is language that supplies us with many different labels for what we are doing. Without the label "gardening" or something similar, we would never pick up a shovel and dig a hole. Without language, the problem that "gardening" solves would never be perceived or discovered as a problem; a problem that incites action and generates knowledge. Add to this the insight that language is fundamentally social and interpersonal, then it can be argued that communication constitutes meaning in such a way that B is always associated with others and every thirdness implies not only an individual doing something, but people doing things together. For Taylor and Van Every (2011: 12) "communication is achieved through the establishment of a 'thirdness,' and [...] it is in and through the continuing reconstruction and reiteration of thirdness in the practices of its many communities that an organization becomes present to us and is thus enabled to exist in our world, socially and materially."

According to Taylor, coorienting communication is the smallest unit of society. When we analyze the social into its most basic and undissolvable elements, then what we find is coorientation through communication, the communicative construction of meaning. The social is nothing other than cooperative action based on cooriented communication. Taking an example which is not from Tayler himself, let us suppose, when A and B get together at a meeting, they ask C to take over graphic design and D to do marketing. They all agree upon a budget including allotments for material resources. During this process, one cooriented communication becomes linked to others and embedded in still others. It could be supposed that A asks B to ask C to carry out a particular task. In this case B and C coorient on the basis of B representing A. It is actually A that initiates the communication, but B represents him. This chain, which Taylor and Van Every call "imbrication" (2011: 29), can become quite long and complicated in large organizations.

Cooriented, imbricated communication can be analyzed into "conversations" and "texts." Conversations use language, but also charts, organograms, images, and so on, which at some point become fixed in protocols, agendas, notes, and contracts. All these forms of fixing in some objective form what A, B, C, and D say to each other in their many individual conversations can be considered as "text" (Taylor 2009: 157). According to Taylor, who refers at this point to the philosophical hermeneutics of Ricoeur, communication is manifested in two ways, "*conversation*, or the to-and-fro construction of a collaborative fabrication of shared talk, and *text*, or forms of communication that may be extended in time and space beyond the bounds of a single time/space setting" (157). A text is a kind of linguistic artifact that has become independent of its author or speaker and takes on a life of its own as an object of interpretation. Anything that has been written down, or transformed into text, becomes a source of meaning independent of the intentions of the author. Based on texts of many kinds, conversations can call upon "others" who are not bodily co-present to an interaction in order to repeat what was said before, legitimate views, authorize speakers, and much more.

Texts, like stone axes and other tools, exist outside the boundaries of individual conversational episodes. They are independent of the momentary, instable conversations that are constantly coming and going. They can therefore exercise a stabilizing influence on fleeting conversations, binding them over time and space to common themes. If there is uncertainty about what was decided at the last meeting, A can read the protocol and remind C that the graphic design is long due. C can reply that the design team has started a project that is waiting for funding and can only be completed next week. In the course of these communicative events, names are given to groups and tasks. For example, A, B, C, and D find themselves speaking not only of "we," but also of their cooperative action as a company with the name, for example, of "APPCO." APPCO must be first to market, must obtain government approval, must secure a partner from the telecom sector, and so on. Collective actors thus appear in communication and begin to say and do things on their own. In this way, structural characteristics such as duration, repeatability, stability, collectivity that look like what we commonly refer to as organization are "constituted." Taylor calls the process in which structures emerge from a chain of communications "imbrication" (2000, 2009: 155, 161ff.). In terms reminiscent of Giddens' structuration theory, Taylor and Van Every summarize the idea of imbrication as follows:

[...] the making of sense, wherever people collaboratively address some task, is intrinsically both acting and structuring. The organization is already present, as what we call the "thirdness" of sensemaking, in all collective activity: understanding our singular experience as an exemplar of our common heritage of constituted meaning. At the simplest level of action, whenever 'you' and 'I' transform ourselves into a 'we,' an organization has formed. There is action but there is also structure and a shared meaning. The most elaborated kind of organization, with thousands of employees, operating in every continent of the globe, is merely an extension of that elementary transformation of agency into organization, the consequence of a scaling up through what we call 'imbrication.' (Taylor/Van Every 2011: 14)

Imbrication is "self-organizing" in the sense of Maturana and Varela's (1980, 1987) theory of autopoiesis. Autopoiesis, literally, "self-production" defines the unique characteristics of biological systems to produce the elements and their interactions such that these elements and interactions continue to produce themselves. A system can be considered to be "autopoietic" when it has clear boundaries distinguishing it from its environment; when the system consists of elements that the system itself has constructed as specific functions for the fulfillment of its own operations; when the operations of the system are directed to maintaining themselves (operational closure on the basis of self-referentiality); and when no information is imported into the system from without (informational closure). Autopoietic systems are self-referential, operationally and informationally closed systems. They are based upon processes of selection, relationing, and steering.[9] When these processes construct elements to perform certain operations, for example, calcium is selected to become bone tissue, it is the function of the skeleton that the system constructs. What is important is the function and not calcium, which theoretically could be replaced by any other substance that fulfills the function of a skeleton. For Taylor this is what imbrication does. It makes it possible to replace a bank teller by an ATM machine, or face-

---

9 | See Krieger/Belliger (2014) for a discussion of the model of autopoietic systems in relation to network theory.

to-face communication with memos and these in turn with email, or delegates commands from the CEO to a manual. Recalling Floridi's third order technology, where artifacts act upon artifacts, the human actor who originally initiated cooriented communication steps into the background and all but disappears. A process or workflow is set up which "automatically" functions. From the point of view of ANT, imbrication amounts to constructing "black boxes," that is, functional input-output devices in which human communication has been "delegated" to intermediaries. This is what gives the impression in some organizations that the employee has become a mere cog in the organizational machine. It is in this sense that organizations become "standardized." As Taylor puts it:

Imbrication, in its organizational application, creates structures that are durable, disciplined and impervious to outside influence [...]. A significant effect of imbrication is to mask the basic power relationships within the organization, and to produce a more stable environment for the carrying on of its business. It could be thought of as infrastructure [...] or institutionalization. (Taylor 2000, without page number)

VENTRILOQUISM – COOREN

Cooren (2004, 2010; Cooren et al. 2011) locates his own approach within what he calls "the Montreal School" of CCO, in which Taylor's work plays a founding role.[10] A distinguishing characteristic of the Montreal School according to Cooren is the explicit reception of actor-network theory.[11] Cooren objects to the four flows model of McPhee and Zaug precisely because they exclude non-human actors from organizational communication. McPhee and Zaug follow Giddens in defining social actors as "conscious, capable agents" (McPhee/Zaug 2009: 28), that is, as human individuals. Cooren and Fairhurst (2009: 199ff.) find this inadequate for several reasons. First, McPhee and Zaug are not consistent

10 | See the Wikipedia article on the School of Montreal https://en.wikipedia.org/wiki/School_of_Montreal

11 | See Cooren (2000) for a discussion of ANT within the context of linguistic philosophy.

in their view of agency. They speak not only of individual human actors, but also of collective agency. The very idea of the four flows is one of organizational communication in the sense that "organizations require distinct types of relations to four 'audiences'" (McPhee/Zaug 2009: 21). Organizations somehow "require" and somehow maintain "relations" to audiences. It seems indisputable that organizations somehow "do" things. IBM "decides" to sell its PC production to Lenovo. Apple "sues" Samsung for patent violations. The Supreme Court of the USA "makes" same sex marriage binding for all 50 states. Of course, there are individual actors within IBM, Apple, and the Supreme Court, but the things that these collective actors do have impact not because of the individuals, but because of the agency of the organization. Samsung has nothing to fear, if Apple does not somehow stand behind, or in front of, or over Tim Cook and stay the same even after Tom Cook has left the company. How are these two kinds of agency linked to each other? How is this undeniable scaling up from individual to collective actors to be understood?

Secondly, for Cooren and Fairhurst, the four flows model does not explain how individual interactions lead to durable social forms that extend in time and space beyond the here and now of face-to-face interaction. Cooren agrees with Taylor that the deductive approach that begins with an already constituted macro organizational form and then asks what kinds of communication this form requires in order to be what it is overlooks the question of how one moves from the "micro organizing processes" (Cooren/Fairhurst 2009: 120) bottom up to arrive at the whole. It is the *"source of stability* that needs to be unveiled" (123) and not what kinds of communication maintain stability once it has been constituted.

Cooren and Fairhurst propose an "association thesis" (123) based on Latour "to depict and analyze how non-human entities tend to not only dislocate interactions, but also stabilize them." The goal is to "identify the properties of communication that enable it to constitute organizations" (124). Communication is described as "a series of actions that *associate* actors with each other" (134). What distinguishes Cooren's approach to CCO from that of Taylor is the broad understanding of communication to include more than conversations and texts. The idea of text does not do justice to the ways in which non-humans enter into and condition communication. Texts can be quoted. They can be recited and referred to. But what is usually perceived as "collective action," that is, the action of a collective actor such as IBM or Apple is not merely a text that is quoted or recited. IBM is more than the sum of texts that somehow name it or refer to it and those conversations in which someone quotes or recites these texts. According to Cooren, a collective actor is much rather a "product of associations" (134).

The example offered by Cooren and Fairhurst (2009: 129ff.) to illustrate these claims is the situation of how visitors entering the lobby of a building in New York go through a security screening. After the events of 9/11 many building administrators moved to implement security measures. Typical security systems included signs informing persons entering a building that they had to register at the reception desk to obtain an electronic entry permit, which allowed visitors to go through an automatic gate, and so on. In this situation, non-human entities such as the sign, the reception desk, the video camera, the permit card, the automatic gate, and so on can be considered agents in that they influence the behavior of persons entering the building. This influence can be said to have "made a difference." Making a difference is the minimal definition of agency that Cooren and Fairhurst (130-1) following Giddens propose. Making a difference in this situation is only possible, when signs, reception desks, registration procedures, video cameras, databases, automated gates, building owners, administrators, occupants, equipment supply companies, etc., are all "associated" with each other in certain more or less stable ways. Indeed, it is the stability and durability of non-humans that allow them to make important differences in this situation. These entities and therefore the associations they may enter into do not exist only in the here and now of any individual interaction in the lobby. They link interactions to actors both human and non-human beyond the immediate space and time of any one interaction. From the point of view of actor network theory, interactions do not take place in the here and now, but in a network that extends almost indefinitely in all spatial and temporal directions. Without these extensions, that is, without the associations and the network that they make up, the interaction could not take place at all.

This is what "technical mediation," as we saw earlier, is all about. Baboons would not be able to successfully organize a security system in any way comparable to this because they only have their bodies to negotiate social relations. Instead of a sign, a desk, a gate, a card, a monkey would have to stand and wave its arms, make noises and so on at exactly the right time and place every time an interaction happened. Baboons do not delegate actions to objects. They do not allow themselves to be translated and enrolled into the programs of action at least partly constituted by the affordances that objects such as a sign or a desk have. Instead of speaking of mediation, translation, enrollment, and programs of action, Cooren speaks of "ventriloquism" (2010, Cooren et al. 2013). The theory of communicative ventriloquism is designed to explain how absent others, including non-humans, can speak through present actors.

So how can we conceive of communication as involving agents other than human ones without neglecting human contributions to what is happening? The notion of ventriloquism provides a useful analytic concept for addressing this question because ventriloquists are people who are skilled in making puppets do and say things without entirely losing their own agency. (Cooren et al. 2013: 262)

Although the usual understanding of ventriloquism assumes that a human agent is manipulating a non-human puppet and that it is only the human who is doing the talking, Cooren claims that "it is also possible to regard the ventriloquist as the one who is being ventriloquized," since ventriloquism "creates a dynamic that transcends both the ventriloquist and the dummy" (263). Latour has often pointed out that the puppet master is also influenced by the puppet. He or she is in the situation of having to do what the puppet "demands." Just as a ventriloquist speaks through the puppet, and the other way round, the puppet suggests, influences, and demands certain actions from the ventriloquist, so do absent actors, individual and collective, human or non-human, "make" local actors who are present to an interaction "speak" for them. Cooren is well aware that ventriloquism is usually thought of as a one-way street. The ventriloquist is the one who actually does the talking and the puppet only appears to speak. Indeed, the art of ventriloquism lies in disguising this fact and creating the illusion that a puppet can speak. Cooren, however, follows Latour in reminding us that the puppet, just like the many non-humans in the lobby of the building in New York, makes a difference.

Not just any puppet can speak in any way whatever. Puppets take on lives of their own. They influence, inspire, and even demand that the puppet master act in a certain way. Upon closer inspection, ventriloquism must therefore be seen as a two-way street. Fundamental concepts of democracy, namely, delegation and representation are based on the possibility that one actor can speak for others, without losing autonomy. The political representative speaks "for" his or her constituency. The "people" are the sovereign that "makes" the representative speak. On the other side, the political office holder demonstrates leadership and legitimacy by speaking also for him or herself. Both puppet and puppet master influence each other. This means, for example, that when justice speaks through the decisions of the judge, neither the judge, nor justice are completely independent from each other. Both play a part. Both are agents. Their association, their mutual mediation is what constitutes a court of law. For Cooren, "ventriloquism proved a useful metaphor for reconceptualizing communication, as human interactants do not only ventriloquize specific figures but are also ventriloquized (animated) by them" (263).

A ventriloquist theory of communication, according to Cooren, can explain how communication constitutes organizations without distinguishing micro and macro levels or agency and structure. These unresolvable dichotomies have posed serious problems for a coherent sociology of organizations. When people speak in the name of the organization, or of a project team, or of the workers union, or any other collective, it appears that they are somehow being transported to another level called social structure or institution. Instead, according to Cooren, they are being ventriloquized by a "figure" (263). A figure is a "form (*figura* in Latin), which needs to be observed in all its occurrences or 'apparitions'" (263). Figures "always 'arrive' with their own history and evolution – like any agent in an interaction" (263). Defining the communication that constitutes organization as a kind of ventriloquism allows organizational theorists to "account for iterability, patterns, and repetitions without losing sight of the details of interactions" (263). Ventriloquism explains how communication constitutes organizations because it explains how figures that are not present at local interactions and who influence and condition local interactions in a consistent way over time and from place to place enter into communication. Theoretically, no macro social structures are necessary, only figurative agents. Following ANT, Cooren argues that figures are ontologically no different from any other agents, since agency is a process of ventriloquizing and being ventriloquized. Individual human actors, non-human actors, collective actors, that is, "figures" are all on the same ontological level, they all exist in communication, and all must play their respective parts if the show is to go on. Nonetheless, the non-humans are dependent on the humans to speak for them, to represent them, to speak in their name, or, to be ventriloquized by them.

CONCLUSION

It is not without significance that the concept of ventriloquism is drawn from dramaturgy and theories of stage performance. When Richard Burton played Hamlet, his performance was good because the actor Burton seemed to disappear and the literary figure Hamlet became embodied, appeared on the stage, and spoke through him. From the point of view of a ventriloquist theory of communication, Burton became the figure of Hamlet and Shakespeare the ventriloquist. Hamlet is a literary figure, just as justice, science, the people, management, etc. can be thought of as social figures. Unlike literary figures such as Hamlet, social figures such as justice, IBM, the President, etc. have no author that ventriloquizes them. They speak, as it were, for themselves and ventriloquize the many representatives that speak in their names. Here again, the two-way street of ventriloquism is apparent. Richard Burton also contributed essentially to who and what Hamlet was, and because of Burton's performance, still is. This is why Burton is good actor. Teachers, judges, scientists, artists, politicians, managers, and entrepreneurs also speak for their organizations, institutions, and ideals. These individual actors make a difference. Despite what the metaphor of ventriloquism seems to suggest, they are not *mere* dummies. A theory of dramaturgical performance could easily agree with Cooren when he says, "human beings are inhabited, concerned, preoccupied, enthused, moved, or impassioned by the figures they ventriloquize, yet which also ventriloquize them" (264).

What Cooren's theory of ventriloquism adds to the insights of McPhee and Zaug and Taylor is the clear statement that communication does not, and cannot, take place in an immediate *hic et nunc* of bodily co-presence. Each contribution to the CCO theoretical endeavor shows in its own way that in order for communication to be constitutive of organizations, it must be extended beyond any particular local place and present time. Recalling the discussion of ANT and technical mediation, we could say that communication is "networked" with many flows, texts, things, people, times, and places that go beyond the here and now of any particular interaction. The theories of the communicative constitution of organizations attempt to explain how this is possible and therefore how organizations, which are forms of cooperative action extended in space and time, can arise from fleeting, unstable encounters. Nonetheless, as the metaphor of ventriloquism shows, CCO remains tied to the idea of an illusion, a kind of theatrical magic in which something greater and other than interactions arises from them. Can the communicative constitution of organizations be effectively theorized as a kind of magic? Are we not exchanging one mystery for another? In addition to this, communication is still the prerogative of humans whose linguistic abilities allow them to become ventriloquists, that is, representatives of non-humans.

The nearness of Cooren's ventriloquist theory of communication to Goffman's dramaturgical theory of social interaction is striking. For Goffman, standardized identities such as CEOs, supervisors, teachers, etc. "speak" in and through the human individuals who "take on" these "persona" (literally "masks"). Furthermore, the space in which interaction takes place is full of props, settings, scripts, signs, texts, and other non-humans that exist beyond the immediate here and now of face-to-face communication. From Goffman's perspective, ventriloquism is a performance based on dramaturgical structures and imperatives. Ventriloquism is therefore not an explanation, but rather something that itself needs to be explained. How does the magic of the theater work? What mechanisms, techniques, and conditions go into making up the illusion of ventriloquism? From the perspective of Goffman's careful studies of interaction, the magic of the theatre and the illusion of ventriloquism are the same. It is therefore reasonable to expect that Goffman's analysis of the techniques by which dramaturgical space is constituted, that is, those techniques that create the magic of a (ventriloquist) performance can illuminate how communication can constitute organizations. We therefore turn now to a closer look at Goffman's dramaturgical theory of social interaction.

3. Staging and Narrative — Localizing and Globalizing

THE SOCIOLOGY OF INTERACTION — GOFFMAN

The sociology of interaction is often referred to as "micro" sociology since it focuses on face-to-face communication, which is traditionally thought of as the smallest unit of social reality. *The Presentation of Self in Everyday Life* (1959), *Behavior in Public Places* (1963), *Interaction Ritual* (1967), *Frame Analysis* (1974), and other studies are classics in the sociology of interaction. Among the most influential of Goffman's theoretical achievements is his description of social interaction as a dramaturgical event. Metaphors of the theater, the stage, role-playing, masks, stage settings, and similar categories drawn from dramaturgy have long been applied to social life. Sources for Goffman's dramaturgical theory are Durkheim, Kenneth Burke, Marcel Mauss, and perhaps even Shakespeare, who's famous line "All the world's a stage and all the men and women merely players [...]" (*As You Like It*) has become a classic reference for social theory. With Goffman's work, metaphors drawn from theater entered into the foundations of social theory. In the following, we will attempt to interpret some aspects of Goffman's dramaturgical theory of interaction from the point of view of actor-network theory. The goal is not to give a complete or exact interpretation of Goffman's *oeuvre*, but to reconstruct his theory of social interaction from the point of view of what was said above about technical mediation and the communicative constitution of organizations.[1] Our aim is not to be faithful to Goffman, but to explore the possibility that

---

1 | The editor of an influential collection of essays on Goffman points out that Goffman's work almost „obliges readers to be creators in their own right and fashion their personal vision of his multi-layered theory" (Riggins 1990: 1).

Goffman's work can be faithful to ANT. If this is possible, it could show how we can avoid some of the lingering difficulties in approaches to the communicative constitution of organizations, which despite references to ANT, still remain indebted to linguistic philosophy and to traditional assumptions of the primacy of intentional speech acts. CCO theories are not entirely clear about the status of non-human actors, the implicit dualism of micro/macro levels, the lingering tensions between agency and structure, and the dependence on language. Furthermore, the recourse to illusion (ventriloquism) as ground of explanation is problematic. Our goal in bringing Goffman into the story is to try to get a better grasp on how so-called face-to-face communication is dependent upon many actors both human and non-human who are not physically present at the moment of interaction, indeed, how meaning and sensemaking are enacted, embodied, extended, and embedded in networks.

With the help of Goffman's classical phenomenology of everyday social interaction, we will attempt to show that although society is nothing other than the activities of socializing, communication is always "distributed" in space and time among many actors. Perhaps non-humans do not always need humans to "speak" for them. Communication need not be conceived of as a force that can somehow create social order *ex nihilo*. Instead, communication has its own conditions of possibility. In other words, perhaps communication is always already in specific ways "organized." If it is plausible, as Goffman argues, that the dramaturgical organization of space, time, and meaning constitutes communication, then it is the theater that makes the ventriloquist and not the other way round, or at least, they are so completely mutually dependent that the one cannot exist without the other. According to Goffman, there is a lot of work to be done before the ventriloquist, or the puppet, can begin to speak. Before anybody opens their mouth, whether ventriloquist or puppet, many things have to be put into place, brought into play, and set up and arranged, otherwise the risk is great that what is said will not be understood and therefore will not be able to function as constitutive of any kind of organization. It is to this work of setting up, of putting into place, or bringing into play, that we now turn. In more philosophical terms, it could be said that we are attempting to discover the conditions of the possibility of organizing communication.

For Goffman, a social actor is constantly concerned to insure the success of communication, interaction, and cooperation by means of mobilizing and drawing together many different props, helpers, supports, signs, scripts, artifacts, settings, and texts.[2] This activity we would like to call "staging." Although Goffman does not use this term, or at least not in the technical sense we propose, "staging" refers to all the efforts undertaken by all actors involved in an interaction to define the context, the situation, or "frame" of interaction by means of controlling information.[3] Knowing what is going on, or what game is being played, to echo Wittgenstein's notion of a "language-game," depends not only on what actors say, but *how* they say it, *how* they appear, *where* they choose to interact, and with *what props, costumes, stage-settings*, etc. they attempt to bring into play. All this is information in the sense in which we defined information as technical mediation in Part 1 above. What we see in social interaction is not talking heads or Cartesian subjects creating meaning from their own cognitive abilities, but actors of certain kinds upon stages that are being set in certain ways. Some of the actors involved are human and some are non-human. Some of the actors are "local" in the sense of actually being present at a particular face-to-face interaction. Others, however, are brought into play, or play their parts even though they are far away from the time and place of the concrete interaction. In so doing, they extend the *hic et nunc* of interaction into space and time in such a way, as we will see, that the local builds a continuity with the global. What Goffman's descriptions of interaction show is that immediacy is no more than a myth and that all communication is mediated.

---

2 | In social interaction "we find ourselves with one central obligation: to render our behavior understandably relevant to what the other can come to perceive is going on. Whatever else, our activity must be addressed to the other's mind, that is, to the other's capacity to read our words and actions for evidence of our feelings, thoughts, and intent" (Goffman 1983: 53).

3 | "I assume that definitions of a situation are built up in accordance with principals of organization which govern events [...] and our subjective involvement in them; frame is the word I use to refer to such of these basic elements as I am able to identify" (Goffman 1974: 10-11).

STAGING –
THE DRAMATURGICAL ORGANIZATION OF COMMUNICATION

Goffman views social interaction as a performance, that is, the acting out of socially defined "roles" (e.g., mother, manager, teacher, and student). Each social role is defined by a "script" that describes in narrative form a set of rights, duties, expectations, norms, and behavior a person should fulfill when playing that role. The script describes what is expected from anyone who claims to "be" a certain person and play a certain role in society. Identity is therefore constituted in interaction and not a given.[4] The role theory of social interaction is based upon the fact that in order to cooperate and live together, people must behave in predictable ways, fulfill expectations, and act appropriately with regard to specific contexts, "frames" (Goffman 1974), or situation definitions that describe what is to be done by whom and in which ways. Building upon Peirce, Taylor, as we saw above referred to this as "thirdness," as that which gives meaning to an action and thus distinguishes intentional action from mere behavior. The chief metaphor for Goffman is not the performer, for example, the ventriloquist, but the stage, the theater and all that it implies. Role theory conceptualizes social interaction not as ventriloquism, but as the staging of communication. The speaker is not merely an actor, but also a director, a stage-designer, a door attendant, a prop-assistant, and much more. Furthermore, all the things that are brought into play upon a stage do their parts, play their own roles, and speak, that is, participate in the creation of information, in their own ways. All these activities together is what makes communication possible and not merely the ability to be a ventriloquist, to speak for others, to represent something other than oneself. In terms drawn from ANT, the network is the actor. All these things speak for themselves and not merely through a ventriloquist who magically represents them. This implies that social interaction can best be understood by analyzing the basic structures of dramaturgical action.[5]

---

4 | Goffman understands the self as a social construct, "The self [...] is not an organic thing that has a specific location, whose fundamental fate is to be born, to mature, and to die; it is a dramatic effect arising diffusely from a scene that is presented" (1959: 252-253).

5 | "All the world is not, of course, a stage, but the crucial ways in which it isn't are not easy to specify" (Goffman 1959: 72)

It is important to note that social roles never exist alone. A "father" is only possible, when there also a "son" or "daughter". A "husband" is only possible, when there is also a "wife". Without "students," there could not be "teachers." You cannot "greet" someone, if there is no one who is "greetable" standing near you. Social interaction necessarily consists, even then when one person plays different roles with themselves in front of a mirror, of a plurality of roles that are coordinated with each other. The "frame" (Goffman 1974) or the "setting" (Goffman 1959) of any social interaction is a constellation of roles that are for the most part already adapted to and coordinated with each other. A family consists of mother, father, children, brothers, sisters, aunts and uncles and many more typical roles. None of these roles exists by themselves, but only as coordinated elements of a family system, which of course, is culturally specific. There are modern families, extended families, nuclear families, patchwork families, etc. When social roles are played or acted out in relation to one another the situation or frame of the interaction is "family," "work," "school," etc. The father of a family, however, could also be the head of the family owned company and the sons and daughters could be employees. When they come together at a meeting of the board of directors to close an important deal, they do not play family roles, but business roles. The frame we call "business" is ordering their possibilities for interaction and the mutual expectations they have. The chief financial officer would not accept being treated like the „little brother" when it comes to making company decisions. For the same reason, the meeting of the board of directors does not take place in the family living room or at the dinner table, but in the boardroom at the company offices.

If playing a social role always means being involved in a constellation of coordinated roles involving various actors, the question arises of how this complicated business is organized. It would seem improbable that it just happens by itself without effort. We all know how fragile social relations are and how often misunderstandings occur. When interaction is successful and everything goes smoothly then this is an achievement that must be attributed to the fact that everybody involved worked hard to insure that the interaction did not dissolve into conflict and chaos. If order is to arise from noise, that is, if a situation, a frame, a context is to arise within which not everything is possible, and everyone knows what to do, then how is this done? If the explanation is not to lie in referring to illusion or magic, there must be concrete techniques and practices that contribute to making communication possible. Goffman answered this question by comparing social order to dramaturgical order. He claimed that social interaction is dramaturgically structured. Every social act is to be seen as a "performance" (Goffman 1959: 17). A "performance" is an event in which one person or group of people (the performer or performers) act in a particular way for another person or group of people (the audience). In addition to this, performance implies that activities ought to comply with certain expectations, norms, and standards. An actor on a stage cannot do just anything in any way whatever, but must satisfy the expectations of the audience, otherwise he will be exposed to a scathing critique and nobody will pay to see the show. Similarly, a social role is a script that prescribes certain behavior, just as the script for an actor in the theater prescribes what the actor says and how he or she behaves. This implies that social interaction does not just happen, but must be explicitly or implicitly "staged" just like the performance of an actor on the stage of a theater.

To say that human behavior and social interaction is dramaturgically structured means that it "takes place" under certain conditions and in a certain way. It would be misleading to reduce the complex conditions of social action to merely "playing a role." The social actor, and to a certain extent the actor in the theater also, are not merely actors playing roles, that is, slavishly following scripts, but they are also playwrights, directors, prop-assistants, stage-designers, and much more. It would therefore be more accurate to speak of a theory of "staging" instead of a theory of role playing. Social interaction is made possible by the entire constellation of activities and conditions that make up staging. These activities and conditions can be described as establishing or setting up specific *structural roles* and specific *structural positions*. To speak of "structural" roles and positions means that these roles and positions are general and apply to all performances, regardless of the particular content, it does not mean that they exist somehow independently of the activities of staging. As Goffman put it, "The issues dealt with by stagecraft and stage management are [...] quite general; they seem to occur everywhere in social life, providing a clear-cut dimension for formal sociological analysis" (1959: 15).

Structural Roles

- *Actor without mask*: If social identity is playing a role, this implies that identity is not given, fix, once and for all, but can be changed and varied. Any role that an actor plays is not the only one that they can play. The actor is not the role and the role is not the actor. An actor can play many different roles, as in fact, everyday social interaction shows. We pass more or less smoothly from family roles to work roles to hobby roles, etc. This implies that at a certain point one role stops and another begins. Between roles the actor is not wearing any mask. The social actor is someone who can step out of the limelight, take off one mask, and put on another. It is because social identity is essentially changeable and in fact constantly changing, that we are confronted with the question of identity, of who we "really" are. We exist, as Heidegger said, as a question for ourselves, a question that calls forth many answers, none of which is the final and definitive answer.
- *Actor with mask*: Social interaction consists of actors playing roles, or wearing masks. The actor acting always has some kind of mask on. On stage, before an audience, we are dealing with Hamlet, but not Richard Burton or Anthony Hopkins or anyone else. Of course, Richard Burton is also a social identity of a kind and other persons could pretend to be Richard Burton more or less successfully. As soon as a person is "seen," "observed," "known" in any way they are perceived "as" playing a role, even if they are playing themselves alone in a room for themselves. We always speak through a *persona* (mask) and only because of this are we able to speak at all. If the question of who is speaking cannot be placed or answered, then no one is saying anything, nothing at all is happening.
- *Audience*: In order for a performance to take place there must be an audience, that is, someone must witness the performance and acknowledge that a performance is taking place. The "role" of the audience can also be played by the director of a play or by fellow actors, or by the actor herself who watches her own performance in a mirror, on a video, or in the mind's eye. The audience has the function of acknowledging that a performance is taking place and accepting or rejecting it.
- *Outsiders*: Finally, no performance is for absolutely everybody everywhere, but only has meaning within a certain context, at a certain place and time, in a certain language and so on. This means that a

performance always includes certain people, but also always must ex-clude many other people. The people excluded from a performance, that is, those who do not play roles or participate as an audience can be called "outsiders."

These four types of roles define the kinds of actors that are necessarily involved in any social interaction. Social interaction always consists of actors who can change their masks, actors wearing masks, audiences, and all the rest who could potentially become involved, but for this particular situation for whatever reason are excluded. Corresponding to these general types of actors there are four general "positions" or spaces in which interaction must "take place." The theater exists usually as a kind of building with standard features. Theaters today are modelled on structures that have been known since Greek antiquity. Theaters are made up of special kinds of spaces. They are built so that there are always four distinct areas or positions that can be taken. This structure is what makes any space or building into a theater in the first place. It is what makes it possible for a performance to "take place." Social interaction, insofar as it can be considered a dramatic performance, also needs to "take place" within a structured space. Even if the theatrical space is clearly defined and structured, this must not imply that such spaces and places are limited to certain physical spaces. Experimental theater has shown that dramatic performances can occur anywhere, in the street, on trains or buses, in public places of all kinds. To speak of dramaturgical spaces or positions does not imply any particular kind of physical space such as theater, but, as we shall see, a form of information control that "takes place" anywhere.

Structural Positions

- *Backstage:* There is always some kind of "backstage" where actors prepare for the performance and where masks, props, costumes, and scenery are kept ready for use. The playwright, the director, the prop-assistant and stage designer also take this position, since they do not appear on stage and directly participate in playing a certain role. The audience should not be able to look into this area, since they would see Richard Burton, for example, arguing with the director about how a certain line should be spoken. Seeing Richard Burton and all the others involved in staging the play, would dispel the illusion of Hamlet and ruin the play.

- *Center stage:* There is always an area that functions as "center stage." This is the position where the actor appears with his or her mask on and where the performance takes place. This is where attention is focused. It is where the "spot light" shines.

- *Auditorium/Hall:* There is also an "auditorium" or "hall" where the audience is located. The hall must be clearly distinguished from the stage, otherwise the audience is in the spot light and the actor is invisible, simply one among many. Attention must be directed to the actor and his or her performance and not to the audience. Even if they are not in the spotlight, the audience also plays a role. The audience has the important function of signalizing acceptance or rejection of a performance. For example, they can start booing or get up and leave if they reject a performance; or the audience can applaud or just keep quiet in order to signal that they accept a performance and want the actor to continue.

- *Outside:* Finally, all those who do not and should not witness a performance are banned to an area outside the theater. Either they are not admitted in the first place or, if they sneaked in, they get thrown out. In any case, this area must exist for the performance to be possible. A performance cannot happen everywhere and not everyone is invited. Even if the mass media can create an audience of millions, this is still not everyone, but only a selection of possible viewers and no matter how important a message might be, it does not concern everybody, everywhere.

Although Goffman repeatedly defines interaction as "the reciprocal influence of individuals upon one another's actions when in one another's immediate physical presence" (1959, 15), it is clear that the dramaturgical positions and roles described above are not unique physical spaces. Every social interaction requires that there be a "backstage." This need not be a physical space somehow separated from the center stage by a curtain or otherwise hidden from the view of the audience. The backstage enables the actor to take off a mask. Backstage, the actor is "out" of the role. This is also the "place" where the actor is not merely the actor, but also the director, the playwright, the prop-assistant, and much more. This is the space "in-between" performances. In this space, the actor is no longer "under" the script, but "above" it, no longer "in" the role, but "out" of it. This is the place where the actor can modify the role, or drop it entirely and pick up a different one.[6] The actor can rehearse lines, try on different apparel, etc. When a particular performance comes to an end, the actor can step out of the spot light and return to the backstage. As a social position, the backstage can be thought of as "privacy," that is, the place where society is excluded and where a person can be alone without having to worry about the approval or disapproval of others.[7] The backstage can also be thought of the place of *decision*.[8] For it is here that decisions are made on what role to play and how to play it.

The existence of a backstage is the necessary prerequisite for the ability to play many different social roles and to play them in many different, and perhaps innovative ways. Within the family circle, a woman plays the mother, at work she plays the manager, in church she plays the believer, at the golf club she plays the fellow golfer, etc. If there were no backstage, all these roles could not be held apart from each other; they would constantly be conflicting with each other. As we saw in the discussion of primate social behavior in Part 1, monkeys live in the episodic present and have no backstage in which to hold other roles and activities ready. Primates do not sequentially move from role to role, but must negotiate all roles at

---

6 | Latour's (2013a) critique of Goffman's "role" theory overlooks the possibility created by the backstage for an actor to not simply be "under" a script, but also sequentially "above" it, that is, to move sequentially from in to out of a script and thus be able to change it, or to switch to another script. Furthermore, we would like to read Goffman from the point of view of Weick's understanding of "sensemaking." For Weick (1995) "Sensemaking is less about discovery than is about invention. To engage in sensemaking is to construct, filter, frame, create facticity, and render the subjective into something more tangible" (13).

7 | It has often been noted (see for example, Meyrowitz (1990) that privacy is a subjective, social, cultural, and historical dimension of social existence and that therefore the dramaturgical notion of the backstage cannot be equated with any particular understanding of privacy. Especially new media and the internet have placed traditional notions of privacy in question.

8 | For Luhmann (2000) organizations are decision making systems. Organizational communication is the communication of decisions. In Luhmann's view, if social action consisted of slavishly following scripts, there would be no decisions to communicate and thus no organization.

once. Furthermore, it is because of the backstage, that an actor has the possibility of deciding to play a traditional role in a new way, surprise the audience, and attempt to change the situation. A mother at work in the office, for example, can attempt to change expectations of her coworkers when they walk in while she is arguing with her husband about who should be taking care of the children that afternoon. Instead of being embarrassed, she could display this role as normal for working mothers. Embarrassment is what happens, when the backstage through some mishap becomes visible to the audience. Much of current discussion on issues of privacy and transparency in the network society can be understood as renegotiation of the way the backstage should function in society. In any case, the success of social interaction depends on a backstage of some kind, even if the new media revolution, reality TV, Facebook, etc. are changing the ways in which we set it up and make use of it. We will return to this later when we discuss new media and network norms.

Leaving the backstage implies appearing on center stage. The center stage is the position that an actor takes when performing in a social interaction. When the actor plays a role, he or she is automatically standing in center stage. Just like the back stage, center stage is not a physical place, but a virtual place, a social construction. The center stage is anywhere where the attention of others is focused. The actor "demands" attention for his or her performance. It is important that the actor correctly, convincingly, successfully occupy this position and so hold the attention and gain approval of the audience. If not, then the interaction may fail. People will not know "what is going on" and what is expected of them. If an actor fails to step into center stage no one will pay attention. The actor will not succeed in participating in a social interaction. For example: One meets an acquaintance in the street and attempts to greet the other person. But just as one passes by the acquaintance happens to be talking to someone else. In a situation such as this, it is often difficult to gain the attention of the other person. One has to somehow draw attention to oneself. One has to create a center stage and put the acquaintance in the role and position of the audience in order to be able to play the role of "greeting." This can mean "pushing" the acquaintance out of the center stage they are currently occupying in their discussion with the other person; a risky undertaking that might well fail. Otherwise, one runs the risk of saying hello to no one, which is embarrassing and ridiculous. One stands in the street seemingly talking to no one. Others wonder what you are doing or think you may be talking to yourself.

The "auditorium" or "hall" is the position in which the audience finds itself in all social interactions. As for all dramaturgical spaces, this is also not a real physical place, but a social space that can be defined as that space wherever the center stage and the backstage are not. As with the other dramaturgical positions, this could be anywhere. At the moment when an actor begins to play a role for you, for example, an acquaintance greets you on the street while passing by, you find yourself in the position of being the audience for their performance. If for some reason you do not want to greet the person, you can pretend not to notice them and risk being seen as rude, because you refuse to accept being pushed into the position of the audience. If the other person, however, does manage to get your attention and you take the position of the audience and accept their greeting, then you can take center stage yourself and greet them in return. They then find themselves in the position of the hall, playing the role of being your audience. Center stage and hall are continually being exchanged in the course of a social interaction as the actors take turns playing their respective roles. In every social interaction someone, even if only yourself, must assume the role of audience in the space of "auditorium" or "hall".

Those who are excluded from an interaction are "outside" the dramaturgical space in which the interaction is taking place. A typical example is a crowded restaurant where people are sitting at tables very close to each other. People at every table are carrying on "private" conversations. The people at the surrounding tables are physically very close, perhaps only an arm's length away, but they are nevertheless excluded from the conversation you are having with your partner and that is taking place right next to them. They could easily hear what you are saying. Perhaps they even listen in. However, they cannot let this be seen without causing embarrassment. There are many social situations where being "outside" an interaction does not mean being physically distant or separated by doors, walls, etc. The position of the outside is a necessary condition of all interactions. If one cannot maintain an outside, for example, if one insists upon speaking very loudly in a crowded restaurant, then this will disrupt social communication and lead to conflicts. For this reason, people go to great efforts to set the stage with doors, walls, distance between tables, barriers of all kinds, etc.

Although Goffman often described interaction as taking place within a well-bounded physical space in which participants are physically present in face-to-face communication, the dramaturgical theory does not require physical co-presence. Meyrowitz (1990) has argued convincingly that Goffman's dramaturgical space should be understood as an "information system" (89).

I suggest that a close examination of the dynamics of situations and behavior as described by Goffman indicates that place itself is a subcategory of the more inclusive notion of a perceptual field. For while situations are usually defined in terms of who is in what location, the implicit issue is actually the types of behaviors that are available for other people's scrutiny. [...] The physical location...is not what shapes the nature of the interaction, but the patterns of information flow. Indeed, the analysis of situational definitions can be completely removed from the issue of direct physical presence by focusing only on information access. (Meyrowitz 1990: 88)

He goes on to add that:

Such information comes in many forms including words, gestures, vocalizations, posture, dress, and pace of activity. (ibid: 89)

Meyrowitz bases his "informational" interpretation of Goffman on the fact that communication, even face-to-face communication, is always in some way *mediated*. There is no purely immediate communication any more than there is a pure *hic et nunc* of interaction. A performance always depends on many other things than the actor herself, stripped, as it were, of all props, scripts, texts, accessories, and staging. It is important to note that Meyrowitz views Goffman from the perspective of new media studies. The affordances of new media on communication and social interaction transform one-to-one communication into many-to-many communication in a virtual dimension independent of the usual limitations of space and time. We will return to this aspect of "mediated" communication in Part 4 below. For the moment, we wish to emphasize that staging can be understood as a matter of *information control* in the sense of information defined above as technical mediation. We saw above that when things get out of hand, what we hold on to − and what is holding on to us − is information. This does not imply, as we saw, that the things disappear. On the contrary, they reappear as the links, the associations, the interfaces that allow things to become social actors and participants in interaction. We attempted to show in Part 1 that information should not be too quickly reduced to mental manipulation of linguistic signs. Interfaces, links, associations in the sense of technical mediation are not merely mental constructs, but ways in which humans and non-humans build actor-networks. It is from this perspective that we wish to interpret Goffman's description of how social actors build their relations.

BRINGING THINGS INTO PLAY

The performance of a social role requires setting up and maintaining the dramaturgical space. Setting up and maintaining the dramaturgical space in which social interaction can "take place" is a condition of the possibility of defining the context, the situation, or as Goffman also says, the "frame" of an interaction. Framing is necessary in order for people to be able to understand what is going on, what roles they are expected to play, and what they are allowed to expect from others. In order to successfully set up and maintain a "frame" certain forms of "information control" are important.[9] Not just anything can be said and done in a social situation. Not just anything can happen anywhere at any time. Socialization creates a world constituted by situations or frames, special places and times. We move through this world without thinking about it. This is implicit, practical knowledge, much the same as the practical knowledge that our hominid ancestors acquired when they began to use stone axes in certain situations, and for certain purposes. Using a tool, as we saw, is a complex event involving mediation between the user, the tool, and the effect of the tool. Setting up these links implies selection of the right materials, handling them in the right way, in the right time and place, with a particular purpose or particular effect in view. Not everything that is present is relevant, not everybody that is present is involved and must be attended to, not every possible social interaction is allowed to take place. These constraints are what is meant by social structure, or what Max Weber referred to as an "iron cage." The process view of organizing interprets these constraints as many ongoing choices that are being made

---

9 | Goffman speaks of "impression management" (1959: 30).

in the staging of interaction. As the new institutionalism points out, these choices have become second nature for most of us and are therefore no longer available for conscious deliberation and decision. Social structure emerges as cognitive constraints. ANT would say that much of our behavior has become "black boxed," that is, so tightly translated and enrolled in networks that we no longer have a choice, but simply function according to what is expected of us. Nowhere perhaps do we become more aware of how much of our knowledge is implicit and unconscious as when we find ourselves in a different culture, where nothing we do seems to fit. All the information that we more or less unconsciously rely upon in order to understand how we are supposed to behave seems to lead us astray. Indeed, we are like little children who must go through a process of re-socialization into the foreign culture in order to be able to function as normal social actors. What we learn, or must re-learn, in socialization is how to select and control information, that is, in the language of ANT, to establish associations, links, or interfaces between heterogeneous actors.

From Goffman's many different descriptions of the forms of information control that are used in staging we can identify the following:

1. identification
2. front
3. standardization
4. idealization
5. simplification
6. exclusion
7. selection and segregation of the audience
8. solidarity
9. mystification

These forms of information control aim at setting up the dramaturgical space of social interaction, distributing and assigning roles among actors, and defining the situation, the setting, the context, or Goffman also put it, the "frame." They are all forms of communication that are acquired or internalized during socialization and are performed almost automatically, without taking time to think. This does not imply, however, determinism. When conflicts or uncertainties arise, the entire dramaturgical construction can become explicit, contested, and renegotiated. Black boxes can be opened up. Networks can be deconstructed and reconstructed.

When this happens, it is not the human actors alone who are called into question, but also the many non-humans who are also actively involved in staging. Are the clothes right, the place and time correct, the furniture, the lighting, the room, the building, etc.? What can be done, by whom, how, with what effect? All these issues crop up the moment things don't run smoothly or the frame is questioned. In order to set up the situation in such a way that these questions don't constantly impede communication and cooperative action, actors of all kinds do the following.

Identification

An actor can have very different attitudes to his or her own role in a social interaction. For example, the actor can fully identify with the role or only act "as if." Identification is the result of successful socialization. The role has become internalized and the actor plays the role spontaneously, genuinely, and convincingly. Although we know that our identity is a performance and that in every interaction we are following a script, we are ourselves convinced that we "are" the role we play. This makes the performance "authentic" and believable not only for ourselves, but also for the other people involved. Authenticity is important for the success of social interaction. If others are to accept our performance, then it helps if we believe in it ourselves, or at least, convince them that we are who we pretend to be. Even if everyone knows that the actor is not the mask, successful interaction depends on a minimal conviction among all participants that actors are not lying or being insincere. If an actor does not identify with a role this can lead to mistrust and disrupt the interaction. Of course, we do not identify completely with all the roles we play in all situations. This is usually the case when we do not feel that the situation or the role is "right" for us or do not especially want to participate in a certain situation. Often we must be polite or to do what others expect of us, even when we do not identify with the role we assume or which is expected of us. In these contexts, identification means that we lead others to believe that we are identifying with a role even if we are not. A good actor, such as John Gielgud, can lead others to believe they "are" Hamlet even though everyone knows that they are not.

Front

The "front" consists of all objects, things, clothes, postures, settings, lighting, furnishings, etc. that make up the surroundings of a certain interaction. As commentators have often remarked, the front is like the façade of a building or the stage of a theater. It makes a difference where a certain interaction takes place. The surroundings or "setting" should be controlled and precisely defined.[10] A "doctor's office," "living room," "bar," "court room," "lobby," "class room," "cafeteria," etc., are all set up differently according to established cultural conventions. Everything from the shape of the room, the color or the walls, the kind of floor, the furniture, the paintings or decorations, the lighting, the kind of clothing worn or behavior that is expected; everything can be either "appropriate" or "inappropriate" and support a certain social interaction or disturb it. A businessperson can spend great effort creating the proper settings for an important meeting with partners or customers. A doctor sees to it that her office looks like a doctor's office and not a hotel lobby. Appearance is a major part of the front. Appearance includes clothing, makeup, jewelry and accessories, hairstyle, etc. A woman, but men too, can easily spend hours preparing for a night out. Not only setting and appearance, but also manner, bearing, the way a person talks, moves, positions themselves in a setting, etc. also has an effect on defining the situation. Fronts, including the setting, appearance, and manner are set up, changed, and rehearsed backstage as part of the work done to make social interaction successful.

Standardization

Standardization refers to all attempts to make the role that one is playing unambiguously comply with the expectations of the audience. In order for people to agree quickly on what they are supposed to do together, the various roles that are part of a situation must be easily identifiable.[11] When

---

10 | "First, there is the 'setting,' involving furniture, décor, physical layout, and other background items which supply the scenery and stage props for the spate of human action played out before, within, or upon it" (Goffman 1959: 22).

11 | "A certain bureaucratization of the spirit is expected so that we can be relied upon to give a perfectly homogeneous performance at every appointed time" (Goffman 1959: 56).

we walk into a store, we need to know who the salesperson is and who is merely another customer. Everyone must know as quickly and as easily as possible, what role an actor is playing. The salesperson, for example, will tend to stand by the sales desk, or they will wear clothes displaying the logo of the store. The actor attempts to reduce his or her actions and communications as well as all aspects of the front to a minimum required to identify the role. The actor attempts to play the role in a "typical," easily recognized way, such that misunderstanding and confusion can be avoided. For example, if one plays the role of a teacher, then the success of the performance depends on how quickly and unambiguously everyone involved can see who is the teacher. There is great pressure in society to standardize roles. Settings, situations, or frames must be easily understood by everyone in order to avoid misunderstandings. This is the source of conventional or stereotypical behavior. If one behaves in an unexpected and original way, then the other people involved will become insecure and perhaps not accept the performance. Faced with non-acceptance, an actor must go to extra effort in order to explain what he or she is doing and why he or she is doing things differently and hope that the audience then accepts the role.

Idealization

The willingness of an audience to accept a role depends on how much a role is valued and respected in a society. Actors attempt to "incorporate and exemplify the officially accredited values of the society" (Goffman 1959: 35). The roles of "doctor," "teacher," "mother," etc. are not only standardized, but also highly respected roles, since they can be related to well defined and commonly accepted role-models. An actor therefore usually attempts to idealize the role they are playing and make it recognizably similar to well-known and highly valued models.

Simplification

Simplification is the attempt to keep the situation as simple as possible by not confusing roles and settings.[12] The actor attempts to play only one role at one time in the proper setting, that is, with the proper front, the necessary standardization, and the best idealization available. If a gentleman wants to convincingly appear to a lady as a charming admirer, he will try not to appear in any other way, for example, as an ambitious businessman or a submissive son or an officious bureaucrat. All parties to social interaction try to reduce complexity and exclude, hide, and disguise other roles and other possible situations that could interfere with the frame they are trying to impose on the interaction. If you want to have a romantic dinner with a woman or a man, then you usually do not invite your parents, the neighbors, your tax consultant, or your business partners, and it is embarrassing if they happen to take the table next to you in the restaurant. This would make the situation unnecessarily complex and lead to role conflicts.

Exclusion

The chances that a performance will be accepted are better when everything that does not belong to the performance or could in any way disturb the performance is somehow excluded. Simplification implies not only focusing on a certain situation but also excluding what does not fit.[13] This could mean that one disguises or covers up certain aspects of one's own identity, for example, when men or women lie about their age or their social status.[14] Exclusion is also important to create a "backstage" where the actor can take off his or her mask and appear differently.

---

12 | "First, individuals often foster the impression that the routine they are presently performing is their only routine or at least their most essential one" (Goffman 1959: 48).

13 | Goffman speaks of focusing the interaction, participants grant each other "a special communication license and sustain a special type of mutual activity that can exclude others who are present in the situation" (Goffman 1963: 83)

14 | "While in the presence of others, the individual typically infuses his activity with signs which dramatically highlight and portray confirmatory facts that might otherwise remain unapparent or obscure" (Goffman 1959: 30).

Selection and Segregation of the Audience

An important factor for the success of social interactions is the control of the audience. Not everyone should be allowed to participate in a performance, but only the "right" people. The businessperson who wants to impress prospective customers will try to exclude his mother, his children, his neighbors, his competitors and many others so that his or her role as a reliable, competent, dedicated businessperson will readily be accepted. This means that he or she must control the information in a social interaction by means of setting up a front, simplifying, idealizing, standardizing, and excluding such that only the right people participate in his performance. This can mean setting up a room, changing furniture and decorations, arranging to meet at a certain place, and much more.

Solidarity

Only when communication is based on solidarity can misunderstandings, conflicts, and uncertainties be overcome and a common ground for cooperation be found. All social interaction depends in the final analysis on a willingness of participants to cooperate. Even if a performance is not what is expected or if it is unclear what frame is applicable, a basic solidarity among participants prevents the outbreak of open conflict or even violence. Frames and situation definitions can only be communicatively set up, maintained or transformed on the basis of solidarity. As a form of information control, solidarity can be signalized and experienced in many ways. From the point of view of ANT, it could be argued that solidarity is based on the awareness that the actor is the network and that isolation or non-cooperation endangers one's own identity and ability to act in society.

Mystification

Common experience, a shared understanding of the situation and acceptance by an audience are only one side of the coin. An actor must also be able to create an aesthetic "distance" between the audience and the social stage upon which he or she appears. The success of the performance depends on putting oneself in the spotlight and pushing all others into the darkness of the auditorium, that is, into the role of being viewers. Those who accept a social performance also accept being pushed aside so that the actor can perform his or her role. Turn taking in conversation is an example. Each person gets to have their moment in the spotlight. One person "steps forward" into the center of attention and the others "step back" and become the audience. Although a certain willingness on the part of most people to step back and let others take center stage can be presumed, one must nonetheless often assert oneself and make others pay attention. Theatrical performance is always in some way a mystification.[15] The "magic" of the theater consists in the ability to create a distance between the "real" world and the world of the performance. Every theater lives from the mystification of the stage. As we saw above in the discussion of Cooren's theory of ventriloquism, an actor is always more than what is physically present at a certain moment. Every real teacher who stands before a class of pupils calls up the authority of the ideal and mythical "teacher," or as Cooren would say, the "figure" of the teacher, who in some way "speaks" through the real physical teacher. The CEO is ventriloquized by the company, for whom he or she speaks. The judge speaks for the law. This may be called "mystification" because the weaknesses of the actor are covered up and his or her competence is over-emphasized and extended in space and time beyond the here and now of interaction. The magic of the theatre depends on the magic of bringing many things and actors into play that are not really present or even could be. But the theater is much more than mere magic. Many different actors participate in order to make mystification possible.

All of the methods of information control mentioned above serve the purpose of allowing what is not present at the moment of interaction to become involved and influence what is happening. Many of these "actors" that are brought into play by staging can be considered as "texts" in the sense in which Taylor uses this term. This means, and Taylor would surely agree, that the success of social interaction is not a matter of simply relying upon the good will of all participants and their sensemaking activities in conversational episodes. Often there is very little good will and great efforts must be spent on information control by recourse to texts in order to insure that communication succeeds and sense is made. Mutual understanding, consensus, and cooperation are less probable than misunderstanding and conflict. Everyday life in society presupposes many communication skills

---

15 | "The audience senses secret mysteries and powers behind the performance [...]" (Goffman 1959: 70).

and a detailed knowledge of many different social roles. Setting up and maintaining the dramaturgical space in which a social interaction can "take place" is a matter of bringing many non-present and non-human actors into play so that it becomes increasingly difficult to change settings, renegotiate frames, challenge idealizations, and open up the question of what game is being played. Interaction is therefore based more on "co-regulation" than "coorientation."[16] This may well be experienced as constraint, as a macro social structure that conditions and limits who we are, what we can do, and how we can organize our common endeavors. Nevertheless, without these various forms of information control, Taylor's texts would have no effect, and Cooren's ventriloquist would have trouble gaining the attention of anybody long enough in order to get them interested in his or her performance. It is not that nobody would care; they simply would not understand what was going on and what was expected of them. The more human and non-human actors have been mobilized and translated into a certain situation, the more it becomes increasingly difficult to move them and to change the constellation into which they have been arranged. This is what gives organizations, which are large assemblages of actors associated in certain ways, the appearance of being somehow "macro," that is, beyond individuals, overpowering them and forcing them into ways of being that are distinctly social.

Recalling what was said above in Part 1 about technical mediation, if we follow the somewhat unusual terminology of ANT, staging is nothing other than "mediating," that is, "translating" and "enrolling" human activity into the activity of a hybrid actor, a network made up of humans and non-humans.[17] Latour views interaction as a network effect.

---

16 | Cognitive research (see Fogel 1993: 29ff.) speaks of "co-regulation" instead of "co-orientation" (Taylor). Since Fogel bases his interpretation of interaction on systems theory, meaning is seen as an "emergent" property of interaction situations.
17 | Goffman's phenomenological descriptions of interaction have been confirmed by recent socio-cognitive research (Fogel 1993; King, 2004; Popova 2015), which uses the metaphor of a "dance" rather than theater. Citing King (2004) Popova (2015: 166) says that "social interaction should be considered as a dance, in which each partner must participate, moment by moment, in creating the coordination, which then will create a Gestalt effect [...]". As Fogel (1993: 29) puts it, interaction is a "continuous unfolding of individual action that is susceptible to being continuously modified by the continuously changing actions of the partner."

We say, without giving the matter too much thought, that we engage in 'face-to-face' interactions. Indeed we do, but the clothing that we are wearing comes from elsewhere and was manufactured a long time ago; the words we use were not formed for this occasion; the walls we have been leaning on were designed by an architect for a client, and constructed by workers – people who are absent today, although their action continues to make itself felt. The very person we are addressing is a product of a history that goes far beyond the framework of our relationship. If one attempted to draw a spatio-temporal map of what is present in the interaction, and to draw up a list of everyone who in one form or another were present, one would not sketch out a well-demarcated frame, but a convoluted network with a multiplicity of highly diverse dates, places and people. (Latour 1996: 231)

No actor appears on the social stage without the props, scripts, settings, etc. that make him or her into the person that he or she is in a social situation. All these humans and non-humans influence what is going on. No social situation is a pure interaction somehow taking place in a mythical *hic et nunc* of face-to-face co-presence. This does not mean that in the place of immediate interactions we must put macro social structures. On the contrary, Goffman's social actors are not isolated individuals, but scalable actor-networks, that is, hybrid actors more or less "distributed" in space and time. John Law made this point succinctly when he remarked:

If you took away my computer, my colleagues, my office, my books, my desk, my telephone I wouldn't be a sociologist writing papers, delivering lectures, and producing 'knowledge'. I'd be something quite other – and the same is true for all of us. So the analytical question is this. Is an agent an agent primarily because he or she inhabits a body that carries knowledges, skills, values, and all the rest? Or is an agent an agent because he or she inhabits a set of elements (including, of course, a body) that stretches out into the network of materials, somatic and otherwise, that surrounds each body? (1992: 382)

From the point of view of Goffman's dramaturgical theory of social interaction, we would presumably have to answer this question positively. The social actor is indeed someone who "inhabits a set of elements" that "stretches out into the network of materials, somatic and otherwise." *The dramaturgical construction of identity amounts to setting up an actor-network, that is, constructively engaging in processes of translation and enrollment on the basis of a program of action that is defined by negotiations involving all participants.* Who John Law is as a "sociologist writing papers, delivering lectures [...]," etc. is a question that his laptop, his office, his colleagues, etc. also contribute to answering. Obviously, the Cartesian concept of the self as a unified series of conscious states or mental representations is not very useful to describe what it means to be a social actor. Not isolated individuals, but networks are actors. If the network is also considered to be the basic form of social order, and therefore also the basic form of organization, then the relevance of Goffman's theory to organizational studies becomes apparent.

What is less apparent is the reason why Goffman's work, although its foundational significance for organization theory is acknowledged by all, has been subsumed under the tradition of symbolic interactionism, the linguistic turn, and a cognitive science that excludes anything beyond mental processes within the brain from the realm of meaning. Of course, one reason for this could well be that until recently there simply were no plausible alternatives to understanding how social order can be constructed apart from language and communication. The Cartesian view of mind and cognition as mental states within the brain dominated much of philosophy, psychology, and cognitive science for decades. Until recently, there were no convincing models of cognition that went beyond the brain. Meaning, language, and communication were understood as processes within the brain. Even if social constructivism attempted to modify this view, it was still a matter of individuals working together to construct social meaning. This situation is now changing. Actor-network theory is surely one example of a broader view of meaning and action. Another can be found in the new non-Cartesian cognitive science, which understands mind as embodied, embedded, enacted, and extended, that is, as beyond the confines of the brain. Our claim is that insights gained from ANT and from Goffman's dramaturgical theory of interaction provide a basis for understanding Weick's "sensemaking" as constitutive of organizations in a way that extends and enriches the work done by the CCO school of thought.

If communication is understood as networking and networking as staging, then sensemaking cannot be a merely linguistic or mental activity. If sensemaking is not a merely linguistic or mental activity, then there is no gap to be bridged between interaction and organization, between individual and society. Interactions, in the extended sense described above, are the social and as such they are constantly organizing. What seems to be standing in the way of an adequate theory of the communicative constitution of organizations is an inadequate concept of communication itself. So long as communication is not understood to be embodied, embedded, enacted, and extended, there will always be a gap that needs to be bridged, there will always be a tension between agency and structure. In order to sketch out a definition of communication that not merely bridges a supposed gap between micro interaction and macro structure, but eliminates it altogether, we turn to a discussion of that form of communication which is often placed at the center of organizational studies, namely, the concept of "narrative."

SENSEMAKING AND NARRATIVE

In recent years, many social scientists including organizational theorists have come to see narrative as that form of communication that orders human action.[18] Why is storytelling so interesting for understanding organizations? To begin with, narrative communication constitutes social actors within a context of temporally interdependent events. From the point of view of narrative, if anything is to do anything at all in a meaningful way, it has to take on a an identity, that is, a certain role in relation to other actors in a coherent series of activities and occurrences. Some claim that it is only through narrative that agency can appear at all.[19] If there is no story, there are no actors, and nothing happens. Without narrative, nothing is done or accomplished. No nation, no people, no city, no company, no association, no organization, and even no individual actor could exist without being able to tell "their" story. Identity, both personal and collective, appears to be a narrative construct.[20]

The idea of the communicative constitution of organizations, as we saw above, can be traced back largely to Karl Weick's idea of "sensemaking."

---

18 | See not only the foundational work of Weick (1969, 1995), but more recently Czarniawska (1998).

19 | See for example the foundational work of Brunner (1986) on narrative and identity.

20 | The literature on narrative is inexhaustible. For questions of identity, see for example Brunner (1986), Mackenzie/Atkins (2008).

Weick not only understood organizations to be processes of sensemaking, but saw sensemaking as storytelling.

To focus on sensemaking is to portray organizing as the experience of being thrown in an ongoing, unknowable, unpredictable streaming of experience in search of answers to the question 'what's the story'. (Weick et al. 2005: 410)

Sensemaking is storytelling because it is the story that makes sense of what is going on, that assigns roles to actors, sets goals, and thus organizes action. Weick is careful to point out that it is not a matter of merely interpreting a script that already exists. Storytelling for Weick is not just interpretation of texts, but a creative process. For Weick, the process of organizing is a creative narrative process.

A focus on sensemaking induces a mindset to focus on process, whereas this is less true with interpretation (= product) [...]. The act of interpreting implies that something is there, a text in the world, waiting to be discovered or approximated. Sensemaking, however, is less about discovery than is about invention. To engage in sensemaking is to construct, filter, frame, create facticity, and render the subjective into something more tangible. [...] The concept of sensemaking is valuable because it highlights the invention that precedes interpretation. It is also valuable because it implies a higher level of engagement by the actor [...]. A failure in sensemaking is consequential as well as existential. It throws into question the nature of the self and the world [...]. Whenever the sense is lost (= failure of efforts to replace one sense of the world with another), the loss is deeply troubling, whereas the loss of an interpretation is more like a nuisance (= interpretations can be added or dropped with less effect on one's self-perceptions). (Weick 1995: 13-14)

Despite the emphasis on creativity, invention, and process, Weick knows very well that sensemaking cannot be creation *ex nihilo*. Stories that make sense are based upon stories that have already made sense in some form and have already been told and which are therefore known and more or less accepted by all involved in the sensemaking process. For this reason, sensemaking is not only forward-looking and inventive, but also retrospective. Apart from the temporal dynamic of linking past, present, and future, there are other constitutive characteristics of storytelling. Weick (1995: 17) lists seven defining characteristics of sensemaking, which indicate the breadth, as well as the complexity, of how sensemaking works.

Sensemaking is understood as a process that is:
1. Grounded in identity construction
2. Retrospective
3. Enactive of sensible environments
4. Social
5. Ongoing
6. Focused on and by extracted cues
7. Driven by plausibility rather than accuracy

The reception of Weick's work by Taylor, McPhee, Zaug, Cooren and other thinkers within the CCO School did not, with the exception of Czarniawska (1998, 2004, 2008) focus on narrative.[21] Instead, different kinds of information flow, interdependence of conversations and texts, or ventriloquism take center stage. The CCO School tends to ask the right question, namely, how communication constitutes organizations, but focuses primarily on forms of communication that are linguistic and discursive. This interpretation of Weick's seminal concept of sensemaking is understandable considering the influence of the linguistic turn in philosophy and in the social sciences. Nonetheless, it tends to neglect the material, embodied, and enacted aspects of Weick's original idea. In order to open up the possibility of understanding sensemaking in a broader way, we have taken a detour through Goffman's dramaturgical theory of interaction. For Goffman, as we saw above, not only do material things play an important role in enabling communication, but the dramaturgical metaphor suggests a close relation between role playing and storytelling. Perhaps Goffman's description of staging can serve as a basis for interpreting Weick's notion of sensemaking in a more enacted and material way, and thus lay the foundation for a more adequate understanding of the role of narrative in organizing.

Acting out a role in a dramaturgical setting is at once performance and narrative. When we witness a performance on stage it is the actions and the setting, and not only the language or script, that tell the story. As Goffman might have put it, the social actor is also a storyteller. This is also

---

21 | For a review of literature on sensemaking see Maitlis/Christianson (2014).

what Weick meant, when he claimed that sensemaking amounts to finding a good story. Although Weick seldom refers to Goffman when explaining sensemaking, we will argue that sensemaking and staging have much in common. If we look more closely at the seven defining characteristics of sensemaking cited above, it can be argued that sensemaking in organizations as Weick describes it and the staging of social interactions in Goffman's dramaturgical theory are in fact the same process. If this is the case, there is no fundamental difference between interaction and organizing, that is, between micro and macro levels or between agency and structure. Interaction is organizing, and organizations consist of nothing other than interactions. According to Weick, organizations arise in and are maintained and transformed by means of sensemaking. When Goffman described social interactions, he was explicitly not looking for organizations or even interested in how organizations are constituted. Nonetheless, Goffman's description of staging may well be a useful description of that process by which social order, including organizations, is enacted. we will attempt to make this claim plausible by comparing sensemaking to staging. An important link in the argument will be offered by the significance of narrative.

For Weick, the first and most important characteristic of sensemaking is the construction of identity. Identity is not only a matter of who is doing what, but also of what the situation is in which actors play roles.

Identities are constituted out of the process of interaction. To shift among interactions is to shift among definitions of self. Thus the sensemaker is himself or herself an ongoing puzzle undergoing continual redefinition, coincident with presenting some self to others and trying to decide which self is appropriate. Depending on who I am, my definition of what is 'out there' will also change. Whenever I define self, I define 'it,' but to define it is also to define self. Once I know who I am then I know what is out there. But the direction of causality flows just as often from the situation to a definition of self as it does the other way. And this is why the establishment and maintenance of identity is a core preoccupation in sensemaking [...]. (Weick 1995: 20)

From Goffman's perspective, this amounts to the taking on a role by means of identification and attempting to establish the setting. The actor must put on a mask, take on a role, and attempt to internalize or identify as much as possible with the role. This is only possible, if the role also fits the situation, the frame in which it is being proposed. Organizing activities in organizations and social interaction both require that actors find out who they are and what role they are to play by means of making associations and attempting to fit actions, words, settings, props, appearances, etc. together in a meaningful way. McPhee and Zaug's four flows model could be understood to describe typical frames that are repeatedly used by actors to situate their sensemaking activities in certain kinds of organizations. The stories that are told often appear as membership negotiation, self-structuring, institutional positioning, or activity coordination. Standardized roles, goals, settings, scripts, etc. are available for use, but cannot be seen as dominant structures dictating what the story is. The answer to the question, "What's the story," relies on given scenarios, but is nonetheless an outcome of ongoing negotiations.

Identification, for Goffman, is supported by reference to "standardized" expectations about the situation on the part of those involved in the interaction. This requires what Weick calls a "retrospective" view about what is taking place. Organizing activities begin with a question, a problem, a situation that calls for action of some kind. Actors ask themselves: What has happened that has led to this particular situation? Who was involved? What were they doing? All these questions imply a retrospective reconstruction of actors and events. Weick is careful to point out that retrospective definition of a situation is not a matter of attempting to find out as objectively as possible what might have happened in the past. On the contrary, the past is constructed on the basis of present actions and decisions. Actors set priorities, make decisions about relevance and goals and then retrospectively explain, account for, and legitimate what they are doing in the present. Weick refers to Garfinkel's (1967: 104ff.) classic study of how jurors make sense of evidence and arguments in a trial. They do not as expected attempt to find out what happened, but first make decisions about what happened and then retrospectively go back and attempt to justify their decisions by selecting what they consider to be relevant evidence and arguments. Weick generalizes this procedure for sensemaking in organizational settings.

The important point is that retrospective sensemaking is an activity in which many possible meanings may need to be synthesized, because many different projects are under way at the time reflection takes place [...]. The problem is that there are too many meanings, not too few. [...] The problem is confusion, not ignorance. I emphasize this because those investigators who favor the metaphor of information processing [...] often view sensemaking, as they do most other problems, as a setting where people need more information. That is not what people need when they are overwhelmed by equivocality. Instead, they need values, priorities, and clarity about preferences to help them be clear about which projects matter. Clarity on values clarifies what is important in elapsed experience, which finally gives some sense of what that elapsed experience means constructed retrospectively on the basis of what is supposed to have happened and what is expected to happen in the future. (Weick 1995: 27-28)

In terms of staging, when an actor puts on a mask and takes her place on a stage that she has set up, she makes every effort to select what is relevant and important in order to make it clear to others what the situation is about and what role she is attempting to play. This means setting priorities, making decisions about goals, defining possible options, and envisioning future outcomes. Present decisions, therefore, condition what is claimed to have been going on in the past and what is understood to have led to this present action.[22]

The third characteristic of sensemaking according to Weick is that it is enactive, embodied, and material. Weick speaks of sensemaking as being "enactive of sensible environments." Quite in keeping with "embodied" and "enacted" cognitive science, which we will discuss later, Weick emphasizes that "the concept of sensemaking keeps action and cognition together" (30). This corresponds to what Goffman calls setting the stage, the front, appearance, and manner. Sensemaking, just as setting the stage, takes place by means of interventions into the environment, manipulating material things, moving about physical objects, etc. Weick is very clear about this. "I use the word *enactment* to preserve the fact that, in organizational life, people often produce part of the environment they face..." (30). Enactment means that the situation, the frame, the context in which actors appear and attempt to do things is not fixed and determined, but an ongoing process of the actors themselves.

---

22 | The fact that it is decisions in the present made on expectations of future outcomes that come before retrospective sensemaking has led to the idea of "prospective" sensemaking (cf. Gioia/Corley/Fabbri 2002; Boje 2011).

[...] there is not some kind of monolithic, singular, fixed environment that exists detached from and external to these people. Instead, in each case the people are very much a part of their own environments. They act, and in doing so create the materials that become the constraints and opportunities they face. There is not some impersonal 'they' who puts these environments in front of passive people. Instead, the 'they' is people who are more active. (Weick 1995: 31)

This can also be said of all the activities that actors perform in order to make their role understandable and acceptable to their audience. Setting the stage for social interaction means making many decisions about place, props, appearance, and manner that require action. This can also be seen as the locus of *power* in social relations. Performance is always an attempt to make a certain definition of a situation be accepted by others. In terms of actor-network theory, the translation and enrollment of actors is always guided by the attempt to realize a certain program of action often against the resistance of other actors, who have their own programs of action. To the extent that an actor is successful in setting the stage, or enacting her program of action, this then becomes a constraint on the other actors involved. It appears as a macro structure determining what they are to think and do. That which Taylor calls "texts" are the products of enactment and staging. Here again, it should be kept in mind, that not only humans are doing the acting, but also non-humans.

The fourth defining characteristic of sensemaking for Weick is that it is always social. Making sense is an intersubjective construction of meaning for the sake of enabling interaction and cooperation. This is of course what Goffman's theory is all about. The social actor is never alone, even if no other people are present at the moment. The actor is always also the audience. Weick (38) cites Walsh and Ungson (1991: 60) who clearly state that an organization is "a network of intersubjectively shared meanings that are sustained through the development and use of a common language and everyday social interaction." For Weick (39) the social dimension of sensemaking derives from the fact that "Conduct is contingent on the conduct of others, whether those others are imagined or physically present." This point hardly needs to be emphasized when comparing sensemaking to Goffman's theory of staging. After all, interaction is by definition social.

The fifth characteristic of sensemaking is that it is an ongoing process and not a fixed state of being. Weick emphasizes that sensemaking "never stops" and "never starts" (43). Organizing is a matter of always being in the middle of things. One situation leads to another. Sense is never made, but always "in the making." Goffman would agree that frames and interactions are constantly changing, being modified, and open to contestation and renegotiation. Indeed, the construction of meaning, as philosophical hermeneutics (Dilthey, Heidegger, Gadamer, Ricoeur) has long said, is a circular movement that continually spirals into time. In order to explain what this means, Weick cites the interpretation of Heidegger's hermeneutical circle by Winograd and Flores (1986: 34-36):

1. You cannot avoid acting: Your actions affect the situation and yourself, often against your will.
2. You cannot step back and reflect on your actions: You are thrown on your intuitions and have to deal with whatever comes up as it comes up.
3. The effects of action cannot be predicted: The dynamic nature of social conduct precludes accurate prediction.
4. You do not have a stable representation of the situation: Patterns may be evident after the fact, but at the time the flow unfolds there is nothing but arbitrary fragments capable of being organized into a host of different patterns or possibly no pattern whatsoever.
5. Every representation is an interpretation: There is no way to settle that any interpretation is right or wrong, which means an 'objective analysis' of that into which one was thrown, is impossible.
6. Language is action: Whenever people say something, they create rather than describe a situation, which means it is impossible to stay detached from whatever emerges unless you say nothing, which is such a strange way to react that the situation is deflected anyway.

The sixth characteristic of Weick's sensemaking is also to be found in Goffman's staging in that the selection of cues, objects, appearance, manners, etc. is always biased, incomplete, subjective, and guided by divergent interests. What Goffman refers to as idealization, simplification, and exclusion all aim to reduce the complexity of a situation, filter out what could confuse other actors, and steer activities in a certain direction. Actors attempt to establish a context, or frame for the interaction. The frame is at once a product of cues and that which conditions which cues are selected or preferred. As Weick puts it, "Extracted cues are simple, familiar structures that are seeds from which people develop a larger sense of what may be occurring" (50). The important thing about selected cues is that they work. Sensemaking takes hold of cues in the midst of uncertainty and attempts to use them to construct order and meaning out of a situation. The ongoing, social, enacted, retrospective construction of identity and meaning uses cues that it at once selects and is selected by.

Finally, sensemaking, just as storytelling, is driven by plausibility, coherence, and acceptability instead of objective factuality. The story has to be good, but not necessarily objectively true. This corresponds to Goffman's idea of "mystification." Mystification is what makes an actor's performance convincing and believable. If sense is always in the making, then the best sense that can be made out of a situation is never determined by what is already known with certainty. In an ongoing process there is always uncertainty and incomplete information. There is no objective, accurate knowledge of so-called facts.

The strength of sensemaking as a perspective derives from the fact that it does not rely on accuracy and its model is not object perception. Instead, sensemaking is about plausibility, pragmatics, coherence, reasonableness, creation, invention, and instrumentality. (Weick 1995: 57)

Accuracy and factuality which are expected of scientific knowledge are in any case unattainable in the process of organizing, since information is always selected and filtered by the interests of actors participating in a situation. There is no such thing as complete and accurate knowledge of any real-life situation. In organizing, decisions must be made, usually in a hurry, on the basis of incomplete and uncertain information. For the manager, as well as the actor in a social interaction, creating belief and inspiring consent and cooperation is the most important thing, and objective truth comes later, if at all. In any case, the social and ongoing nature of sensemaking implies that there will always be different interpretations, points of view, and perspectives on any state of affairs. To insist upon accuracy would mean that practically speaking, no decision could ever be made. This brings us to the significance or narrative in sensemaking.

If accuracy is nice but not necessary in sensemaking, then what is necessary? The answer is, something that preserves plausibility and coherence, something that is reasonable and memorable, something that embodies past experience and expectations, something that resonates with other people, something that can be constructed retrospectively but also can be used prospectively, something that captures both feeling and thought, something that allows for embellishment to fit current oddities, something that is fun to construct. In short, what is necessary in sensemaking is a good story. (Weick 1995: 60-61)

NARRATIVE AND COGNITIVE SCIENCE

Despite the many references to action, embodiment, and environment in Weick's description of sensemaking, it seems to culminate in language, discourse, and narrative. The reception of Weick's concept of sensemaking, at least within the CCO school, has largely understood it to be primarily a linguistic and cognitive activity. As Taylor and Van Every (2000: 40) put it, "sensemaking involves turning circumstances into a situation that is comprehended explicitly in words." So also the opinion of Gephart (1993: 1485), "Sensemaking has been defined as the discursive process of constructing and interpreting the social world." Similarly, Hill and Levenhagen (1995: 1057) understand sensemaking as "a vision or mental model of how the environment works." Finally, for Balogun and Johnson (2005: 1576), "Sensemaking is primarily a conversational and narrative process...involving a variety of communication genre [...] both spoken and written, and formal and informal." Although there are interpretations of sensemaking that include non-verbal communication and action, the emphasis on language and mental processes in theorizing sensemaking and storytelling is apparent.

The dominant interpretation of sensemaking emphasizes linguistic and discursive activities. Even if stories help construct identity and are social in nature, they are no different from any other communication, namely, linguistic entities that come from the brains of individual human beings. Understanding sensemaking as networking and as staging, however, makes it at least plausible to claim that what for Taylor appear to be episodic micro-conversations or for Cooren as ventriloquism could better be understood as the activity of networking, that is, of bringing many non-human actors onto the stage of social interaction and extending interaction beyond the *hic et nunc* of face-to-face communication. If we take a broader view of sensemaking to include networking and staging, the gap between micro and macro disappears and therefore no longer needs to be bridged or explained away. The question is no longer how do we get from micro interaction to macro social structures, from conversations around a cup of coffee to decisions of the board of directors. Instead, what needs to be explained is how interaction and sensemaking are embodied, embedded, enacted, and extended in the environment and no longer something that happens first and foremost in the heads of individual humans. To equate sensemaking with storytelling calls for an understanding of language and cognition that is no longer based on a Cartesian mind/body or subject/object dualism. In case this is possible and plausible, it can indeed be claimed that narrative is that form of communication that organizes actors into organizations (Czarniawska 1998, 2004) and we can better explain how communication constitutes organizations.

The concept of storytelling is admittedly confusing. On the one hand, it emphasizes language, writing, and communication, that is, something that is authored by humans. Stories are artifacts. Narratives are things that someone has produced and put out into the world in form of texts, as Taylor would say. On the other hand, narrative is said to construct identities, actors, and bind human actors into associations with things. In this view, narrative is the process of organizing in much the same way as we have defined networking. On the one side, storytelling is a linguistic expression of mental representations. On the other side, narrative is the process of translating, enrolling, mediation, making associations, and building actor-networks. Narrative seems at once to lie beneath and above human control and decision. As social actors, we find ourselves at once under the script that describes the roles we have to play and above the script as playwrights, changing the roles and all associated props to fit the current situation. It is this paradoxical character of narrative to at once shape and be shaped by actors both human and non-human that prompts Latour (2013a; 2013b, 381ff.) to link storytelling and organization so closely together that they form a unique "mode of existence." Like the links, interfaces, and information that made a primitive actor-network out of the hand and the stone in the example of the stone axe discussed in Part 1, the "script," as Latour (2013b: 391) puts it, "holds on" to the actor, binds her into expectations, associations, and activities, while at the same time she is the one who is doing the telling and playing the role.[23]

Instead of speaking of the communicative constitution of organizations, the challenge seems to lie in a theory of the *narrative constitution of organizations*. The problem that immediately presents itself, if we take this suggestion seriously, is that narrative seems to be a monologue and not a social event, and it seems to be merely linguistic and not enacted and extended into the environment. This situation is not helped by the fact that narrative theory is based upon textual hermeneutics, literary theory, linguistics, and psychology. Often cited as sources of narrative theory in the social sciences are Russian formalism, the New Criticism in the USA, French structuralism, and German hermeneutics (Polkinghorne 1987, Czarniawska 2004). All of these approaches to narrative assume that storytelling is a universal and primordial form in which humans organize experience, make meaning of otherwise chaotic and meaningless events, and mediate their social relations. The way in which humans do this is by making use of their unique cognitive abilities. The emphasis is on language and the cognitive processes of a big brain. Story telling is something humans do first of all in their heads, that is, by using the cognitive abilities of the mind and which is then expressed in language, whether spoken or written. This view is reflected in the typical definitions of narrative that Herman (2007: 23ff.) lists:

One will define narrative without difficulty as the representation of an event or of a sequence of events. (Genette 1982: 127)

The representation [...] of one or more real or fictive events communicated by one, two or several [...] narrators [...] to one, two or several narratees. (Prince, 2003: 58)

Narrative is the representation of events, consisting of story and narrative discourse, story is an event or sequence of events (the action), and narrative discourse is those events as represented. (Abbott 2002: 16)

---

23 | In order to emphasize the dynamic, future orientation of narrative, Boje (2011) introduces the concept of "antenarratives." "Antenarratives are a bridging of past narratives stuck in place with emergent living stories. [...] This exchange is what shapes the future of organizations" (3, 4).

Narrative is the representation of at least two real or fictive events in a time sequence, neither of which presupposes or entails the other. (Prince 1982: 4)

The semiotic representation of a sequence of events, meaningfully connected in a temporal and causal way. (Onega/Landa 1996: 3)

Herman (2007: 24) points out that many of the terms used in these definitions imply other key concepts. To speak of events implies not only temporal sequence and relation, but also action, which implies agents, which further implies intentions or motivations. In addition to this, when agents are motivated to do things, they usually are trying to solve problems or settle conflicts of some kind. Furthermore, all of these definitions make certain assumptions, namely, that narrative is "a form of mental representation, a type of textual or semiotic artifact, and a resource for communicative interaction" (Herman 2009, 2). Narrative theory is obviously conditioned by its heritage from literary studies and textual hermeneutics. This is understandable, after all, telling a story is something that happens in language, spoken or written by someone for someone with a certain purpose and constrained by formal and cultural understandings, such as genre, about what counts as a story, and how such things as stories are to be understood.

It may seem surprising that storytelling and narrative have come to play such an important role in the social sciences. The attractiveness of narrative theory for the social sciences, despite its basis in texts and language, comes from its clear rejection of positivism and the so-called "behavioral" approach to the social world. The phenomenological and hermeneutical tradition in the human sciences had always resisted the idea that human life can become the object of a value-free, objective way of knowing modeled upon the natural sciences. Meaningful action, as opposed to mere behavior, depends upon actors having intentions and reasons for what they do and upon their ability to give good reasons for their actions.[24] An appropriate methodology for the human sciences would therefore be based on "understanding" of

---

24 | "Within the logical-scientific mode of knowing, an explanation is achieved by recognizing an event as an instance of a general law, or as belonging to a certain category. Within the narrative mode of knowing, an explanation consists in relating an event to a human project [...]" (Czarniawska 2004: 8).

intentions and not on "explanation" of behavior.[25] The non-positivist self-understanding of the human sciences, including organizational studies, has largely been determined by the attempt to define both its proper object of study and its proper methodology in opposition to the natural sciences. This program has led to an emphasis on texts, language, and intentionality, which in turn is supported by the typically modern split between subject and object and between the social and the natural realms of being. Under the influence of this "modern constitution" (Latour 1993: 13ff.), it becomes almost inevitable to understand sensemaking and storytelling as mental activities undertaken by Cartesian subjects and expressed in spoken language and written texts. Our claim is that this situation has led to an understanding of communication and narrative that is no longer fruitful for a contemporary theory of organizations. If organizations are to be understood as being constituted by processes of sensemaking, understood as networking and staging, then narrative must be understood not only linguistically, but also as material, embodied, enacted, and extended in the environment. The question now becomes, *how must narrative be conceived in order to serve as a foundational concept for a network theory of organizations.*

A new approach to narrative that is less dependent on the assumptions of modernity comes from new directions in cognitive science. Under the title of "distributed cognition," "extended mind," or "enacted mind," current research has pointed to the constitutive link between embodiment, action, material objects, and cognitive processes.[26] According to this view, cognition is always already extended into the material world.[27] This means that there is no gap to bridge between a Cartesian subject on the one side and the world of non-humans on the other side. The subject is already always objectified, a "quasi-subject" as Latour puts it. The object is always already in some way an actor, a mediator, a partner

---

25 | See Apel (1988) for a detailed discussion of the classic conflict between hermeneutics and positivism.

26 | See Herman (2013) and Popova (2015) for a discussion of non-Cartesian cognitive science applied to narrative.

27 | Cognition refers to the following tasks: "(1) perceiving (visually, aurally, etc.) the world, (2) remembering perceived information, (3) reasoning on the basis of information perceived or remembered, and (4) expressing this information, or listening to information expressed by others, in the form of language." (Rowlands 2010: 16)

in sensemaking. Latour speaks therefore not only of quasi-subjects, that is, subjects that are also objects, but "quasi-objects," or objects that are also actors. This is what technical mediation, as described in Part 1, is all about. If we recall what was said in Part 1 about how technical mediation can be considered the construction of information, the claim is that information, whether perceived, remembered, processed, or expressed, is not something exclusively in the heads of those primates with brains big enough to somehow hold on to it. According to ANT, information is distributed among the actors in an actor-network. It is not the human alone, not the stone alone, and not the wood alone that makes a "builder using a stone axe." All contribute to the actor-network. The interfaces that mediate hand, stone, and wood, may be understood as information. They are cognitive, but belong to the network and not exclusively to any of the individual components in the network.

This insight is the basis of what has come to be called "non-Cartesian cognitive science" (Rowlands 2010). This new model of cognition has become a viable alternative to the traditional computational model. Cartesian cognitive science is also known as the computational model of cognition. According to this traditional view, cognition is like a computer. The brain is the hardware, the mental processes that go on in the brain are the software, the data that is processed come from the sense organs, and the output is language and action. A non-Cartesian cognitive science rejects the computational model and extends cognition beyond the brain. "The starting point for non-Cartesian cognitive science is the extent to which we make use of things around us in order to solve problems and get things done" (Rowlands 2010: 13). What the new cognitive science shows is that cognition is an attribute of the actor-network not of the individual actors. It is the actor-network that is intelligent, that learns, that acts and not the individuals that make it up. Otherwise known as the "4e model," this new paradigm of cognitive science sees cognition not as something that exclusively happens in the brains of humans, but something that happens in the interactions of humans with non-humans. Mind is said to be "embodied," "embedded," "extended," and "enacted" (3).

To claim that cognition is *embodied* amounts to recognizing bodily processes and structures as partly constitutive of mental processes. It is not enough, as Rowlands makes clear, to claim that cognitive processes depend on bodily structures, such as in the case of audio perception, the distance between the ears is used in order to calculate the direction of a sound source. If this is theorized merely as a dependence, it leaves cognitive processes within the brain, even though the brain is dependent on a body for obtaining the data it processes. The thesis of the embodied mind is only a challenge for Cartesian views if bodily structures "constitute" or "compose" cognitive processes.

According to this [...] interpretation, cognitive processes are not restricted to structures and operations instantiated in the brain, but incorporate wider bodily structures and processes. These wider bodily structures and processes in part constitute – are constituents of – cognitive processes. (Rowlands 2010: 57)

Although Rowlands limits his discussion of embodiment to research done on visual and audio perception (see Shapiro 2004), this basic insight could easily be adapted to Kubrick's ape, and the example of the hand, the stone, and the wood that we described as technical mediation in Part 1. The shape and functionality of the hand, the strength of the arm, all these bodily structures contributed to the link, the interface that made the stone axe possible. The ape in Kubrick's film did not first sit down and think about using the bone in this or that particular way and then form a mental representation of these uses which was expressed in language or action. On the contrary, cognition happens in the links between hand, bone, and the skulls of the enemies, or, in our less violent example of the stone axe, in the interfaces between hand, stone, and wood. It is the network that creates information. It is the network that is intelligent. The thesis of the embodied mind amounts to claiming that the body also thinks and not merely the brain.

The concept of the "extended mind" can be traced back to Clark and Chalmers (1998) seminal article of the same title. Going beyond the thesis of embodied mind, the thesis of the extended mind claims that cognitive processes are distributed not only in the body, but also in the environment.

The actions that the organism performs on the world around it are ones of manipulating, exploiting, and/or transforming external structures. What is distinctive of these structures is that they carry information relevant to accomplishing a given cognitive task. And by acting on these structures in suitable ways, the cognizing organism is able to make that information available to itself and to its subsequent cognitive operations. (Rowlands 2010: 58)

Latour's description of technical mediation via processes of translation and enrollment could easily be appealed to in order to explain what the extended mind thesis is all about. The difference between Rowlands' interpretation and Latour's theory of technical mediation is that for Rowlands the role of things is limited to merely making information "present" (58) and not actively mediating interfaces, links, and associations. ANT assigns to things a more active role in the construction of information than do current theories of the extended mind. It could, of course be argued that making information present and available for humans to appropriate is already an activity on the part of entities. It is nonetheless unclear what is meant by information in Rowlands' account. Rowlands model of extended cognition implies four claims:

1. The world is an external store of information relevant to processes such as perceiving, remembering, reasoning [...] (and possibly) experiencing.
2. Cognitive processes are hybrid – they straddle both internal and external operations.
3. The external operations take the form of action, broadly construed: the manipulation, exploitation, and transformation of environmental structures – ones that carry information relevant to the accomplishing of a given task.
4. At least some of the internal processes are ones concerned with supplying the subject with the ability to appropriately use relevant structures in its environment. (Rowlands 2010: 59)

It would seem that Rowlands understands information as something that is somehow present in things awaiting human agents who know how to access and use this information for their own purposes. The world appears as an "external store of information," much like a library full of books. Humans do things, that is, "manipulation, exploitation, and transformation" in order to access information that is "carried" in external objects. An example of such action would be going to the library, checking out the book, holding it properly in the hand and reading it.[28] This view of information seems to think of information as some kind of entity that

---

28 | This is in fact very similar to the example of Otto using his notebook to find instructions to get to the museum that is discussed by Clark/Chalmers (1998).

can be present in the world. If information, as we argue, is conceived of as a relation, a difference, a link, or interface, then it cannot be present apart from the mediating activities of actors in a network. Indeed, information *is* this activity of mediating. Information in this view is not at all like data stored on disks, or in books, that can be called up and processed by computer-like brains.

Rowlands' account of extended cognition seems not to take account of the way information is constituted as mediation, translation, and enrollment of actors within an actor-network. Information understood as technical mediation is not *in* anything, it does not lie about in the environment waiting to be discovered. This implies also, as Rowlands would agree, that information cannot be a cognitive state. It is not a substance, not even a mental substance, but a relation, a difference, a mediation. Information is what is constructed when humans and non-humans become translated and enrolled into an actor-network. It is the glue that holds the network together. Information is an interface that points in two directions at once. In the relation between the hand and the stone, for example, both contribute something to make such a thing as a stone axe, a hunter, or a builder. Information is a product of both human and non-human agency. It is perhaps best defined as that which agency, that is, mediation, is. This broader concept of agency and information is not denied by the thesis of the extended mind. Rowlands (67) is careful to say that the extended mind thesis does not refer to cognitive "states," but to cognitive "processes." There is therefore no reason why the thesis of extended mind could not be interpreted from an ANT perspective. Our claim will be that interpreting cognitive science from the point of view of ANT contributes to a theory of narrative capable of showing how narrative is more like networking and staging than like the authoring and reading of literary texts.

The third of the four "e"s is the idea that cognition is *embedded*. The thesis of the embedded mind claims that not only bodily processes and structures, but also processes and structures outside the body in the environment are at least party constitutive of cognition. This view can be distinguished from the thesis of the extended mind by virtue of the idea of "off-loading" cognitive tasks onto to structures in the environment. As Rowlands puts it:

In general, the guiding idea underlying the thesis of the embedded mind is that in accomplishing cognitive tasks, an organism can utilize structures in its environment in such a way that the amount of internal processing it must perform is reduced. Some of the complexity of the task is, thereby, off-loaded onto the environment, given that the organism has the ability to appropriately exploit that environment. (2011: 69)

In this view, the brain must no longer carry the entire burden of the work when processing information. Cognitive tasks can be shared with external structures. Mind can thus be claimed to be "embedded" in an environment in which some cognitive tasks have been off-loaded. The environment becomes a "scaffold" or support structure for cognition. In the course of evolution cognition has become "dependent" upon such external structures. This dependence is an historical and contingent fact. The claim is therefore not that the mind must off-load information processing onto external structures, but simply that the mind has evolved in such way that this is the case. Rowlands (69f.) argues that the thesis of the embedded mind does not go far enough, since it only claims "dependency" on external factors and does not assert the "constitution" of cognition by external factors. The cognitive contributions of external factors come originally from the brain. There is no constitutive agency of non-humans. In this way, so Rowlands, the idea of the embedded mind still leaves the door open for Cartesian claims that real cognition happens only in the brain.

If we apply the idea of dependency on external factors to Goffman's description of how actors depend on staging in order to accomplish interactional performances, it could be argued that props, fronts, appearances, etc. are *necessary conditions* of the possibility of social performance and therefore also of sensemaking in Weick's terms. In a review of Hutchins' (1995) theory of "distributed cognition," Latour summarizes the idea of embeddedness as follows: "Thinking becomes an ingenious way of constantly shifting from one medium to the other until one reaches 'simpler' or 'easier' tasks by delegating more and more tasks to other actors in the setting, either humans or non-humans" (1996b: 57). This strategy, of course, can only work if the external structures or the non-humans actors actually do something and carry their burden of the work. If the stone did not do its share of the work, the hand could not cut the wood. Despite Rowlands' reservations, the thesis of the embedded mind could well be integrated into the concept of networking and also the idea of extended mind. The embedded mind can be interpreted such that it not only makes use of external supports, but can only do so, because things do their part of the cognitive work.

The fourth thesis of the new non-Cartesian cognitive science is that the mind is not only embodied, extended, and embedded, but also "enacted." This view of mind refers explicitly to the phenomenological tradition (Husserl; Merleau-Ponty) and was developed by Mackay (1967), Noë (2004) and Thompson (2007). Based on descriptions drawn from the phenomenology of perception it is argued that when we see something, what we see is not a product of mental constructs based on incomplete perceptual data, but something that can only be derived from bodily activities. For example, when we look at a tomato we do not have data of the entire three-dimensional form, but only of one limited perspective. Instead of assuming that when we see the three dimensional tomato we are making a mental construction on the basis of limited visual data, it is more reasonable to assume that we are seeing what bodily activities of holding the tomato in the hand and turning it around, etc. have produced. Generalizing this insight, knowledge about the world is a product of bodily activities. Knowledge is not "constructed," it is enacted. Knowledge is not merely a representation produced in the brain, but a practical activity. Knowing is doing.[29] If we add to this the claim that doing, or agency, is distributed in an actor-network among humans and non-humans, for example, that the stone also does something in order to become a stone axe in the hand of a hunter, then the enacted mind thesis is compatible with ANT. From the point of view of ANT, the answer to Rowlands' critically intended rhetorical question, "Is our ability to probe and explore environmental structures extended into, or distributed onto, the world" (75) is clearly "yes." Without the agency of things, human activities would not last longer than the moment these things were held in the hand and we would still be on the primate level of social organization. For ANT, the entire network is the actor and not merely the human part of it. Furthermore, and perhaps most importantly, the thesis of the enacted mind supports evolutionary theories of the development of cognition

---

29 | Recall the discussion above of Weick's notion of sensemaking as including enactment. Weick emphasizes, "the concept of sensemaking keeps action and cognition together" (1995: 30).

through practical knowledge. As we saw in Part 1, hominids used tools long before language, as we know it today, evolved. Donald (1991) referred to this ability as "mimetic culture." Actor-networks were more like "action-networks" in which humans and non-humans played different roles and pursued different goals in such a way that these activities themselves communicated what they were, how they were to be done, who could participate and so on. For almost a million years, language was not needed, even if much later on with the rise of *Homo sapiens* it became a decisive evolutionary advantage.

The reader has probably begun to ask what all this has to do with narrative and storytelling. Cognitive science was brought into the discussion in order to help explain why narrative is not merely something that goes on in the heads of humans and is expressed in language. If organizations are to be explained on the basis of communication, it would seem that talking heads is not enough. This becomes plausible the moment Latour's networking, Goffman's staging, and finally Weick's complex definition of sensemaking is taken into account. The important work done recently on the communicative constitution of organizations by McPhee, Zaug, Taylor, Cooren, and others would profit from an understanding of communication that is at least as embodied, embedded, enacted, and extended as non-Cartesian cognitive science proposes. Even if much contemporary theory on organizational communication still adheres to the talking heads model, the new cognitive science supports not only many of Weick's own statements about the embodied and enacted aspects of sensemaking, but also the comparison of sensemaking to ANT's concept of networking and Goffman's description of staging. In order to make it plausible, that communication is more than mental processes and language, we turn now to recent work on narrative from the perspective of non-Cartesian cognitive science.

The discussion of the new non-Cartesian cognitive science admits of at least two interpretations of storytelling. Narrative can be an artifact or a structure in the environment upon which information and cognitive tasks have been "off-loaded." Just as books in the library can be thought of as external sources of information that support cognitive processes, the texts, scripts, and stories used by actors in sensemaking and organizing can be seen as external cognitive scaffolds. Herman (2013) discusses this view of narrative in detail in his important book on *Story Telling and the Sciences of the Mind*. The second possible interpretation is that sensemaking, staging, and networking do not merely make use of narrative structures that language has put into the environment, but instead are themselves narratively structured. Networking, staging, and sensemaking *are* storytelling and not merely an activity that makes use of stories, scripts, and texts. This view claims that experience and action are narratively structured and that it is because of this that language can and does create narrative texts, both spoken and written. Narrative artifacts add variety, complexity, and quantity to actor-networks that are always already narratively structured. Popova (2015) and Lindblom (2007) have applied insights from non-Cartesian cognitive science to a theory of interaction and narrative that tends in this direction. Let us begin with the first alternative; narrative as artifact and then turn to the idea that networking and sensemaking are themselves narrative.

Under the title of "storying the world," Herman (2013) discusses "recent work in cognitive science as a resource for sense making" (4). Herman (227ff.) sees five ways in which narrative can be said to "scaffold intelligent activity," that is to say, be used as a tool. First, whether told, written, or enacted, narrative reduces the complexity of the world to segments of experience or manageable "chunks" (232ff.) Only certain things that happen are taken up by the story and many other things that are simultaneously going on in the world are excluded. At any moment the world is made up of an endless continuum of events. Not everything can be perceived, attended to, and made sense of. As already Weick pointed out, selection is necessary in order to reduce the infinite complexity of the world to manageable proportions. And as we saw in the discussion of primate social relations, monkeys are constantly confronted by the entire spectrum of social relations and must episodically and *ad hoc* negotiate what is happening at every moment. Narrative functions like a filter that allows only certain things to be perceived as relevant and filters out all the rest. Second, narrative constructs causal relations between the chunks of experience, which can then appear as "events" or "actions" carried out by actors with specific purposes. As Herman puts it, "narrative allows a constellation of events to be grasped as a series of actions grounded in a causal network" (237). When something happens, then something else has led to this event and something else will follow upon it. When something happens, this is because some actor, whether human or non-human, has done something. Stories select only those events that are meaningful, that is, an actor has done something that will lead to, influence, and condition what will happen next and what other actors will do. To speak of causal relationing in narrative does not imply a mechanical or deterministic causality, but much rather intentionality. The actor who does something, does it for a purpose. This is necessary in order to link up actors to events and events to each other in a meaningful way. It is often pointed out that a narrative is different from a mere list of events. This is precisely because it links one event to another in a chain of causal influence.

Third, not only does narrative break up a chaotic continuum of experience into chunks and relate these as events, but events that are linked to each other with regard to a certain outcome can be compared to expectations or established patterns so that problems and solutions appear. As Heidegger said, human existence is "thrown" into a historical world already structured by events, meanings, and projects. It is because of existing patterns and expectations that we can perceive "problems" and know when something does not behave as expected. Narrative therefore not only tells a particular story, but tells it within a world horizon of possible other stories. If things happen in a certain way, they could have happened otherwise. Narrative accounts for the possibility to make judgments not only about meaningfulness and credibility, but also about appropriateness, correctness, and fittingness. This in turn means that narrative is the basis of classification, categorization, and what has come to be called "ontologies." Things first appear in stories and only later can they be listed in classificatory systems and become items in inventories. Narrative makes it possible to discover norms, types, standards, contexts, and frames. The normal, the expected, appear as background against the unexpected, surprising, unusual, and abnormal. As we saw, when describing Goffman's dramaturgical theory of interaction, social actors are always concerned to meet expectations of appropriateness for the roles they attempt to play and these expectations are based on a world that is ordered in a certain way.

Narrative structure can be said to reduce the complexity of the world, link up actors and events in causal relations, and allow for the discovery of problems and solutions against the background of types and norms, but this is not all. The fourth characteristic of narrative according to Herman is that it assigns actors to roles within the scheme of events and discovers thereby "protocols for sequencing actions – that is, for figuring out exactly what one should do, where, when, and in what order" (243). This is what Goffman would call a "script." Greeting someone passing by on the street cannot be done in any way one might wish, that is, if one expects to be recognized and greeted in return. Narrative is procedural and normative in that it not only describes what happens, but also prescribes how things are to be done. This refers not only to the events in the story, which have a model character that can be imitated, but to the action of telling the story itself. The social actor goes to great trouble to set the stage for her performance. There are cues, efforts to select the audience, attempts to have the proper appearance, manner, props, and many more things that are mobilized such that other social actors are able to make sense of what is going on and participate. In words very similar to Weick and Goffman, Herman points out that

> [...] it is important to stress that narrative communication is not tantamount to activity on the part of the teller and passivity on the part of the interlocutor (or group of interlocutors). Rather, stories require a dovetailing of sequencing strategies by interpreters as well as producers of narrative. All parties must actively enable the production of the narrative via an intercalated sequence of actions performed and actions withheld. (Herman 2013: 244)

Finally, Herman argues that narrative can be described as "storying the world," that is, "as an instrument for distributing intelligence" (248). This means that narrative "off-loads" cognitive processes onto things and actors in the environment. Narrative itself can function as an off-loaded artifact when it becomes text in Taylor's sense of the term. It creates and becomes part of an environment that is made up of other actors, scripts, tools, events, norms, and patterns. Narrative constructs "agents-within-an-environment" (248), which Herman explicitly links to the ideas of distributed intelligence and embedded mind derived from cognitive science.

To say that stories, texts, or enactments are cognitive tools in which intelligence has been off-loaded is quite different from the view of narrative as the original form of action and experience that was discussed in Part 1 under the title of "technical mediation" and of "networking." From the point of view of networking, narrative is not a part of the environment, a mere tool or an artifact that can support cognitive processes, but instead, narrative is that which makes these processes possible. A story told or written is indeed an artifact, like the stone axe. It is a linguistic thing, which can also become an actor in an actor-network, for example, when managers develop a vision and a strategy for a company that is eventually expressed in protocols, statements, and documents and which in processes of sensemaking can be called upon to help solve problems. *The question we are asking is whether it is only possible to create narrative artifacts and texts, such as those that Taylor discusses, and which he claims are constitutive of organizations, or whether the reason this is possible is because experience is already narratively structured.* This more basic understanding of narrative as a condition of the possibility of texts, leads to a broader view that goes beyond thinking of stories as artefacts or tools that may or may not be available in the environment. Instead, narrative becomes inseparable from the activity of constructing an actor-network. Narrative is no longer an artifact that has certain affordances. It is of course true that narrative artifacts do have affordances. This is what Taylor describes as texts. These artifacts, or texts, tend to shape human action and experience. Herman also seems to argue that narrative is a tool for sensemaking, something sensemaking can make use of, but not sensemaking itself. A story is like the stone axe, a part of an actor-network, but not the activity of networking itself. Herman's concept of "storying the world," however, points to another interpretation of narrative as the way in which intelligence first becomes distributed, embedded, and extended. This is closer to Weick's view of sensemaking as organizing. In this view, narrative is networking, staging, and sensemaking itself and not merely a tool, one among others, that helps in these activities.

In certain passages, Herman seems to go beyond the idea that narrative is a part of the environment, and compares narrative structure to the environment itself, that is, to the entire intelligent ecosystem in which humans and non-humans interact. Citing Vygotsky, Hutchins, Clark, and others who defend the thesis of distributed cognition and extended mind, Herman compares narrative structure to a cognitive ecosystem – Latour of course would speak of an actor-network – in which "individual components of the system take on properties or capacities because of their participation in the larger whole to which they contribute" (260). Narrative is not the part, but the whole. Herman (263ff.) locates this important characteristic of narrative in its scalability. Despite the influence of the Aristotelian tradition in literary theory, stories are not in fact isolated units, always with a clear beginning, middle, and end. Stories are usually embedded within other stories. They link one set of roles, expectations, events, and outcomes with any number or others that take place outside the constraints of coherence imposed by any one setting or frame. Stories are not isolated frames, no more than any social interaction is isolated from others that have occurred before it and can occur after it is finished, or could occur instead of it. Narrative is therefore not only a specific story or frame, but that which also allows social actors to be able to switch from one frame to another, operate in different frames at the same time, make sense of different roles and expectations, without sacrificing continuity of identity. This is the decisive characteristic of narrative that makes what we call "history" possible. Without narrative, no actor, whether individual or collective, would be able to have a history that assimilates many different situations, roles, and expectations within an open horizon of potential meaning. From this point of view, narrative is not only *local*, but also *global*,[30] that is, all-encompassing.

The discussion of narrative from the perspective of cognitive science up to this point has opened up the question of whether stories are mere artifacts, or the condition of the possibility of artifacts. Is storytelling part of what organizing does, or the very nature of organizing itself? How can narrative be conceived of as the condition of the possibility of experience and not merely a useful tool for certain kinds of experience? In order to answer these questions, we turn to a discussion of action from the point of view of cognitive science. Does action and not merely what we say about actors and events have a narrative structure? Lindblom (2007) develops a theoretical framework for the "embodied nature of social interaction and cognition" (191ff.). She bases her argument not on the idea of distributed intelligence, but on the thesis of *embodied* and *enacted* mind. In keeping with the embodied mind thesis, she argues that "embodied actions should not be regarded as appendages of the thinking 'mind' [...]" (195). Embodied action is itself a cognitive process and must not wait upon linguistic expression in order to become meaningful.

For Lindblom, the thesis of the embodied mind as it is often presented in cognitive science does not address the issue of communication. It may be that mind is embodied, but how is embodied action also communication and therefore able to function as the basis of meaning which is never purely private, but also social? The problem left unanswered by much work on the embodied mind thesis is the social dimension of human life. Lindblom

---

30 | We will return to a discussion of localization and globalization below.

argues that "although the embodied approach has challenged mind/body dualism at the individual level, the dualistic stance between the individual and society is still present" (105). She argues that since an agents actions "are always in relation to others [...], it is literally useless to distinguish between individual and social actions" (196). Citing classic theorists of the social construction of meaning such as Mead (1934) and Vygotsky (1978), she claims that individuals do not first have mental representations and intentions and then enter into contact with an environment and with other social actors, but the other way round, "meaning and intentions are emergent phenomena of these social interactions" (196). If narrative is to be the condition of the possibility of organizing, then it must not be reducible to individual activities, but must be inherently social.

It is important to note that the social interactions Lindblom claims to be constitutive of mind do not include humans alone, but also non-humans. This is because intentions are not in the head, "but instead constructed between people and their surroundings" (196). This perspective enriches the thesis of the embodied mind not only with other bodies, but with things as well. The claim is that cognition is not only embodied, and is a "group event" (196). To speak of embodied mind is therefore to speak of "embodied actions in co-regulated social interaction" (196), which is almost an exact definition of what Goffman described as staging. The basis of co-regulation among social actors, as we saw in the discussion of Goffman's dramaturgical theory, is always the frame, the context, the situation. This defines what is going on, what game is being played, and what roles and expectations apply when questions of fitness, appropriateness, or just plain sense arise. For Lindblom, just as for Goffman, the context of social action is not merely other people, but also "external structures such as the different tools, artifacts and etc. that we use as scaffolds, offering important resources to social and cognitive action" (197). Finally, Lindblom is careful to point out that embodied social interaction unfolds in a temporal dimension and has a process character.[31]

Lindblom's argument is important for understanding narrative because it adds a *communicative dimension* to embodiment. The embodied mind is constituted in interactions with the environment, for example,

---

31 | "Interacting socially through embodied actions is a dynamical process that unfolds at a temporal horizon, which means that cognition should be considered a process rather than a static object of content." (Lindblom 2007: 197)

by using a stone axe to chop wood. The question is how this action is also communicative and therefore a force for establishing social relations. Recalling Donald's idea of a "mimetic culture" that characterizes prehumans long before *Homo sapiens* with linguistic abilities evolved, it can be supposed that social order was based on practical activities and not on linguistic communication. This implies that *actions in themselves have a communicative function*. When Kubrick's hominid used a bone tool this action not only did something, but also *showed* what it did. It *communicated* what was going on to others in the group. According to Lindblom (143), this possibility implies the following four fundamental functions of embodied action:

- The body functions as a social resonance mechanism
- The body functions as a means and end in social interaction
- Embodied actions and experiences function as a helping hand in shaping, expressing and sharing thoughts
- The body functions as a representational device.

What does this mean? It means that "there is a strong relation between embodied and cognitive states in social interaction, since the bi-directional exchange between these states as well as between the interacting partners, occur automatically without any higher knowledge structure" (144). In other words, *doing is communicating and not only knowing*. Support for this is to be found, according to Lindblom, in what has come to be known as "mirror neurons." "Mirror neurons are certain kinds of neurons that become activated both when performing a specific action and when observing the same goal-directed movements of an experimenter" (125). The same neurons are activated when an action is performed and when the action is merely observed. The mirror neurons are interpreted to be a kind of "resonance mechanism" that links observed activities to the subject's own activities by means of activating or simulating the observed action via the subject's own sensorimotor processes. When an activity is observed, this information is linked automatically and directly to the sensorimotor processes of the observer and not first sent to the brain to be encoded linguistically. The observer literally experiences or, as is often argued, "simulates" the action and thus can understand what is being done. The observer can not only mimic the activity, but also understand what is being done, for example, understand that the activity being observed is "chopping wood," or "hunting," or "building."[32] This view corresponds well with Donald's account of mimetic culture among hominids. Citing Rizzolatti (2005) and Fadiga et al. (1995), Lindblom says that "the linking between action and perception offers an 'intuitive' understanding of the observed action, i.e., what it means to do it and what the action really is about [...]" (126). She concludes:

Consequently, mirror neurons enable the agent to perceive and understand the meaning of the observed action, and its system is subsequently considered the neurobiological and embodied underpinning of social experience, social interaction as well as even mind-reading and ToM [Theory of Mind]. Apparently, the close linkage between first-hand and third-hand aspects of social interaction implies that the body and its sensorimotor processes are 'cognitive' in themselves, and not only bounded by the brain. The central issue here is 'action-understanding', which means that in order to recognize an action, besides activating the perceptual (e.g., visual or auditory) system, the motor system is also activated. (Lindblom 2007: 144)

The embodied mind becomes a social mind the moment activities themselves become communicative. If actions not only do something, but also communicate what is being done, this would explain why Kubrick's ape was special and also account for how the use of stone tools by prehumans did not remain merely episodic and individual, but were able to constitute social order. It also offers an explanatory basis, as Lindblom explicitly claims, for the emergence of language. Entities, gestures, sounds etc. could be used as signs and symbols that then could be linked into and added onto the actor-network. Let us recall at this point that actors, actions, and events that unfold in a temporal dynamic are constitutive characteristics of narrative. Narrative and social interaction seem to share many of the same constitutive characteristics. Is this sufficient reason to declare that they are similar or even identical? Can it be plausibly argued that the embodied and enacted mind is narratively structured? Are building actor-networks, staging, and sensemaking as we have previously

---

32 | Iacoboni (2005) describes a study in which mirror neurons were able to discern whether a person picking up a cup of tea intended to drink it or to clear it from the table.

described them also to be seen as narrative processes? If so, in what ways is narrative at once artifact and process?

In order to attempt to answer these questions, we turn to Popova's important work on *Stories, Meaning, and Experience, Narrativity and Enaction* (2015). Popova does not rely on neuroscience or a theory of simulation in order to explain the narrative structure of experience. Instead, she departs from Albert Michotte's (1946/1963) experiments on the perception of causality. Michotte set out to show that the philosopher David Hume was wrong in interpreting the concept of causality as a supposition created by the mind and not based on perception of reality. Against Hume, who was the person who Kant claimed awakened him from his "dogmatic slumber," Michotte was able to show that subjects directly perceive causal relations and intentionality. Kant's Cartesian and constructivist solution is not the only way to answer Hume's skepticism. If we are convinced that we experience an ordered work in which events are causally related to each other in a meaningful way, then this is not an illusion, as Hume would have us believe. This is reality and not merely a construction of mental acts. Popova summarizes the meaning of Michotte's work as follows; "causal interaction can be directly perceived by the mind in the same sense as that in which we perceive shape or movement, that is, as a low-level perceptual event" (15). Causality, order, necessity, and even meaning – all of which are essential characteristics of narrative – are therefore not unwarranted assumptions based on a contingent series of unconnected perceptions. In experiments with billiard balls or with abstract moving dots on a screen, subjects ascribed causal relations and agency to their movements and did not perceive unrelated perceptual events. In a passage reminiscent of our example of the stone axe in Part 1 as well as of Lindblom's discussion of the communicative function of action above, Popova (16) cites Michotte:

I quoted various examples in this connection, e.g. that of a hammer driving a nail into a plank, and that of a knife cutting a slice of bread. The question that arises is this: when we observe these operations, is our perception limited to the impression of two movements spatially and temporally coordinated, such as the advance of the knife and the cutting of the bread? Or rather, do we directly perceive the action as such – do we actually see the knife cut the bread? The answer does not seem to me to admit of any doubt. (Michotte, 1946/1963: 15)

Equally important as "dynamic causal structure" for understanding the narrative constitution of experience is for Popova "participatory sense-making" (5). The "enactive paradigm of cognition," developed by Varela, Thompson, and Rosch (1991), Thompson (2007), and De Jaegher and Di Paolo (1997), assumes that "embodied situatedness in a social world is the source, if not the limit, of all human knowledge" (4). This means that meaningful actions are not only directly perceived as such, as Michotte showed, but that they are also perceived as communication. In a way quite similar to Lindblom, who emphasizes the communicative aspect of action, Popova understands enactment as not only showing, but also telling. A narrative is always a story that is in some way told by a storyteller to someone who is a listener or reader. For Popova, "a key aspect of understanding narrative is to stop treating it as an abstract structure, as a representation in the manner of classical narratology, and seeing it, instead, as a pattern of experiential and intersubjective sense-making" (6). This does not mean, however, as one might expect when tellers and listeners are said to be constitutive of narrative, that it must be conceived of as a linguistic artifact. "I reject the claim that narrativity exists exclusively in language. Narrative, grounded as it is, by our definition, in perception and cognition, cannot be studied as a mere linguistic artifact" (8).

Popova sees "enactment" in the same way that Lindblom understands embodiment "as broadly comparable to communication" (8). Narrative is therefore to be seen as "an interactional process of co-constructing a story world with a narrator" (9). This implies that whenever humans (and perhaps prehumans also) do something, they not only do it, they intentionally *show* it. What makes networking, staging, and sensemaking special is that they are constituted by a unique *double intentionality, to do and to show*. Communication is an intentional action with its own purposes and procedures. Enacted narrative is not merely storytelling, but also always story-doing as well. The mere perception of a sequence of causally related events or of ascribed intentionality for an action is not enough. What is needed is also an ascription of the intention to show and tell something. According to Popova, "the mediated causality of a story requires in equal measure an ascription of intentionality to a narrating consciousness" (30). Furthermore, it implies that the "enaction" of the narrator's intention, as described by reference to mirror neurons, is not mere simulation, an automatic transfer of information, but an *interpretation* that emerges from a process of negotiation between storyteller and listener or reader. What is happening is therefore a question that can only be answered by a process of negotiation between actor and perceiver understood as teller and listener. Recalling Kubrick's ape, picking up the bone and using it as a weapon was not merely an action, but also, and this is the important part, a story told to the others in the group. Using a stone axe not only enacts a story, but also tells/shows it for others to see and follow. Popova's definition of narrative follows directly from this view of acting as also a telling:

[...] a minimal narrative is understood as at least two causally linked events, accompanied by a clear ascription of intentionality to a narrating consciousness, realized either verbally or visually, which is enacted by a reader in the process of narrative understanding. (Popova 2015: 38)

How does this help answer the question of the significance of narrative for sensemaking and organizing? Our question was: Is narrative the foundational form of ordering social relations as well as organizing? Can storytelling be understood as the condition of the possibility of experience, communication, and cooperation? On the basis of the important ideas of Herman, Lindblom, and Popova a positive answer to these questions becomes at least plausible. As Popova puts it, "The main point that we have been making is that we do not experience the world in some chaotic, undifferentiated way, but that narrative structure [...] is already part of our very perception of reality" (42). When narrative structure not only includes sequencing of events, intentionality, actors and actions, typologies and norms, but also an open horizon of interpretable meaning on the basis of communication between actor and perceiver, or "teller" and "listener," then narrative must be understood as an "intersubjective process of sense-making" (72). Popova concludes:

[...] stories are not static or inert cultural artifacts; they become the expressions of intersubjective meaningful action and participatory sense-making between tellers (narrators) and readers. In other words, they are interactive processes in their own right, as opposed to formal structures (as assumed in structuralist narratology) or individualistic (monologic) processes of reader interpretation (as taken up in discourse studies or pragmatic theories of communication). Narratives are simultaneously the processes leading to, and the end products of, such joint activity. (75)

Let us return to what was said above about Karl Weick's notion of sensemaking. For Weick, as for Goffman and even for Latour's concept of technical mediation as well, social order and therefore organization is constituted by communicative processes that link humans and non-humans into relatively stable associations. Insofar as these associations can be termed organizations, the question of the communicative constitution of organizations finds a plausible answer in the description of narrative as embodied, enacted, extended, and embedded cognition. What Herman called "storying the world" could be compared to Weick's definition of organizing in the sense of "finding answers to the question 'what's the story'" (Weick et al. 2005: 410). As Popova says, "stories do not happen in individual minds, either those of tellers or readers, but in the dynamic interaction between them" (89), and, recalling ANT, we would like to add to this that interaction does not occur without the mediating agency of non-humans.

We claim that on the basis of the new non-Cartesian cognitive science as it is applied to the theory of narrative, it is plausible to assume that technical mediation or what we have termed networking, Goffman's staging, and Karl Weick's sensemaking are narratively structured. This implies that the communicative constitution of organizations occurs through enacted narrative. It is narrative communication in the above specified sense that can be said to "constitute" organizations.[33] Stories constitute organizations, because narrative is the fundamental form of organizing anything. Nonetheless, if we look at organizations what we see are usually not stories. As McPhee and Zaug pointed out in their analysis of the different typical forms of communication in organizations, what we see are employees being on-boarded in processes of membership negotiation, we see how collective identity is created by self-structuring, how external communication with suppliers, customers, regulators, and competitors is being managed, and how internal processes and workflows are established and transformed. McPhee and Zaug claim that these four flows of information are constitutive of organizations because in some way or another every organization must differentiate itself from its environment, regulate its internal operations, relate

---

33 | This "praxeological" view of narrative is supported by Lorino/Tricard (2012) although they base it on Dewey, Peirce, and Ricoeur and not directly on non-Cartesian cognitive science.

to other organizations beyond its boundaries, and be able to identify itself. The question immediately arises: How are these various forms of communication – even structurally – comparable to narratives such as Tolstoy's War and Peace or The Little Prince? How are the managers and workers involved in these different tasks aided or guided by the idea that what is going on is storytelling? Even if the thesis of the narrative constitution of organizations is theoretically coherent and of heuristic value for management and organization science, what good is the theory for practical managerial concerns? In order to bring the discussion back to what might be seen as the main concern of organization studies, we turn now to a discussion of the scalability of networks and narratives. We will try to show how little stories with few characters and a simple plot can become big stories in which many different tasks are being done. Our claim will be that narratives, both large and small, accomplish what is necessary in order to constitute organizations. In order to make this claim plausible we turn to a discussion of localizing and globalizing.

LOCALIZING AND GLOBALIZING

Networking, sensemaking, staging, and enacted narrative are different words for one thing, organizing. Stories with few actors and few events are local narratives and small organizations. Stories, however, can become very long and complicated. They can consist of many smaller stories, on-boarding stories, work process stories, marketing stories, etc. As the stories get longer, local organizing is extended and becomes large organizing. This is accomplished by means of adding more and more human and non-human actors such as documents, office buildings, a diversified work force, logistical infrastructure, research staff, development laboratories, marketing departments, etc. What once was a small organization becomes larger and larger until one even begins to speak of global organizations. Latour speaks of "localizing" and "globalizing" in order to explain how actor-networks are scalable and continuous.

The ideas of scalability and continuity imply that interactions and organizations are not on distinct ontological levels, as traditional sociology supposed, but much rather on a continuum from the local to the global. Neither is agency something individual nor is structure something collective. Individuals are always already collective actors, that is, actor-networks. Individuals are always already structured as networks. For this reason there are always constraints on choice. Kubrick's ape could not just pick up any bone and have success in battle. Hominids could not use just any stones as tools. Stones and other things constrain what hands and arms can do when it comes to building, hunting, fighting, etc. What the discussion up until now has attempted to make clear is that interactionism and institutionalism do not describe different things. Bottom up and top down approaches to social order are not ontological or even epistemological choices, that is, choices about different things and the appropriate ways to study them, but choices about how much of a network one wishes to describe. Localizing and globalizing may be said to be the ways in which narrative scales up and scales down actor-networks. The more one scales up, the more it may seem that constraints to individual choice increase. The more one scales down, it may appear that choices, freedom, and contingency increase. In either case, it is a matter of more or less, and not a matter of a qualitative jump to another ontological level.

When employees constantly switch between speaking for themselves or speaking in the name of the organization, and when managers start talking in the name of the strategic goals of the company, shareholder value, or the culture of the organization, they are not jumping to a higher ontological level, but simply adding more actors to the network. The more actors one has to translate, enroll, and mobilize in order to get a job done, the more effort it takes. Once a network is set up to do a job, it takes a correspondingly large effort to change how things work. Anyone who has attempted to introduce new processes and procedures into an organization knows this. Attempting to do things differently usually amounts to running into a wall of resistance. This is why "change management" is an important topic and organizations spend large amounts on efforts for reorganization. This does not mean, of course, that networks are the same in the ways that actors are added or subtracted, or in the ways actors or mediaries move through the network, or what the trajectory of the network is, and in the ways of translating, enrolling, and black-boxing that go on.

Many different factors influence the kind of network that at any time is being enacted. Latour (2013) speaks of different kinds of networks as different "modes of being." When different kinds of networks are extended to the global dimension, they appear as different modes of being, different domains, or as different functional subsystems of society.

This explains why society is not only made up of individual actors or even individual organizations, but also clusters or types of organizing such as "science," "politics," "religion," "art," "law," "business," etc. Doing politics is different from doing business, or at least it should be. Science is not the same as education, even if both forms of networking cross each other and at many points overlap. Despite these undeniable differences, what is going on in all domains is networking. Differences in ways of networking, the kinds of actors involved, and ways of translating, enrolling, and mobilizing do not constitute different ontological levels or the social that characterizes traditional sociology. From the point of view of traditional sociology, it may seem that interactions aggregate and merge into a higher level or macro-structures. The other way round, it may seem, as the new institutionalism assumes, that social systems, domains, norms, culture, values, customs, and ideologies influence individuals. Following ANT, our claim is that both bottom up and top down approaches are describing the same thing, namely, networking, even if globalized networks often appear substantially different from each other and from interactions. It is admittedly contra-intuitive to not recognize domains such as law, politics, business, education, art, religion, healthcare, and so on and to claim that they are all the same, as well as no different from the individual interactions that are going on "within" them.[34] ANT appears to want to say the same thing about everything and disregard basic distinctions upon which sociology has long been based. This strategy can only be considered reasonable when there is something to be gained by it. Does talk about localizing and globalizing explain the differences in scale and kind of organizing with which society presents us?

According to ANT, what may seem like ephemeral face-to-face interactions on the one side and like macro social structures or domains of society on the other side can instead be understood as *processes of localizing and globalizing*. No amount of aggregating individual conversational episodes or laying them on top of one another leads to macro structures, not even by taking the detour of producing and using what Taylor calls "texts." Global stories do not "emerge" out of a chaotic multitude of ephemeral interactions and purely personal stories. Personal stories,

---

34 | Latour (2013b) has recognized this difficulty and therefore set out upon An Inquiry into Modes of Existence (AIME) in order to describe the differences between forms of networking.

as Goffman showed, are always networks of many different actors. If two people agree to meet to discuss a project next Monday at the office, then, as we have seen from the above discussion of networking, staging, sensemaking, and narrative, there are many more actors involved than these two individuals. The office plays a role, the project, organizational goals, budgets, norms, cultural values, and so on. If any of these things are uncertain or cannot be taken for granted at the time and place when and where the two people speak to each other, then usually a question is asked, a telephone call is made, a time-table is consulted, a protocol is read, that is, someone or something that is not immediately present is called in to participate and brought into play.

Cooren, as we saw above in the discussion of the communicative constitution of organizations, speaks of "ventriloquism" to account for how distant actors can speak in a local interaction. McPhee and Zaug point to typical kinds of problems that need to be solved such as settling the question of who is involved, what they should be doing, in the name of what, and so on. Taylor argues for the importance of texts, documents, inscribed decisions, and for Weick, this is all narrative sensemaking. In one way or another, it appears that organizing is not constrained by space and time and by demands for co-presence in face-to-face encounters. On the contrary, organizing is constrained by the many heterogeneous actors involved in negotiating programs of action that go beyond any *hic-et-nunc* interaction. The more actors involved, the more potential conflicts of interest, efforts to mobilize others, and attempts to functionalize or "black-box" entire chains of associations. Scalability is not only an important characteristic of networks, but also, as Herman noted, of narratives. Because of scalability, building social order from small to large can be seen as a process of aggregation, of linking up stories and connecting them to each other. Again, this does not need to be understood as a jump to a higher ontological level. Actor-networks are not macro social structures, or what new institutionalism calls institutions, operating behind the backs of the actors. There is no super actor called society and no mini-actors called individuals that live within it, who either are determined by it or are burdened with the impossible task of somehow creating, criticizing, and transforming it. Instead, there are a multitude of more or less connected stories consisting of many different and often conflicting actors, goals, events, and processes. As Latour puts it:

For humans, an abyss seems to separate individual action from the weight of a transcendent society. But this is not an original separation that some social theory concept could span and which might serve to distinguish us radically from other primates. It is an artifact created by the forgetting of all practical activities for localizing and globalizing. (Latour 1996: 234)

What are these "practical activities" of localizing and globalizing, which are to replace the usual partitioning of the social into micro interactions on the one side and macro structures on the other? Latour is rather cryptic when it comes to describing what localizing and globalizing consist of.

Neither individual action nor structure are thinkable without the work of *rendering local* – through channeling, partition, focusing, reduction – and without the work of *rendering global* – through instrumentation, compilation, punctualization, amplification. (Latour 1996: 234).

Instead of agency and structure, instead of the chicken and the egg along with the question of which comes first, we have "channeling, partition, focusing, reduction" on the one side and "instrumentation, compilation, punctualization, amplification" on the other. How is this to be understood? Latour places the entire discussion of social relations not under the title of "intersubjectivity" as is usually done. He speaks instead of "interobjectivity" (1996). For baboons, as we saw in Part 1, social relations are purely intersubjective. Primates have only their bodies and their physical co-presence in the here and now with which to construct social relations and they therefore must re-construct these relations anew at every moment. This makes their social life very complex, because the entire spectrum of social behavior is potentially present at any moment. Every episode of life is filled with the entire spectrum of social options. A troop of baboons living in the savannah are "looking incessantly at each other so as to know where the troop is going, who is with whom, who is grooming whom, who is attacking or defending whom" (Latour 1996: 231). As we saw in the discussion of Goffman, humans do not interact in this way. Humans go to great effort to enlist the help of many non-humans in order to *reduce* the complexity of any event. Human social order differs from that of apes because "for an interaction to take place one must first reduce the relationship so that it does not, step by step, mobilize all social life, with which it would otherwise end up being co-extensive" (230).

Reducing all possible social relations to just one at a time is what Goffman describes as framing. Establishing a frame for social action is done by the work of selection and exclusion, partitioning, setting up boundaries, channeling who and what can participate, and focusing on only certain options to the exclusion of all others. This can be understood as information control. In order to do this, as we saw, non-humans are brought into play. Human interactions are framed interactions. A kitchen, a classroom, a doctor's office, a courtroom are set up differently so that information is channeled, activities are partitioned off from others, attention is focused on specific tasks, and the complexity of social life is reduced to manageable size. Paradoxically, in order to reduce the complexity of social life to manageable proportions, that is, to one local activity at a time, a network of associations between humans and non-humans must be constructed that extends far beyond any particular place and time. Latour speaks of the "contradictory forms" of human interaction. On the one hand, action is framed, reduced, partitioned off from all that is not specifically relevant to a certain task. On the other hand, frames are made up of a network of people and things that extend far beyond any specific time and place. This means that although complexity is reduced, although this particular time and place are framed so that only one specific activity, for example, teaching in a classroom, can take place, the many props that frame this setting, the school, the desks, the blackboard, the text books, the media, the curricula, testing procedures, etc., link this specific interaction to actors, events, decisions, artifacts, and so on that go far beyond this classroom and this particular lesson. In a passage that deserves to be quoted again, Latour explains:

We say, without giving the matter too much thought, that we engage in 'face-to-face' interactions. Indeed we do, but the clothing that we are wearing comes from elsewhere and was manufactured a long time ago; the words we use were not formed for this occasion; the walls we have been leaning on were designed by an architect for a client, and constructed by workers – people who are absent today, although their action continues to make itself felt. The very person we are addressing is a product of a history that goes far beyond the framework of our relationship. If one attempted to draw a spatio-temporal map of what is present in the interaction, and to draw up a list of everyone who in one form or another were present, one would not sketch out a well-demarcated frame, but a convoluted network with a multiplicity of highly diverse dates, places and people. (1996: 231)

What this amounts to is that the *frame* is one thing and the *network* is another. Framing or localizing *reduces, channels, partitions, and focuses.* However, it can only do this because the network has *instrumentalized* heterogeneous actors, *compiled* them into associations of many different kinds, *amplified* these associations in chains whose trajectories extend in all directions in space and time, and *punctualized* or segmented the social world into a myriad of different tasks, actions, goals, actors, and processes that are, as Taylor would say, "imbricated" with each other.[35] Networking makes interacting, at least in the way humans do it, possible. Networking is not "intersubjective," but as Latour would say, "interobjective." It is the objects, the non-humans, for example, the schoolhouse, the classroom, the desks, the textbooks, the blackboard, etc., that allow "teaching" to be more easily and efficiently localized. Enacted narrative is what does this. It erects the walls, installs the desks and the blackboard, plans the curriculum, provides the textbooks, etc. All these things would not be "present" to the activity of teaching, if enactive narrative had not arranged them in spatial and temporal order. Life would indeed be very complex if we did not have all these props at our disposal. However, it is precisely all these things that not only frame action, but link up to activities, places, and times that are not present, that exist and play roles beyond the momentary interaction. Schoolhouses, for example, are linked not only to classrooms and teachers, students, and teaching, but also to educational budgets, political agendas, fire departments, building codes, etc. Textbooks are linked to publishers, book sellers, and the scientific production of information. Teachers are linked to professional associations, pedagogical theories, developmental psychology, certifying procedures, labor unions, etc. The network of heterogeneous actors that appears as education goes in all directions in space and time, and crosses over into other domains such as politics or science. Networking uses these resources to narratively frame one activity at a time in a causal sequence of events with identifiable actors pursuing intentional goals. Stories, as Herman put it, are embedded or linked up to myriad other stories. Framing is enacted narrative. As any narrative must do, framing partitions events into a sequence of activities, focuses on specific goals, in a setting reduced to what is relevant and channeled

---

35 | For Callon "the process of punctualization thus converts an entire network into a single point or node in another network" (Callon 1991: 153).

or steered by the intentions of identifiable actors. Let us recall at this point what Karl Weick said about organizing:

To focus on sensemaking is to portray organizing as the experience of being thrown in an ongoing, unknowable, unpredictable streaming of experience in search of answers to the question 'what's the story'. (Weick et al. 2005: 410)

It is because the local frame is built in and out of the global network that frames are effective for getting things done and also can be changed and extended almost indefinitely. Teaching can move from the classroom to the teacher's room, and from there on to the teacher's conference, to the board of education, to the streets when protesting against cutting funds or protesting for environmental protection, and so on. Each time a different frame is localized from the global network.[36] As we will see below in the discussion of organizing networks in business, education, healthcare, and civil society, localizing always has access to the global network and therefore does not amount to creating closed systems or constructing social domains. If politics is not business, this is a question of how localizing is getting specific jobs done, and not a boundary that cannot be crossed once new and different jobs need to be done. Localizing reduces, focuses, channels, and partitions what networking has amplified, compiled, instrumentalized, and punctuated. This is not merely a linguistic matter. It is done by building walls, setting up classrooms, buying textbooks, producing media, raising taxes, hiring teachers, planning curricula, etc. With regard to the question of what is gained by overlooking traditional distinctions between domains and levels, it can be argued that all these activities are indeed the same and it is theoretically acceptable to say the same thing about them. *All these activities involve both human and non-human actors in processes that, as we have seen, can best be theorized as enacted narrative, as networking, staging, and sensemaking.* Localizing is not the same as agency any more than globalizing is the same as structure. Localizing does not necessarily have to be *either* political, *or* economic,

---

36 | As Arsenault (2011: 260) puts it, "Because networks can be constructed out of many smaller networks, it is generally more instructive to think of networks as embedded within a network of networks rather than one or several separate networks. It is for precisely this reason, that some theorists (most notably Castells [1996]) have posited the emergence of a 'network society'."

or scientific, *or* educational, etc. It can, should need arise, cross local boundaries and draw upon resources throughout the global network. Localizing is not a micro interaction any more than globalizing is a macro institution. Both localizing and globalizing do the same thing, namely find the answer to the question, 'what's the story'. Localizing tells a short story and globalizing tells a long story.

CONCLUSION

With regard to the question of organizations, who is to say where a particular kind of organization, for example, education begins and where it ends? Is the organization of education different from identifiable educational organizations, such as schools, universities, or corporate training centers? Does organizing education take place in the schoolhouse, in the educational system from kindergarten to university, in corporate training, in informal or on the job learning, in political decisions on the local or national levels, or in funding drives, or even parent-teacher organizations? Of course, any part of the network can be localized for a specific purpose. Different stories can be told for the neighborhood school, the university, corporate training, etc. All these local stories, however, can and often must be embedded in each other, linked up to one another in longer and more complicated stories and thus globalized. What does this mean for the question of organizing and organizations? Organizing and organizations, both small and large, can be understood as being communicatively constituted by localizing and globalizing narratives. *Our claim is that the problem of the communicative constitution of organizations can be posed as the problem of localizing and globalizing narratives, that is, when narrative is theorized as networking, staging, and sensemaking.* Posing the problem in this way could have heuristic value when it comes to dealing with questions of organizational change and scalability. Specifically with regard to organizations and trends, we will take this up below in Part 5.

It is important, however, to recall at this point in our discussion that the concept of "narrative" that we use does not refer to a linguistic artifact, but to the embodied, embedded, extended, and enacted construction of information in the sense of technical mediation. Speaking of localizing and globalizing narratives refers to how things play significant roles in ordering human activities and how humans build networks together with non-humans. Narrative is networking, staging, and sensemaking, all of which symmetrically include non-humans as partners and actors. These non-humans make their own contributions to the network. The influence of artifacts and technologies on forms of organization is a longstanding topic of management and organization studies. Although this topic has mostly been dealt with in economics or political economy, ANT, as well as the new non-Cartesian cognitive science, have contributed to a new understanding of the role of technology and non-humans in society. Perhaps the most important technological innovation that in recent years has dominated discussions of the relation of technology to society are the so-called "new media." Not only does the computer and computer networks represent a technology that has come to play an important role in all areas of life, but also it is a technology of communication and information. If social order and organizations are constituted by communication, it is reasonable to expect that a technological revolution in communication will have a significant impact on society and be of great relevance for organization theory. If things are important, then those things that we use every day in everything we do have an influence on what we do and who we are. We turn now to a discussion of the significance of our most significant non-human other. We will take a closer look at information and communication technologies in order to better understand the communicative construction of organizations in today's global network society.

4. The New Media Revolution and the Network Society

We have followed ANT in defining human social order in terms of "technical mediation" instead of linguistic mediation and "interobjectivity" instead of intersubjectivity. These concepts emphasize the role that things, artifacts, and technologies play in constituting and sustaining human social order. They also emphasize the role things play in organizing and organizations. The work done in organization theory under the title of "communicative constitution of organizations," as we saw in the discussion of the work of McPhee, Zaug, Taylor, and Cooren in Part 3 above, emphasizes the role of communication in organizing, but tends to favor a purely linguistic understanding of communicative action. We reinterpreted Goffman's theory of interaction and took a closer look at Karl Weick's idea of sensemaking in order to show that not only language, but also enactment and embodiment are important aspects of communication, especially that form of communication which is decisive for organizing, namely, narrative communication. We reviewed current ideas from the new non-Cartesian cognitive science that support the view that cognition is embodied, enacted, embedded, and extended in the environment. We argued that processes of embodying, embedding, enacting, and extending cognition could be understood as narrative in that they follow a narrative structure. Narrative includes much more than merely language, that is, telling stories. It includes entering into relations with things and building actor-networks. Communication, including storytelling, is something quite unusual. It is embodied and enacted. It involves non-humans as well as humans. It is a process of networking, setting up associations, linking heterogeneous actors together with regard to divergent programs of action. In short, it creates information. This raises the question: If entities, things, artifacts, and technologies are essentially part of the stories we tell, what exactly do they do? What difference do they make? What influence do technologies have on how narrative organizing is done and therefore on how society is organized? If technologies have an important influence on human social order, to what kinds of artifacts and technologies should we look if we want to understand how enacted narrative communication constitutes organizations in today's technological world? We will attempt to answer these questions by looking at the impact of new information and communication technologies (ICTs) on society.[1]

A perspective that has come to be called "technological determinism" often guides sociological discussions of the impact of technologies on society. The succinct definition of the term by the Wikipedia editors make it clear what is meant: "Technological determinism is a reductionist theory that presumes that a society's technology drives the development of its social structure and cultural values."[2] A classic technological determinist theory is Marxism, which as is well known argues that the technologies of industrial production determine social structure, for example, the emergence of a working class. With regard to media technologies, Walter Ong (1982) argued that the invention of writing radically changed the course of human history and institutions. In the same vein, Marshall McLuhan (1964) proclaimed the media to be the message and saw the influence of mass media technology at the basis of social change. Much discussion today of the influence of so-called "new media" on all areas of society seems to reflect McLuhan's technological determinism. Talk of a digital media revolution (Manovich 2001), a second media age (Poster 1995; Negroponte 1995; Rheingold 2000), or a global network society (Castells 1996) tends to support the suspicion that much of new media discourse is informed by technological determinism.

As we saw in the discussion of actor-network theory in Part 1, *technical mediation* should not be confused with *technological determinism. Mediating* is not the same as *determining.* The stone does not determine the hand to use it as an axe. The hand also must contribute its part and play its role.

---

1 | Choosing ANT as the theoretical basis for asking the question of the influence of ICTs on society means neglecting other interesting theoretical approaches. See Mingers/Willcocks (2004) for an overview of different approaches. For a discussion of ANT in relation to other major social theories, see Krieger/Belliger (2014). For a general discussion of technology and society see Volti (2014).

2 | https://en.wikipedia.org/wiki/Technological_determinism

Kubrick's ape did his (or her) part when turning the bone into a weapon. Mediation is not determination, since in order for one thing to determine another thing in a causal way, there must at least be two independent things. When Kubrick's ape crossed the line from the simian world into the human world, it left behind for ever the world of things, that is, an unmediated, episodic, and independent form of being and entered a world of interfaces, relations, and information. Neither artifacts nor humans are independent entities that can influence each other in a causally deterministic way. Mediation, as Floridi (2014) put it, is an "interface" that points in two directions and goes both ways. It is *information* and not causal determinacy. In order to explain what this means, we cited Latour's notion of "irreduction."[3]

Contrary to the age-old assumptions of Western metaphysics, the human world consists not of substances, but of mediations. Being is mediation, relation, and therefore information. ANT proposes a *relational ontology*. An actor-network is held together by, or rather, made up of information. The network can become the actor precisely because only networks are capable of meaning. This is not what apes do. They live in the immediacy of the moment. In the human world, there are no unmediated actors. The hominid with a bone weapon is not the ape alone and not the bone alone, that is, there is no situation in which one could causally determine the other. The hominid with a bone is already an actor-network. The builder or hunter with a stone axe is a different actor than if the stone axe were not involved. For this reason, ANT cannot be interpreted as a theory of technological determinism any more than it can be understood as a theory of social determinism. Neither does technology determine society, nor does society determine technology, because both are the same. There is no such thing as society on the one side and nature on the other and therefore no possibility of there being any way that society could "determine" technology or artifacts could "determine" social relations the way in which one billiard ball determines the course of another billiard ball upon impact. Artifacts *are* social relations and social relations *are* associations with artifacts. This is what distinguishes the human world from that of baboons. This is why cognition is enacted, embodied, embedded, and extended. If we accept this view, even if only for the sake

---

3 | Latour (1993: 158), "nothing is, by itself, either reducible or irreducible to anything else."

of argument, then the role that new media play in the networks that we are becoming can be seen in a different way. This is what we propose to attempt to do in the following description of the affordances of new media in our global network society.[4]

WHAT ARE NEW MEDIA?

There is no unified theory of new media but there is at least a kind of theoretical consensus that new media are "digital" and that the digitalization of information and communication has brought significant changes to society. Hartley, Burgess, and Bruns (2013) offer a definition of new media as "those media that are associated with the postbroadcast era of interactive or participatory communication using networked, digital, online affordances [...]" (3). So significant are the social changes that new media are said to have initiated that Mark Poster (1995) could speak of the "Second Media Age" in distinction to the age of broadcast mass media. In a review of literature on the influence of ICTs on society, Arsenault (2011) proceeds from the assumption that "The digitization of information into the universal language of electronic binary code has blurred the boundary between technological and human interaction" (259). Arsenault points out that this impact has led social scientists to turn their attention "to the ways in which computer networks have facilitated radical changes to societal practices and organization" (259). Despite the fact that there is a wide diversity of approaches to understanding the social impact of new media, one thing is seemingly indisputable, new media have changed and are changing society and therefore have become an important topic in the social sciences as well as in organization studies.[5]

It can be said that there are three major approaches to understanding the influence of ICTs on society. One approach begins from ICTs as technical infrastructure. In this view, typical of the work of Feldman

---

4 | The following discussion of new media is based on the treatment of this topic in Krieger/Belliger (2014) and Belliger/Krieger (2016). For a different view, see the work done under the title of the Social Study of Information Systems https://en.wikipedia.org/wiki/Social_Study_of_Information_Systems.

5 | For a discussion of the impact of new media on organizations, see for example Monge/Contractor (2003).

(1997) and Castells (1996, 1998, 2001), it is computer networks that take center stage and provide key concepts for the interpretation of society. The second approach is based not so much on the technical infrastructure of connectivity as on that which flows through it. Not connectivity, but flow of new media content is the key to understanding the affordances of new media. This view is typical of the work of Lev Manovich (2001, 2013). The central question is what happens to information, once it has been digitalized and networked. In the words of Manovich, it is the "new media object," or that which flows through the network, that takes center stage and offers interpretive keys for unlocking the meaning of social changes. Finally, for the third approach, it is neither connectivity nor flow of information, that is the focus, but usage. This view starts from an analysis of how new media are used, what kinds of practices have emerged on the basis of connectivity and flow. What do people do with new media? How do technologies and users "co-construct" each other?[6] What contribution do users make to the meaning and effects of technologies? How have ICTs changed the values, norms, worldviews, practices, and the culture of users?

This approach leads to an interpretation of social changes as being guided not only by technologies, but also by cultural factors such as values and norms in much the same way as the new institutionalism understands norms as constitutive for organizations and social order. Typical representatives of this approach are Benkler (2006), Shirky (2008), Tapscott (2009) as well as the authors contributing to the representative collection of essays in Oudshoorn and Pinch (2003). As Oudshoorn and Pinch point out, this view is closely associated with ANT. If the first two approaches lean toward a technological determinism in their view of how new media are influencing social change, the third view tends in the opposite direction toward social determinism. It is important to emphasize, however, that all three approaches to new media are significant contributions to understanding today's world. They complement and enrich each other. A sound interpretation of the affordances of new media in today's society should attempt to take account of diverging aspects and different points of view while avoiding the pitfalls of both technological and social determinism.

---

6 | The idea of "co-construction" is intended to avoid the social determinism of the social construction of technology (SCOT) approach. See https://en.wikipedia. org/wiki/Social_construction_of_technology

Let us look more closely at the first approach to new media, that which is based on connectivity. Feldman (1997) begins his analysis from network infrastructure and digital technologies. What makes the new digital media different from the traditional analogue media? The difference lies in their specific technologies of encoding, decoding, and transmission. "The digital revolution is being forged by an accelerating move from a world familiar with analogue media to a world that will be increasingly dominated by digital media" (1997: 1). The key to understanding new media is therefore "a shift from analogue to digital" (1). Technologies of digital encoding and processing of information in computer networks take center stage. What results can be termed "manipulable," "networkable," "dense," "compressible," and "impartial" information. Encoding all forms of information into bits and bytes creates a virtual world made up of nothing but numbers. Numbers are mathematical entities that can be endlessly manipulated. Information is no longer analogically bound by a limited continuum of transformations between information on the one side and physical reality on the other. Instead, it can be infinitely transformed by algorithms. Furthermore, information is no longer bound to perceptual channels such as the auditory or the visual. Analogue media are channel specific. There are separate auditory and visual channels. In the digital realm, there is only one channel, the digital network. In this one channel all forms of information can be distributed anywhere at any time. In addition to this, not only can digital information be manipulated at the point of production, it can be manipulated and transformed at all points of the chain of communication; production, distribution, reception, and repurposing. An image can be downloaded from the internet, transformed by software into something else, integrated into other media, repurposed and then uploaded again. The infrastructure of digital connectivity allows consumers of information to also easily become producers. For Feldman, it is the manipulability of digital information that makes new media characteristically interactive. The traditional sociological concept of "interaction" receives a fundamentally different connotation. Interaction becomes "interactivity," that is a form of human computer communication in which information is principally manipulable by all participants, including automated systems. What in the era of mass media was thought to be impossible, that consumers are also producers, becomes a cornerstone of the digital media world.

A further essential characteristic of digital media according to Feldman is that it is "networkable." "This means that information in digital form can be shared and exchanged by large numbers of users simultaneously" (6). Digital media distribute information in a fundamentally different way than print or broadcast mass media. Instead of top down distribution, network distribution is non-hierarchical and many-to-many. Information is shared by large numbers of people without the costs that burdened and hindered transporting analogue information. Instead of an economy of scarcity for information and knowledge and typically hierarchical top-down communication as the standard for large groups, digital media make it possible for large numbers of people to interact and exchange information at low cost. Traditional sociology has often distinguished between interactions at the level of face-to-face communication among two or more people in small groups and the need for centralized, top-down communication as soon as a group becomes larger than a handful of people.[7] For Castells (1996, 2001) networked media are the distinguishing characteristic of todays' society. Global networks in today's society have reached a level of connectivity that allows for the flows of information that moves in them to become detached from the limiting conditions of time and space. There arises a "space of flows," and a "timeless time" (Castells 1996: 407ff., 460ff.) in which knowing and acting take place in a global simultaneity.

Another distinguishing characteristic of digital media is what Feldman calls "density." Since bits and bytes take up practically no space, and micro-electronics such as transistors are very small, great amounts of information can be squeezed into a very small physical space. This has implications for the amount of information that can be stored, distributed, and made available. Entire libraries can be stored on a present day micro stick and the tendency is toward even greater storage capacities in smaller physical units, as well as toward ever greater amounts of data that can be distributed in ever shorter time spans. Density is related to the further characteristic of digital media, that is, information "compressibility." What density is to data storage, compressibility is to data transfer. There

---

7 | See Shirky (2008) and Krieger/Belliger (2014) for a discussion of the impact of networked many-to-many communication on social relations.

appears to be no limit to how much data can be compressed in ever smaller units and how fast it can be transmitted through digital networks. Density and compressibility have resulted in a situation in which the amount of information produced, stored, and transmitted doubles in ever shorter time periods. IDC predicts that by 2020 there will be 40 zettabytes (ZB) of data available[8] and some claim that the amount of knowledge added by the internet of things will double almost daily. The sheer quantity of data and information and its global accessibility create an entirely new situation in a world that had based its economy on print and broadcast media.

According to Weinberger (2012), this changes the very structure of knowledge from a *pyramid* into a *cloud*. Hierarchical communication symbolized by the pyramid is based upon an economy of scarcity. Because the amount of information that can be stored and distributed in print form is limited by the physical attributes of the medium and the costs of production, distribution, and storage, information must be limited both in quantity and access. It cannot be made accessible to all. Society organizes this situation by instituting a small number of experts and authorities who stand, as it were, at the top of the pyramid and whose job is to control the flow of information down to the masses who are at the bottom. At each step on the way up or down the pyramid there are barriers and gateways, rules of inclusion and exclusion. This makes the pyramid a communication structure that is characterized by limitation, exclusion, and restricted access. According to Weinberger, after the digital revolution, knowledge is more like a cloud than a pyramid in that it is non-hierarchical, inclusive, connected, complex, and public. There is no limit to the amount of information that can be produced, stored, distributed, and accessed. Instead of a stable edifice of truth built on indisputable facts certified by experts, there is an unlimited amount of information on all conceivable topics available to everyone everywhere and therefore everything has become negotiable. The digital revolution has created an unbounded, heterogeneous, and uncoordinated network of links and associations.

---

8 | A zettabyte is equal to 1,024 exabytes, that is, 2 to the 70th power bytes, which is approximately 10 to the 21st power (1,000,000,000,000,000,000,000) bytes.

Finally, Feldman points out that digital media are "impartial" to content. Anything and everything can be digitalized and transformed into information. Once digitalized, it can be combined, re-combined, and re-purposed at will. Traditional media were restricted to specific information channels designed for different modes of perception. New media bring a "convergence" of different forms of media into one format and one channel.[9] Kittler (1999) claimed that "the general digitalization of channels and information erases the differences among individual media […], sound and image, voice and text are reduced to surface effects" (1). This means that "a total media link on a digital base will erase the very concept of medium" (2). Along this line, Chaffee and Metzger (2001) find concepts like "media content," "media audiences," "media effects," and other typical characteristics of mass media no longer useful. Clemens and Nash (2015) go so far as to proclaim the end of media. "The age of media is over, for there is now only one medium; and one medium is no medium at all" (11).[10]

Once information has been encoded into bits and bytes, it is all the same, that is, it is "impartial" to its source and to its perceptual specificity. It makes no difference for encoding, storing, processing, and distributing if it is a matter of images, text, music, video, code, software, or any combination thereof. This unique characteristic of digital media has been called "media convergence," that is, the integration of different forms of content and distribution that previously required different forms of encoding and transmission. Another popular term for convergence is multi-media, the combination of text, audio, video in one media product. Add interactivity to this and you have a digital media revolution that is changing not only the world of traditional mass media, but also business, politics, education, and every other area of life.[11] ICTs not only give us multimedial, interactive ebooks, but also navigate automobiles, carry out financial transactions, steer automated factories, coordinate supply chains, regulate transporta-

---

9 | See Jenkins (2006) on "convergence culture."

10 | See Belliger/Krieger (2016b) for a discussion of the end of media thesis and its significance for media studies.

11 | "Media convergence is more than simply a technological shift. Convergence alters the relationship between existing technologies, industries, markets, genres, and audiences. Convergence alters the logic by which media industries operate and by which media consumers process news and entertainment." (Jenkins 2006: 5-16)

tion systems, energy grids, and enable new forms of political participation. Castells (1996), as noted above, has taken this fact as an indication that we have entered a new era, the global network society. The outcome of the connectivity of digital networks is a culture of convergence.

The second approach to understanding new media proceeds not from media infrastructure, but from media content. This approach is represented by the work of Lev Manovich. In *The Language of New Media* (2001) and *Software Takes Command* (2013) Manovich has influentially argued that technologies and practices of creating digital information have changed our relation to information, commodities, and cultural objects. More than the technologies of connectivity, it is algorithms, the software, that fundamentally alters the character and meaning of information in that it creates "new media objects." New media objects are the key to understanding contemporary society. For Manovich "the world [...] is now defined not by heavy industrial machines that change infrequently, but by software that is always in flux" (2013: 1-2). From this point of view

[...] when you play a video game, explore an interactive installation in a museum, design a building, create special effects for a feature film, design a website, use a mobile phone to read a movie review or to view the actual movie, and carry out thousands of other cultural activities, in practical terms, you are doing the same thing – using software. Software has become our interface to the world, to others, to our memory and our imagination – a universal language through which the world speaks, and a universal engine on which the world runs. What electricity and the combustion engine were to the early twentieth century, software is to the early twenty-first century. (Manovich 2013: 2)

Software, of course, depends on network infrastructure. However, it is not connectivity, not the networks, not glass fiber cable, satellites, gateways, routers, switches, bridges, wireless access points, hubs, repeaters, proxy servers, firewalls, etc., but what flows through the networks that is important. New media, according to Manovich, can best be understood by the kind of objects they mediate. The "new media object" (2001: 49ff.), is first of all digital in much the same sense as Feldman described the virtualizing effect of transforming information into binary code. New media objects are "numerical representations." They are numbers, code, products of algorithms, devoid of analogue materiality. This leads directly to the second characteristic of new media objects. They are "modular."

Modularity means that once digitalized, content can be broken down into independent elements that can be used for other purposes. Modules can be recombined with other modules to create new content or new processes. This is not only true of content, but also of the software programs that manipulate content.[12] As the example of object oriented programming or also modular programming suggests, software can consist of functional modules that can be integrated into more complex applications. Modularity is characteristic of all digital objects. Images, for example, can be broken into layers, where one layer consists of a blue background, another of a text, another of a faces or other images. The layers can be used to construct other images and combined at will. For example, one can set up a database of different kinds of fog or mist that can be used in many different landscape images, movies, etc.

Numerical representation and modularity are accompanied by a third principle of new media objects. Manovich calls this "automation." Algorithms process information for specific tasks automatically. An image processing program has many different filters that automatically alter an image. Word processing software will change the font of hundreds of pages of text in a few seconds. Automation goes beyond these relatively simple applications into complex domains of artificial intelligence, robotics, intelligent agents, etc. Automation makes it possible to create intelligent agents and cybernetic control systems for the internet of things and industrial production. A fourth principle of new media objects is "variability." Digital, modular, and automated objects can exist in infinite variations and combinations. There is no difference between original and copy. There is no privileged instantiation of a new media object. There is no limit on the amount of copies that can be produced. Furthermore, any new media object can be transformed into something else. There is hardly any photograph today that has not been run through image processing software and transformed into something other than what has come through the lens of the camera. More and more, this happens already in the camera itself, which has long since become a computer with its own software. There is nothing that cannot be visualized and nothing that is visualized today has not gone through digital processes. In addition to this, big data analytics and user profiling have made it cheap and easy to

---

12 | See for example "modular programming" https://en.wikipedia.org/wiki/Modular_programming

offer media products on a personalized basis or involve user preferences in the creation of media products. This is diametrically opposed to the practices of traditional mass media and analogue culture, which were based on restricted access to information as well as to the production of information resulting in standard products for typical consumer groups.

The fifth and for Manovich "the most substantial consequence of the computerization of media" (2001: 45) is called "transcoding." The term "transcoding" usually refers to the conversion of one data format into another. For Manovich, however, this term describes how "the logic of a computer can be expected to significantly influence the traditional cultural logic of media; that is, we may expect that the computer layer will affect the cultural layer" (45). The computer, software, and digital networks become metaphors for understanding society and even reconceptualizing what it means to be human. The discourse of "cyberculture," "internet culture," or "being digital" relies upon understanding society, culture, and human existence from the point of view of ICTs. The computer serves as a metaphorical key to understanding cognition, communication, cooperation, and many other aspects of society. When Castells speaks of a "network society" this can be seen as an example of transcoding. Transcoding means that new media objects are not "media" objects at all; they are the only objects we have and have become a mirror of ourselves. The principles that constitute new media objects, such as numerical representation, modularity, variability, and automation, become keys to understanding all other areas of reality. Recalling McLuhan's dictum, the media is the message, the language of new media interprets and explains cultural and social life in general. Taking Manovich's idea to its logical consequence, we could say that society and human life are being "transcoded" into new media objects. Society and everything that is a part of it is becoming numerically representable, modular, automated, and variable. Manovich's claim is that "cultural categories or concepts are substituted, on the level of meaning and/or language, by new ones that derive from the computers ontology, epistemology, and pragmatics" (2001: 47).

THE SOCIO-TECHNICAL ENSEMBLE

The third approach to understanding new media can be generally, although to a certain extent misleadingly, classified under the title of the "social construction of technology" (SCOT). The SCOT approach is usually considered part of Science and Technology Studies (STS) with which actor-network theory is also associated.[13] The central thesis is that it is less the influences of technological artifacts that lead to social change than it is the appropriation of technologies by users. Many SCOT studies showed that technologies need not be used for the purposes they were intended by the designers, and also not for the purposes that they themselves suggest, but for purposes that users discover for them through appropriation, resistance, and refunctioning. New and unexpected uses of technologies can then be integrated into development and design thus influencing how technologies are changed and adapted. Whether a technology will be accepted and widely used and in what form depends upon social conditions that are political, economic, cultural and not primarily upon the technology itself. A typical statement of the SCOT program is the following:

It is the social dynamics at work between potential users and those in their social environment (their household, their social networks), as well as between users and other stakeholders such as engineers and designers, producers, policy makers and managers, that shape which ICTs will be used, how they will be used and what type of society will emerge. (Haddon et al. 2008: 1)

SCOT arose as a corrective to technological determinism and for that reason tends to position itself as a theory of social determinism. However, as Oudshoorn and Pinch (2003) point out, recent work on user-technology relations have moved toward a view of these relations as "co-construction." "Users and technology are seen as two sides of the same problem – as co-constructed" (3). This is a middle road between technical and social determinism and speaks of "sociotechnical ensembles" (3) in order to conceptualize "the co-construction or mutual shaping of social groups and technologies" (Bijker 1995). From this perspective, there is neither

---

13 | See Bijker et al. (1987), Pinch/Biker (1984) for programmatic statements of SCOT with corresponding empirical studies.

technologies on the one side and users on the other, much like the producers and consumers of the industrial era, but rather a sociotechnical ensemble in which both users and technologies are mutually conditioning each other and whose characteristics as a whole are what needs to be described. Neither technology nor society should be seen as one-sidedly determining factors, but both together. Even though Castells is often seen as a technological determinist, in his later work he also emphasizes mutual interdependence; "I have conceptualized as the network society the social structure resulting from the interaction between the new technological paradigm and social organization at large" (Castells 2005: 3).

It is against this theoretical background of a mutual shaping or co-construction of social practices and technologies that the third approach seeks to understand the sociotechnical ensemble of which ICTs are an integral part. One of the most striking characteristics of new media is that age-old communicative practices are being transformed.[14] The digital media revolution is transforming traditional forms of human communication, not only because of the affordances of ICTs, but because users have made ICTs serve their own purposes. Throughout history, human society has known only two forms of communication, either one-to-one interaction or, as soon as the number of people involved in interaction no longer permits everyone to speak to everyone, by top-down, one-to-many communication. One-to-one, or face-to-face communication does quite well to organize social relations as long as only a few people are involved. As soon as more and more people become involved, more space and more time is needed for everyone to be able to talk to everyone else in order to coordination activities. At a certain point, the limitations imposed by space and time do not allow for everyone to speak to everyone on a face-to-face basis and another form of communication must take over the task of coordinating activities. Castells sees this as the basis for the distinction between interaction and organization.

Networks throughout history had a major advantage and a major problem vis-a-vis other forms of social organization. On the one hand, they are the most adaptable and flexible organizational forms [...]. On the other hand, in the past they could not master and coordinate the resources needed to accomplish a given task or

---

14 | See Shirky (2008) for a discussion of ICTs as transformative force in communication.

fulfill a project beyond a certain size and complexity of the organization required to perform the task. Thus, in the historical record, networks were the domain of the private life, while the world of production, power, and war was occupied by large, vertical organizations, such as states, churches, armies, and corporations that could marshal vast pools of resources around the purpose defined by a central authority. (Castells 2005: 4)

When small talk no longer gets the job done, and big talk becomes necessary, someone must stand up and speak to everyone else. This someone becomes the chief, the leader, the king or queen, the president, or the boss. When large groups are necessary to get a job done, hierarchical, one-to-many communication takes over and organizes cooperative action. This situation was typical for social organization until only recently. Mass media or broadcast media change nothing is this structure, since only a few have access to the means of information production and distribution. The digital media revolution may be considered revolutionary precisely because asymmetric, one-to-many communication and the hierarchical social structures which for centuries have been a precondition of cooperative action in larger groups is no longer the only means of constructing social order. One-to-one communication as well as one-to-many are being replaced in all areas by *many-to-many* communication. This is changing business, science, education, and politics. As Benkler puts it:

The fundamental elements of the difference between the networked information economy and the mass media are network architecture and the cost of becoming a speaker. The first element is the shift from a hub-and-spoke architecture with unidirectional links to the end points in the mass media, to distributed architecture with multidirectional connections among all nodes in the networked information environment. The second is the practical elimination of communications costs as a barrier to speaking across associational boundaries. Together, these characteristics have fundamentally altered the capacity of individuals, acting alone or with others, to be active participants in the public sphere as opposed to its passive readers, listeners, or viewers. (Benkler 2006: 212)

For Benkler and many other theoreticians of the network society, many-to-many, networked communication creates a new information economy in which new kinds of wealth with new forms of business, science, education, etc. become possible. This means that in many areas hierarchical, one-to-many communication is becoming increasingly inefficient (Tapscott/Williams 2006; Jenkins 2006; Shirky 2008; Weinberger 2012). Above the level of face-to-face interaction, that is, on the levels of groups, organizations, institutions, and social systems, communication need no longer be hierarchical and one-to-many. Castells (1996, 2005) has identified a number of processes that create new organizational forms. Large organizations "decentralize themselves as networks of semi-autonomous units," whereas small or medium sized organizations "form business networks" and "become providers and subcontractors to a variety of large corporations" (Castells 2005: 9). In addition to this, these new networked organizations "engage in strategic partnerships on various projects," whereby the networks built around projects dissolve at the end of a project and flexibly recombine for other projects. Castells is careful to emphasize that the firm or company does not simply disappear. The firm "continues to be the legal unit [...], but the operational unit is the business network" (9). The firm "is simply a connecting node between the networks of production built around business projects and the networks of accumulation organized around global finance" (9).

One of the defining characteristics of the global network society besides ICTs and the new organizational forms they make possible is the "transformation of labor" (Castells 2005: 8). Networked organizations are made up of networked actors, that is, "highly educated, autonomous labor that is able to innovate and adapt to a constantly changing global and local economy" (8). The affordances of digital media and the sociotechnical ensemble of networked communication and cooperative action make it possible for social structures no longer to be built along vertical processes for producing, distributing, and controlling information. This changes the way work of all kinds is done and how information is used by people in all areas. Jenkins et al. (2005) speak of a "participatory culture".

A participatory culture is a culture with relatively low barriers to artistic expression and civic engagement, strong support for creating and sharing creations, and some type of informal mentorship whereby experienced participants pass along knowledge to novices. In a participatory culture, members also believe their contributions matter and feel some degree of social connection with one another (at the least, members care about others' opinions of what they have created). (Jenkins et al. 2005: xii)

Forms of participatory culture go far beyond artistic expression. They include communities of practice, collaborative problem solving, user generated content, open source software, open educational resources, Wikipedia, crowdsourcing, sharing economy, social networking, and much more. According to Jenkins, all these contribute to enabling "peer-to-peer learning, a changed attitude toward intellectual property, the diversification of cultural expression, the development of skills valued in the modern workplace, and a more empowered conception of citizenship" (xii).

Tapscott (2009) has investigated the impact of ICTs on a whole generation that has grown up with new media. Contrary to the usual technology assessment studies that single out specific technologies and investigate relatively limited and clearly circumscribed user groups, Tapscott chooses the Internet and ICTs in general as the technology to investigate. He choose not one specific user group, but an entire generation of young people who are growing up and already have grown up with these new technologies. The question to be answered is what impact new media are having on an entire generation. He called these people the "Net Generation" (Tapscott 1997). In 2007, Tapscott's team interviewed 9,442 people divided into different generations from 12 different countries and conducted deep-dive ethnographic studies of 30 Net-Gens in their homes. The results are eight "net generation norms," that is, clusters "of attitudes and behaviors that define the generation" (Tapscott 2009: 34).[15] For Tapscott the net generation norms are "central to understanding how this generation is changing work, markets, learning, the family, and society" (34). The first can be called "freedom." Freedom refers to the value for and ability to deal with diversity, choice, and information overload. Whereas earlier generations are overwhelmed and uncertain when facing millions of hits in an internet search, the net generation sees this as a chance. Furthermore, they expect similar chances in choosing when and where

---

15 | In a similar vein Jenkins (2009) identifies „new media literacies," that is "a set of cultural competencies and social skills that young people need in the new media landscape" (xiii). These are: play, performance, simulation, appropriation, multitasking, distributed cognition, collective intelligence, judgment, transmedia navigation, networking, negotiation.

they learn and work. "They use technology to escape traditional office constraints and integrate their work lives with their home and social lives" (34).

The second net generation norm could be termed "personalization." The net generation is the first to grow up with convergent media and in a participatory culture. They expect to obtain and modify information tailored to their personal interests. They do not want standard solutions for all. Third, the net generation values "transparency." They want to know who stands behind information, where it comes from, what it is good for, and they want to be able to participate in quality control by publicly rating, commenting, and correcting information of all kinds. Fourth, they value "integrity" and open communication. "The Internet, and other information and communication technologies, strip away the barriers between companies and their various constituencies, including consumers, activists, and shareholders" (35). The fifth norm concerns entertainment or play. Having grown up with interactive computer games, this generation expects surprises, options, being able to find many ways to solve a problem, and expects to take initiative as well as become involved in collaboration when doing so. Collaboration, cooperation, teamwork, sharing, and social engagement, all these make up the sixth norm. The seventh norm may be termed "speed" and refers to the accelerated production, distribution, and use of information typical of new media. "In a world where speed characterizes the flow of information among vast networks of people, communication with friends, colleagues, and superiors takes place faster than ever" (35). Finally, the net generation values innovation, change, surprise, and the unexpected. Whereas earlier generations valued stability, the Net Generation values "flexibility."

Tapscott is not the only one to pose the question of how the affordances of new media are changing basic social and cultural norms. Many authors have asked this question with regard to how organizing is being done in business, education, research, health care, and other areas of society. Surowiecki (2004), Benkler (2006), Shirky (2008), Anderson (2006), Howe (2008), Tapscott and Williams (2006), to mention only a few, have analyzed and described the ways in which organizing is changing in the Internet age. Surowiecki's *Wisdom of the Crowds* (2004) and Howe's *Crowdsourcing* (2006) showed how access to media production and networked communication has made it cheap and efficient to involve consumers or the public in quality control, content generation, decision making, and problem solving within business, government, science, health care, and other branches. Shirky's *Here Comes Everybody* (2008) documented the changes occurring when transaction costs sink to almost nothing and it becomes easy and cheap to bring people together and coordinate activities. Anderson's *The Long Tail* (2006) described how new media have created a global market within reach of small players who can now profitably produce and distribute non-standard products. Benkler (2006) demonstrated the possibilities of new forms of networked business and organization in describing the *Wealth of Networks*. Under the title of *Wikinomics*, Tapscott and Williams summarize these tendencies as follows:

Throughout history corporations have organized themselves according to strict hierarchical lines of authority. Everyone was a subordinate to someone else employees versus managers, marketers versus customers, producers versus supply chain subcontractors, companies versus the community. There was always someone or some company in charge, controlling things, at the 'top' of the food chain. While hierarchies are not vanishing, profound changes in the nature of technology, demographics, and the global economy are giving rise to powerful new models of production based on community, collaboration, and self-organization rather than on hierarchy and control. (Tapscott/Williams 2006: 1)

NETWORK NORMS

The social effects that have been ascribed to new media can be understood as attempts to understand and to document the ways in which organizing in the global network society is changing. In contemporary organization theory the new institutionalism is concerned to relate organizations to norms and values influencing practices of organizing. Without accepting the results of the new institutionalism, it can be claimed that the kinds of stories that are making sense and creating networks today are different from in the industrial age. This difference, we claim, is due to principles characteristic of networking and networks. These principles can be described as "network norms." Although it would be premature and counter-productive to attempt to offer an exhaustive and final analysis of "network norms," it is nonetheless possible to list some of the most important normative principles that guide networking and sensemaking today.[16]

One of the most important effects of the digital media revolution has been identified and analyzed under the title of media "convergence." Convergence can be related to the fundamental norm of *connectivity*. Connectivity is a defining characteristic of networking. It is perhaps the most important of the norms that characterize the sociotechnical ensemble of the global network society. Connectivity means that it is imperative to link up all sources, producers, and users of information. Nothing should be excluded from the network. Here we explicitly subscribe to a network concept that is quite different from that of Castells. Castells (2004) asserts that "networks work on a binary logic: inclusion/exclusion, [...] thus, networks are self-reconfigurable, complex structures of communication that ensure, at the same time, unity of purpose and flexibility of its execution by the capacity to adapt to the operating environment" (4). From the point of view of ANT, this description of networks confuses networks with systems.[17] Systems are defined by a constitutive difference between the system and its environment. A system comes into being by processes of selecting certain elements from the environment that are related to each other by the organization of the system in certain ways so that a specific goal can be attained by the operations of the system. A system cannot consist of everything. It cannot do everything. It must exclude most of the world in order to pursue only certain goals effectively. Networks, on the contrary, can consist of everything and they can pursue multiple goals. The Internet is itself a good example of this principle. Connectivity means not only that networks are decentralized, but also heterogeneous, open, and therefore, as we shall see, flexible with regard to operations and goals. The emerging Internet of Things, which turns objects of all kinds into nodes in the network that produce and distribute information, is a further indication of the influence of the norm of connectivity. From the point of view of the new institutionalism, one could argue that connectivity is a

---

16 | For a discussion of network norms, see Krieger/Belliger (2014).

17 | See Krieger/Belliger (2014: 53-88) for a discussion of the differences between systems and networks.

new kind of institution, a fundamental socio-cultural-technical norm in the global network society.[18]

Just as a participatory culture has arisen on the basis of media convergence and the linking up of everything to everything, so one can say that the *flow* of information has become a primary value and a network norm. Connectivity and flow are imperatives that inform all aspects of society today. Castells (1996: 460) characterizes the network society as a "space of flows." For Castells (2004) "networks process flows, [...] flows are streams of information between nodes circulating through the channels of connection between nodes" (3). In distinction to Castells, however, we do not define flows as restricted by a "program" that "assigns the network its goals and its rules of performance" (3). Again, Castells seems here to rely more on a systems model than a network model. From the point of view of ANT, flow is a network norm that expresses the imperative of unforeseeable, unpredictable, and uncontrollable movement of information, people, goods, money, etc., through global networks. If every node in the network is a participating link, generating, modifying, and distributing content, then, as Weinberger (2012) points out, it is in principle impossible to enforce hierarchical, exclusive, and restrictive forms of communication. It is impossible to channel information in only certain directions, and to effectively restrict access to information. It is the imperative of flow that prevents "programs," in Castells sense of the

---

18 | Emphasizing connectivity, some researchers have begun to speak of a "ubiquitous network society." "The vision of a Ubiquitous Network Society pervades academic inquiry and policy goals. Several related research paradigms focus on the growing presence of heterogeneous computational devices in daily life. The key characteristics of a Ubiquitous Network Society include: (1) The geographic spread of the Internet, with more places becoming networked via fixed or mobile connections; (2) a shift from a one-to-many relationship between humans and computers to one where each person, on average, has many; (3) the embedding of computational intelligence into many aspects of everyday life, enhanced by the miniaturization, increased processing power, and reduced cost of computers; (4) the growth of technical standards enabling machine-to-machine (M2M) intelligence and the subsequent emergence of the Semantic Web [...], a web of interlinked data that can be processed and analyzed by computers without direct human intervention; and (5) the emergence of new ways that humans interact with computers, other humans, and the environment." (Winter/Ono 2015: 3)

term, from steering networks and defining their functions. Networks, as opposed to systems, are neither exclusively nor primarily defined by functionality. From the point of view of ANT, and with regard to the affordances of ICTs, networking is defined by the principles of connectivity and flow. This makes it difficult to maintain, as Castells proposes, a theory of "network power" built upon traditional assumptions of the abilities of elites to exclude, manipulate, indoctrinate, and exploit the masses.[19] We will return to this important difference between Castells' concept of networks and that of ANT when discussing organizing networks in civil society and politics below. For the moment, our concern is to outline the most important of the network norms that can be said to influence networking today.

In addition to connectivity and flow, it is apparent that *communication* has become an institution, a norm, and a value influencing organizing. The preoccupation with the communicative constitution of organizations discussed in Part 2 above illustrates the central importance of communication in organization theory. Of course, it is difficult to describe any kind of human endeavor that is not communicative. It would seem irrelevant and a commonplace to elevate something that is obvious and necessary to the status of an institution. After all, as Watzlawick famously put it, one cannot not communicate. However, in the sense of a network norm and an organizational institution, "communication" refers to the specific many-to-many interaction that characterizes networks after the digital revolution. The network norm of communication refers neither to face-to-face, nor to one-to-many communication. It does not describe a gap between individuals and organizations. It "prescribes" on the contrary, a form of many-to-many interaction and a specific social space that is typical of networks under the affordances of digital media.[20] Sensemaking, organizing, and networking will only be successful when communication is done in certain ways. It is possible – against Watzlawick – to avoid networked communication. Within the sociotechnical ensemble of today's world, however, it would be risky and almost certainly counterproductive.

Together with connectivity, flow, and communication, further network norms are *transparency* and *authenticity*. In a connected world

---

19 | See Castells (2009; 2011).

20 | For a discussion of the social space opened up by networked communication under the title of the "socio-sphere" see Krieger/Belliger (2014: 144ff.).

characterized by unpredictable flows and many-to-many communication, it is almost impossible to keep secrets, attempt to manipulate opinion, or to market ideas or products by means of hype. Furthermore, it is usually counterproductive even to try. As the many rating platforms, whistle blowers, leaks, scandals, and so on have shown, communication in a network society must be open and transparent. Tapscott's long-term study of the net generation showed that Net-Gens want to know who stands behind information, where it comes from, and what it is good for. They want to be able to participate in quality control by publicly rating, commenting, and correcting information of all kinds. Wikipedia and the many rating portals for products and services of all kinds illustrate the importance of the network norms of transparency, authenticity, and participation. These norms are important criteria for sensemaking. Narratives of privacy, secrecy, knowledge as power, and the value of withholding information have become dysfunctional. In the global network society one does not make sense, bring people together, and create value by attempting to steer, block, censure, or misuse information.

Here again, we must take issue with Castells' theory of network power. For Castells, networks are always "programed" by elites who have power to shape what is communicated and how communication takes place in a particular network. Furthermore, since networks are decentralized and plural, network power also lies in the ability of elites to link up networks for the pursuit of certain goals or programs. Power is defined as "the structural capacity to impose one's own will over another's will" (2004: 31). It is the network programmers and those who switch between networks and connect networks to each other who exercise power:

In a world of networks, the ability to exercise control over others depends on two basic mechanisms: the ability to program/reprogram the network(s) in terms of the goals assigned to the network; and the ability to connect different networks to ensure their cooperation by sharing common goals and increasing resources. I call the holders of the first power position the 'programmers,' and the holders of the second power position the 'switchers.' (Castells 2004: 32)

Programming amounts to "the ability to create an effective process of communication and persuasion along lines that favor the projects of the would-be programmers" (33). This is nothing new to networks. It has been the dream of every MadMan, that is, every Madison Avenue advertising executive since the birth of mass consumerism. It is odd that in order to maintain a theory of power Castells seems to find it necessary to reinstate exactly that form of communication that networks did away with. The digital transformation of mass media into many-to-many and participatory media did away with hype, the manipulation of public opinion by mass media, and the one-to-many communication of hierarchies. As the *Clue Train Manifesto* (Levine et al. 1999)[21] proclaimed, the age of hype is over and markets have become "conversational." Not persuasion, not manipulation of opinion, not hype, but authentic and transparent communication is what characterizes networks. This is true for marketing no less than for political or academic communication. Castells' concept of networks as programmable systems breaks down at this point. When networks can no longer be programmed, they cannot be governed by rules of inclusion/exclusion and can also no longer be isolated areas of influence and power that could be connected, or "switched" to each other. It is exactly the programmers and the switchers who have been put out of work by the digital media revolution. It is of course true, that networks link up many organizations and areas of endeavor that previously were more or less isolated. This, however, is not switching in the sense in which Castells uses the term. The various undeniable associations between science, business, politics, religion, etc. need not be conceptualized as "switches," controlled by elites. Instead, they are forms of networking that are subject to the norms and conditions of networking and sensemaking that constitute social order today.[22] It may well be that a theory of networks does not need a theory of power at all, since every form of mediation is also a negotiation, a conflict of interpretations, and a struggle for order.

Connectivity, the free flow of information, and communication are only effective on the basis of trust, and trust demands transparency. Furthermore, transparency is only credible and effective when it is coupled with *authenticity*. In the early days of the Internet, it was fashionable to experiment with alternative identities. In the meantime, it has become very difficult to disguise anything, all the more, who one is. Profiles in social

---

21 | https://en.wikipedia.org/wiki/The_Cluetrain_Manifesto

22 | What Castells terms "switching" could just as well be interpreted in terms of Luhmann's (1989) idea of "structural coupling," for "resonance" between semi-autonomous social subsystems, or Latour's (2013b) idea of "cross-overs," among modes of existence.

networking sites such as Xing or LinkedIn have become central forces in job seeking and professional development. Software as a service in all forms as well as ecommerce of any kind demand secure identification. Most networked communication is guided by the imperative of honesty and authenticity. As the saying goes, who you are in Facebook, is pretty much who you are. If this is not the case, one cannot participate efficiently in organizing anything, not even a dinner party. For this reason, as Tapscott discovered, Net-Gens value integrity and open communication not only between persons, but also between organizations. "The Internet, and other information and communication technologies, strip away the barriers between companies and their various constituencies, including consumers, activists, and shareholders" (Tapscott 2009: 35). Communication in the market place as well as in the public sphere has become a "naked conversation."[23]

Other important network norms are *participation* and *flexibility*. Needless to say, a participatory culture encourages and even prescribes that social actors get involved. Getting involved and participating in a network means that one serves as a node in the network. Not merely computers are nodes in global networks, but also people and organizations. Nodes not only receive and pass on information, they modify and enrich it, and they make choices about what is done with the information, where it goes, and for what purposes. When every actor, both human and non-human, is participating in the network, the network is constantly changing, reconfiguring itself, adding new links, generating new content, forming new clusters, dropping others, and branching out in unforeseeable directions. This is not merely a fact; it is a value, a norm that can be called *flexibility*. Flexibility should not be confused with adaptation. Adaptation is what systems do in order to maintain their operations as a reaction to changes in the environment. Networks, however, do not have environments; they have stronger or weaker ties. Networks do not adapt, they reconfigure. When major reconfigurations take place, organizations that are well networked are less in danger of disappearing. They are able to change. Even if structures and processes change, relations always remain. It is no secret that change and innovation are major values in today's world. For the industrial age, stability was important. In the global network society, flexibility has become the norm.

---

23 | See Scoble/Israel (2006).

CONCLUSION

Summarizing what has been said about the affordances of new media with regard to sensemaking, networking, staging, and enacted narrative, it is reasonable to assume that new "institutions" in the form of "network norms" have emerged. These guide, influence, steer, and condition how organizing is done and what kinds of organizations will be successful in the sociotechnical ensemble of the global network society. They do this not because they are macro social structures that operate behind the backs of individual actors, but because actors, both human and non-human are mediating, translating, and enrolling each other in specific ways that are conditioned by the affordances of ICTs. The network norms describe how networking is being done under the affordances of ICTs. The question of *what* organizations are has become a *how* question. How is organizing being done? Organizations are what happens when connectivity, flow, communication, participation, transparency, authenticity, and flexibility guide networking, staging, and sensemaking. When norms such as these guide organizing, what consequences does this have for questions of management? Since organizing also means *managing*, the question arises, how *management practices* change in the network society. We will now turn to this question.

5. Organizing Networks in the Digital Age

The affordances of new media and ICTs affect all areas of society including business, education, health care, science, politics, and NGOs and NPOs. One way to understand this influence is in terms of network norms. The network norms of connectivity, flow, communication, transparency, participation, authenticity, and flexibility influence sensemaking and organizing in all these areas and in many different ways. Networking, in one form or the other, has become an imperative for organizations. The network norms can serve as a helpful guide to describing various forms of organizing and networking as well as the many new challenges to management that they pose. Although it is possible, and from a theoretical point of view necessary, to analyze and describe the various network norms individually,[1] it should be clearly stated that they collectively and interdependently influence society and organizations. In the following, we will take a closer look at some of the more important trends and challenges that characterize organizing in the global network society.

We will describe some of the developments in education, health care, business, government, and civil society that illustrate what organizing networks can mean today. We admit that the examples we have chosen may not be well chosen. We admit that the list is neither exhaustive, nor even representative of what networking can mean. Nonetheless, we have attempted to pick out typical examples of how networking is being done. We will use them as illustrations of how the network norms are influencing networking. Every form of networking, of course, is influenced by all the norms collectively. For example, when we discuss big data analytics in education, one or two norms may come to the fore, but this should not be

---

1 | See Krieger/Belliger (2014) for a detailed discussion of the individual network norms.

taken to imply that the other norms have no influence on the many uses of big data in education as well as other areas. From the point of view of management practices, this means that the network norms are guiding, influencing, and conditioning management practices in many different ways. Nonetheless, it is useful for purposes of illustration to single out certain norms as exemplary influences on particular practices or trends. The purpose of the analysis is to show how the digital transformation is guided by ways of networking that are in turn guided, influenced, conditioned, and informed by the network norms that we have derived from the affordances of ICTs and described above. It should, however, always be kept in mind that norms are normative and not determinative. Networking activities do not necessarily have to follow the norms. There will be many examples of networks that attempt to limit connectivity, restrict the flow of information, block participation, refuse transparency, and so on, but our claim is that such networks will not in the long run be successful and sustainable.

Organizing Networks in Business

A recent discussion of the new environment for 21st century management recalls Castells' description of the characteristics of the global network society and describes the challenges managers and decision-makers are facing today:

> Managers today face major strategic discontinuities that are changing the nature of competition. [...] For instance, the digital revolution in the form of electronic business processes conducted via the Internet is altering the fundamentals of how companies run their businesses. The recent strategic discontinuities include the elimination of industry boundaries, coalescence between industrial and service businesses, computer-aided design and communication, and the opening of global markets. (Kollman/Stöckmann 2008: 11)

Where once organizations found themselves conditioned by the norms of either markets or bureaucratic hierarchies, networks have now become one the most significant forms or organizing. This means that management assumptions and practices that had proven successful in the industrial era are no longer efficient. Kollmann and Stöckmann warn that "Change and uncertainty may cause serious problems to those companies, which rely on the time-tested behavior of the past [...]" (12). The affordances of new media have put organizations of all kinds into a situation characterized by globalization, digital infrastructure, ubiquitous connectivity, crowdsourcing, open innovation, social media, co-creation, semantic web, collective intelligence, intelligent agents, prosumers instead of consumers, conversational markets, learning organizations, informational overload, open educational resources, flows, knowledge workers, identity management, distributed cognition, connectivism, virtual organizations, the cloud, platform effects, knowledge management, decentralization, self-organization, viral communication, and much more. The phenomena that these terms describe do not refer exclusively to high-tech or media organizations, nor exclusively to companies in the private sector. New management practices are not reserved for Silicon Valley, but are part and parcel of organizations in all areas of society, whether directly concerned with ICTs or not. This includes businesses and organizations in education, healthcare, science, politics, social services administration, art, law, and civil society. Perhaps it is tempting to dismiss these ideas as superficial buzz or merely the latest hype. If we resist this temptation, then these ideas can be understood to describe a fundamental shift in the way networking is done, the kind of stories that are being told, and how sensemaking is organizing social relations today.

Network Management Framework

In the last decades, much effort has been made to describe the challenges of "21st century management."[2] A central topic that has emerged from this research is leadership and management of networked organizations.[3] Although explicitly concerned with interorganizational networks, the framework of network leadership and management that Saz-Carranza et al. (2008) develop can be applied to networks of all kinds. As often remarked (Powel 1990), networks appear as a form of order somewhere between the diversity and heterogeneity of markets and the unity of

---

2 | See the classic work of Peter Drucker (1999) and the extensive handbook by Wankel (2008).

3 | See Powel (1990), Jarrillo (1993), Huxham/Vangen (2000), Kickert et al. (1997), Koppenjan/Klijn (2004), and Saz-Carranza et al. (2008).

hierarchical, bureaucratic organizations. Viewing networks as a kind of middle ground between markets and hierarchies with characteristics drawn from both may seem helpful. However, this view is still bound to the dualistic assumptions of agency and structure, or individual and organization typical of traditional organization theory. To say that networks are neither markets nor hierarchies does not necessarily imply that they are some mixture of the two, some kind of middle ground between the opposing forces of agency and structure. On the contrary, networks are neither markets nor hierarchies and neither are they a mixture of the two. They are something entirely different. This does not mean, however, that the task of managing networks successfully has nothing to do with forces of diversity and unity. Saz-Carranza and his colleagues locate the problems of network management in the "inherent paradoxes implied by networks, in particular the need to be simultaneously united and divers" (2008: 292). This implies that "successful networks are simultaneously united and divers" (297). Instead of finding a normative basis in contracts and property rights as do markets, or employer/employee relations, as in hierarchies, networks are based on complementarity, mutual adjustment, and reciprocity. They emerge and act within a "collaborative context" (Chrislip/Larson 1994) characterized by the specific "boundary-crossing nature of collaborations [...], the lack of formal authority and hierarchy, and the blurriness of strategies" (Saz-Carranza et al. 2008: 296). A collaborative context demands different leadership and management practices than those that had become established in the industrial age.

Leadership in collaborative contexts must be necessarily different, focusing largely on process, and has similarities to facilitative, transformative, and servant leadership - that is, to inspire commitment and action, to lead as peer problem solver, to build broad-based involvement, and to sustain hope and participation. (Saz-Carranza et al. 2008: 296)

Citing Huxham and Vangen (2000), Saz-Carranza and colleagues define leadership broadly as "mechanisms that make things happen in a collaboration" (2008: 296). Contrary to much research on leadership, which focuses on individuals conceived of as either leaders or followers, that is, on their skills, roles, competencies, talents, or authority, Saz-Carranza et al. propose focusing on "activities and actions that make things happen" (296). They therefore do not need to draw a clear boundary between management and leadership, since bureaucratic routines and authoritative decisions no longer play important roles. Furthermore, the framework they propose does not focus on leadership and management *within* networks, that is, within network nodes or network partners, but rather describes leadership and management *of* the entire network. This implies that leadership is a "collective phenomenon" (297) which distributes among all participants the task of "generating unity among the network members while preserving their diversity" (297). Enabling networks to be at once diverse and unified is what gives them an advantage over traditional forms of organization. Diversity fosters innovation, adaptability, flexibility, and resilience, while unity allows the diverse partners to coordinate action and to perform cooperatively and effectively.

In sum, the unity/diversity paradox is inherent to networks, which must be diverse to have an added value with respect to hierarchies but united to allow for concerted action of any kind, unlike markets. Leadership is about avoiding diversity and unity to undermine each other by respectively generating disunity and similarity. (297)

On the basis of this understanding of the task that network management must accomplish, Saz-Carranza et al. develop a framework according to which network management practices fall into four categories, *facilitating, framing, activating,* and *mobilizing*.[4]

   Facilitating includes all those management practices and activities that enable and support interaction, equality, motivation, and participation among members of the network. It is not merely a matter of exchange of information, but of inclusive and participatory decision-making. Otherwise, certain members may feel disadvantaged and the network would tend to disintegrate. *Facilitating* is a management practice that can be derived from the network norms of connectivity, flow, and communication. These norms guide networking toward inclusivity, while maintaining diversity, heterogeneity, open communication, and participatory action.

   Framing is the second category of management practices that Saz-Carranza and colleagues identify as peculiar to networked organizations. As the name suggests, framing includes all activities that enable cooperative action with regard to specific goals. This term strongly recalls

---

4 | Saz-Carranza et al. (2008: 297ff.).

Goffman's staging and Weick's sensemaking. It also is closely related to Latour's notion of "localizing," since framing sets up structures, rules, boundaries, etc. that focus, channel, partition, and reduce (Latour 1996: 234) cooperative action. Framing consists of those management practices that operate not primarily for the network as a whole, but for decentralized units, nodes, and partners, who can manage in this way their unique contributions to the entire network. Without framing, the diversity of the network would not be able to become operative, since individual units would not have sufficient freedom and decision-making powers in order to organize their individual activities. Framing can be understood as being guided by the network norms of participation and authenticity. Each partner can and should be responsible to the network in ways that they are themselves are enabled to determine, at least partly. This demands management practices that make participation possible without unnecessarily limited the authentic expression of participants.

Activating is the third form of management practices found in networks. It refers to all management practices that seek to integrate actors into the network. This is very similar to what ANT calls translation and enrollment. The network becomes more powerful and effective to the extent that it can enroll new members that contribute new skills, competencies, ideas, and impulses. Just as translating and enrolling in ANT, activating in the network management framework of Saz-Carranza and colleagues is concerned with network goals, or programs of action into which members can be integrated, and thus it is also concerned with network identity, reputation, and legitimacy. The network norms of connectivity, participation, authenticity, as well as transparency play roles in successful activation, since it is only when all participants in the network are accepted for their unique contributions and information is available to all that the network as a whole can become a collective actor capable of cooperative action with regard to consensual goals.

Finally, *mobilization* refers to management practices that can bring resources and support into the network. The term "mobilization" in the Saz-Carranza framework means much the same as it does for ANT. For ANT, actor-networks "mobilize" as many human and non-human actors as they can in order to create stability, durability, social presence, and power. Translating and enrolling actors into a network becomes mobilizing the moment the goal is to generate network power. For Saz-Carranza and colleagues "Mobilizing essentially builds network power [...]" (298). Summarizing the four aspects of network management, they write:

Sustaining the unity/diversity paradox generates power, which increases the network's effectiveness. The networks sustain the unity/diversity paradox by activating members, facilitating interaction, and framing the structure (procedures, rules, and values). In addition, networks mobilize support. When activating, the network selects and attracts members who share certain experiences, values, and principles, but who are diverse regarding other organizational characteristics. Interaction and open decision making among the diverse members must be facilitated and members united by framing common procedures, rules, and values. (2008: 298-299)

This framework for understanding network management practices distinguishes itself from traditional management models because management in networks is not about decision making, but *facilitating*, *framing*, *activing*, and *mobilizing* decision-making. Decisions are distributed throughout the network and are made by network members. Management does not reduce complexity or uncertainty, but establishes procedures for openness and inclusiveness. Furthermore, management does not control outcomes, but facilitates processes. It does this my means of what Weick would certainly call sensemaking. In words similar to how Weick describes sensemaking, Saz-Carranza et al. understand framing as what "ascribes, interprets, and makes meaning of the outside reality, it constructs the perceptions of actors regarding reality" (299).

The description of network management practices according to the framework of facilitating, framing, activating, and mobilizing can be easily compared to what we have described above as networking, staging, sensemaking, and enacted narrative and can be derived from the network norms. It enables actors to "go through a naming and framing process, which is, basically, meaning making" (299). Organizing networks is a matter of translating, enrolling, and mobilizing actors into networks guided by programs of action and concerned with allowing all actors to have their own voice. In the global network society characterized by the affordances of ICTs management practices of facilitating, framing, activating, and mobilizing can be derived from the norms of connectivity, flow, communication, participation, transparency, authenticity, and flexibility. It would be a mistake to view networking and networked forms of organizing as an idealistic or ideologically motivated activism that ignores the realities of economics and market constraints. On the contrary, networked forms of organizing in all areas, whether public or private, profit or non-profit, can be said to have a competitive advantage over traditional organizations. As Lavie (2008: 324) notes, "firms can no longer be considered simply as independent entities competing for favorable market positons and protecting their core assets from imitation and appropriation." The global network society creates a situation in which "firms have become interconnected in the sense that they engage in multiple simultaneous alliances" (324) which contribute directly to economic success.

Competitive Advantages of Networked Organizing

Lavie (2008) has investigated the "Competitive Advantages of Intercon-nected Firms." He notes that the "emergence of interconnected firms is a contemporary phenomenon" (325) rooted in the economic realities of the global network society. In order to explain why interconnected firms have competitive advantages, he introduces the notion of "network resources" (325). "Network resources reside in alliances in which the interconnected firm is involved rather than within the scope of the firm's organizational boundaries" (2008: 325). Alliances serve various goals. They allow "flexible and more rapid adjustment to changing market conditions," "reduce time to market in response to shortened product life cycles," "assist in bridging national boundaries," and "reduce market uncertainty and stabilize the firm's competitive environment by forming norms of reciprocity that establish commitment and regulate exchange transactions" (325). Furthermore, alliances are not restricted to any one branch or sector. They have proven efficient in research and development, production, and marketing "in almost any industry" (326). As Saz-Carranza and colleagues pointed out, for Lavie also, the interconnected firm is involved in a network that is "dynamically evolving yet durable" (2008: 326). Whereas traditional theories of the firm emphasize interfirm competition, theories of interconnected firms emphasize motivation for joining an alliance, strategies for partner selection, the management of alliances, governance structures, learning dynamics, and the performance of the entire network. This new research departs from the traditional view that the appropriation of value is based on ownership of the value-generating resources. Against this assumption,

Lavie points out that for interconnected firms there is a "direct sharing of resources" and an "indirect transferability of benefits associated with these resources" (328); and he concludes that the "proprietary assumption of the resource-based view prevents an accurate evaluation of an interconnected firm's competitive advantage" (328). This means that networked forms of organization are able to create and appropriate value more because of their ability "to maintain valuable interaction with their partners" (332) and less because of their inner-organizational assets. Lavie concludes:

At the turn of the 21st century, alliances have emerged as a primary vehicle for conducting economic transactions. Once conceived of as independent entities, firms are now considered interconnected in the sense that they engage in multiple alliances with counterpart firms. This phenomenon necessitates a new theory of the firm that incorporates simultaneous competition and collaboration as drivers of value creation and appropriation. [...] Managers need to pay attention not only to the value of resources nurtured by their own firms but also to the resources possessed by their firms' partners. They must evaluate the value of network resources as well as the value of potential combinations of network resources and internal resources. They must collaborate to create value and compete to appropriate their relative share of that value. They must look beyond the immediate scope of alliances and seek to leverage network resources while finding the right balance between resource sharing and the protection of proprietary assets. (2008: 333)

Global Projects

Understanding the advantages of networked organizing from the point of view of sharing and cooperatively using resources also explains the emergence of *global projects* as an important way in which networks today operate. Ainamo (2008) claims that "a new 'logic of organizing' has been spreading in market economies" (482). This new organizational logic is based on "flattening out organizational hierarchies, weakening of firms' boundaries in favor of networks of collaborations, and restructuring of competition between firms within and across industries" (482). This has led to "global projects as new organizational form" (482). As Ainamo notes, "more and more companies are now becoming structured around distinctly global projects" (483).

Organizing highly skilled workers dealing with complex problems to create novel outputs by integrating varied forms of expertise – also across cultures and institutional systems – represents a significant new organizational form. (Ainamo 2008: 483)

If we follow Barney's (1991) definition of resources as "all assets, capabilities, organizational processes, firm attributes, information, knowledge, etc. controlled by the firm" (101), and accept Lavie's (2008) claim that networked sharing of resources adds value and competitive advantage, global projects can be seen as a viable response to the global network society. Ainamo points out that in todays' world "firms are transforming into fluid, overlapping organizational arrangements in which both internal and external boundaries break down, and cooperation with other firms grows" (482). Cooperation among firms or other organizations does not need to take the form of alliances or partnerships. Projects have emerged as a typical form of interorganizational cooperation. Castells (2005) also emphasizes the project-based dynamic of networking:

[...] large corporations, and their ancillary networks, engage in strategic partnerships on various projects concerning products, processes, markets, functions, resources, each one of these projects being specific, and thus building a specific network around such a project, so that at the end of the project, the network dissolves and its components form other networks around other projects. (Castells 2005: 9)

Projects are usually distinguished from organizations in that they are directed to specific goals to be attained within a limited time and with limited resources. Typical management tasks in projects are initiating, planning, executing, controlling and monitoring, and closing.[5] Although these activities usually take place within organizations, in many industries, such as the film industry, the software industry, the construction industry, biotech, research consortia, as well as the consulting and marketing industry, experts from outside any one organization as well as different organizations are often contracted to work together on specific tasks whose

---

5 | See the Guide to the Project Management Body of Knowledge for a representative statement https://en.wikipedia.org/wiki/Project_Management_Body_of_Knowledge

completion also ends the contractual cooperation.[6] Ainamo identifies two basic ways in which organizations form projects. One the one hand, agencies can develop an expertise on carrying out projects within a certain area. The experts remain within the agency and move from one project to another, or work simultaneously on several projects. On the other hand, agencies can also cooperate with external experts or other agencies. This interorganizational and heterogeneous project organization consists of teams that do not usually remain contracted to any one agency after completion of a project. Along with this move to networked projects on a global scale as one of the major ways in which value is created in all areas, there comes a transformation of what work means and what demands are being made upon labor.[7]

The movement of experts, or "knowledge workers," who traditionally were continually employed by one organization, into free contractual relations with the companies they once worked for as well as other companies, included competitors, has often been noted as a characteristic of labor in the knowledge society. Castells (2000: 12) distinguishes between "self-programmable" and "generic" labor. According to Castells, "self-programmable labour is equipped with the ability to retrain itself, and adapt to new tasks, new processes and new sources of information, as technology, demand, and management speed up their rate of change " (12). These are the "knowledge workers." They are the experts that often make up the flexible and heterogeneous project teams responsible for business activities in many areas today.[8] What project forms of organizing show is that flexibility has become imperative for both employers and employees. The major advantage of project-based organizing is the ability to adapt and reconfigure operations, participants, goals, and processes quickly and on a global scale. The influence of the network norms of connectivity participation, and flexibility can be well illustrated by global projects as well as the demands this form of organizing makes upon labor. On the

---

6 | See the discussion of various project-based industries in Ainamo (2008).

7 | We will return to this aspect of the network society when discussing challenges for education below.

8 | Castells (2000) speaks of the "individualization of labour" as the key transformative factor and characterizes this workforce as, "part-time work, temporary work, self-employment, work by contract, informal or semi-formal labour arrangements, and relentless occupational mobility" (12).

side of labor, it is important to emphasize that not everyone is a knowledge worker and possesses the resources to profit from the freedom implied by variable and open networks. There is a growing problem of those who Castells puts into the category of "generic" labor, as well those who fall out of any form of employability. Some of these problems can be addressed by new networked forms of education and civil society that we will discuss below. Many, however, remain as major issues for the network society.

Corporate Entrepreneurship and Innovation Management

Speaking of organizations as "flexible" usually takes place within the framework offered by evolutionary theory and the theory of complex adaptive systems. Organizations are compared to biological organisms that are able to maintain their operations in the face of environmental changes by means of building up internal complexity. The more complex an organism, or organization, the more inner states it has, and thus the more options it has to react to changes in the environment. Since bureaucratic, hierarchical organization does not favor internal complexity, management theories look to systems theory for a model of how organizations can foster innovation. This model is evolutionary adaptation. Flexible organizations are those that tolerate and even systematically support internal complexity, which is often described as "decentralization." Herbert Simon, for example, speaks of "nearly decomposable systems" (1996: 193) that consist of relatively independent specialized elements. "The claim is that the potential for rapid evolution exists in any complex system that consists of a set of stable subsystems, each operating nearly independently of the detailed processes going on within the other subsystems" (193). From the point of view of network theory, flexibility does not need to be achieved by special measures taken to increase internal complexity. It is a characteristic of networks as such.

Networks are structurally opposed to hierarchies because every node in the network has a certain freedom to enter into connections to other nodes, both within and without an existing network. Of course, nodes in a network can be black-boxed into functional units with circumscribed input/output mechanisms. The prevalence of such black boxes everywhere is indisputable. This is why the systems model appears so plausible and convincing. Before the digital transformation, limitations on communication made it necessary to construct black boxes within organizations and sharp boundaries between organizations. Black boxes, however, can be opened and any element of a functional unit can enter into new and unforeseen associations. The affordances of ICTs tend to open black boxes and thus deconstruct system boundaries. This characteristic of network structure today makes complexity and flexibility into "normal" attributes of networks. Networks do not need to be made flexible by extraordinary measures. They are flexible. What from the systems point of view is a difficult and challenging task is for networks a matter of the normal dynamic of connectivity and flow. The more connectivity a network has the more nodes it has and the more information flows through the nodes in unforeseeable ways, which leads to unexpected developments, that is, to innovation and change.

Innovation from the systems theory point of view is a response to an environment that is considered as excluded from the system and therefore is able only to disturb the system. Changes in the environment are always threats to the system. System viability depends on being able to adapt quickly to environmental changes. These adaptations are innovations. This is why innovation has become a central topic in today's business world. Innovation, however, can be conceived as a synergy of organization and environment, a mutual and interdependent exchange.[9] In this view, both the organization and its environment mutually construct each other, which, we would argue, is another way of speaking about networks. Networks do not have an "environment" in the specific sense that complex adaptive systems do. Networks do not "adapt" to an environment in the same way that a biological system does. This has consequences not only for how innovation and organizational change are theorized, but also for what has been called "organizational learning."[10]

James March in a famous article *Exploration and Exploitation in Organizational Learning* (1991) understands innovation as an adaptive process and thus as "learning." Not only individuals learn, but also organizations. Adaptation to environmental changes is in this theoretical

---

9 | "In the 21st century, organizations should not solely respond to preordained environmental conditions, but should instead influence and actually create their environment by innovation" (Kollman/Stöckmann 2008: 12).

10 | For an overview of research on organizational learning and knowledge management, see Easterby-Smith/Lyles (2011).

perspective understood as learning.[11] Although March's distinction between exploration and exploitation is based on the systems model, perhaps it can be helpful also from the network perspective. Instead of beginning from the assumption that organizations can be modelled as complex adaptive systems with the corollary that learning is adaptation, let us ask how organizations actually learn. As we have seen, organizing is done by human and non-human actors building networks. Organizations learn from individuals (cf. human capital, human resources) who "explore" new possibilities, discover unforeseen possibilities, and then influence the organization by integrating these new ideas into the organization by means of "exploiting" old certainties. This process can also be conceptualized as translating and enrolling actors into networks, or in terms of Karl Weick's sensemaking.[12]

In March's terms, "exploration" requires that organizations allow their workers or smaller units some form of uncontrolled and unstructured free-room so that initiative is possible. Furthermore, exploration should not only be possible within an organization, but also formally acknowledged and systematically encouraged.[13] Within the systems model, this is understood as a strategy of increasing internal complexity in order to increase adaptability. This is based on an organizational design similar to Simon's nearly decomposable system. However, networks are not systems and innovation does not need to be conceptualized as adaptation. Systems operate on the basis of a sharp distinction between system and environment and clear rules of exclusion and inclusion. The environment represents a domain of possible disturbances to the system, which depends on its own internal organization in order to be able to adapt to

---

11 | Already Cyert and March (1963) stated that it is through "organizational learning processes (that) [...] the firm adapts to its environment" (84). In subsequent discussions these processes are seen as formal, internal rules on the one hand or as an informal "culture" of open communication and innovation on the other. The latter is often associated with the term "learning organization."

12 | "Sensemaking [...] is less about discovery than is about invention" (Weick 1995: 13).

13 | This is where "knowledge management" comes in as "the planning, organizing, motivating, and controlling of people, processes and systems in the organization to ensure that its knowledge-related assets are improved and effectively employed" (King 2009: 4).

environmental changes. Networks, on the contrary, are defined by the principle of connectivity. Connectivity means that network boundaries are not at all clearly drawn, but deploy along lines of more or less connectivity. Weak connectivity is a boundary area, whereas strong connectivity tends to be seen as within a network. The principle of connectivity, as we saw above, does not exclude, it includes everything, but on a continuum of more or less and not on the basis of a binary logic of inclusion/exclusion. In order to explain why the network perspective offers a basis for rethinking such important issues as innovation and organizational change, we propose taking a closer look at what has come to called "organizational entrepreneurship."[14]

Entrepreneurs are usually considered to be those individuals who create organizations and not as organizations themselves. An established organization is normally not entrepreneurial, but busy with exploiting the ideas and resources that it has built up and acquired after successfully leaving the exploratory "start-up" phase. This means that entrepreneurs are for the most part not positioned as employees of an organization, but as independent risk-takers and innovators.[15] To speak of "organizational entrepreneurship" is therefore almost an oxymoron.[16] Nonetheless, in the quickly changing and highly competitive setting of the global network society, organizations are increasingly becoming involved in entrepreneurship. This means that management must make place for the unforeseeable and unexpected and attempt to institutionalize what March called "exploration" and which has also come to be understood as organizational learning.

Research into organizational entrepreneurship has identified at least two typical forms in which organizations attempt to institutionalize

---

14 | See Katz/Shepherd (2004); Kollmann/Stöckmann (2008); Gundry (2008); Hjorth (2012).

15 | Citing Schumpeter, Kollmann and Stöckmann (2008) point out that "the transition form a new venture to an established firm is associated with a descent of entrepreneurial spirit and an ascent of bureaucratic management" (11).

16 | "In their pure forms [...] entrepreneurship and organization are bipolar opposites and blending the two in a single form seems nearly impossible" (Kollmann/Stöckmann 2008: 14).

exploration and innovation.[17] One solution is to set up special units such as new business development units. This strategy has the advantage of systematically bringing creative individuals together in small, flexible working-groups that are shielded from the restrictions of bureaucracy that obtain for the rest of the organization. These units can also connect up to resources outside the organization and form learning alliances, research and development networks, and joint ventures. The second approach is to instill a culture of entrepreneurial thinking throughout the entire organization. In this approach every employee is encouraged, expected, and empowered to participate in developing new products, services, and business possibilities. As Kollmann and Stöckmann (2008) put it, "the underlying assumption of this approach is that each employee has the capacity of both entrepreneurial and managerial behavior" (14). This also implies that the organizational design is "characterized by both informal and formal communication across divisional (even hierarchical) boundaries" and that "a sense of autonomy gives employees the freedom to take initiative and act" (15). Regardless of which approach an organization takes, whether specialized entrepreneurial units within the firm or an organization wide culture of entrepreneurship, management must change established routines and discard traditional assumptions.

Various forms of entrepreneurial management have been identified. Stevenson (1983) speaks of "entrepreneurial management," Miller (1983) and Lumpkin and Dess (1996), as well as Dess and Lumpkin (2005) prefer the idea of an "entrepreneurial orientation," whereas Gibson and Birkenshaw (2004) use the idea of organizational "ambidexterity." In all these views, certain common characteristics of organizational entrepreneurship are apparent. An entrepreneurial organization is oriented toward opportunity instead of consolidation. It commits resources in a flexible and uncomplicated way to exploring uncertain opportunities instead of carefully assessing all risks first. Furthermore, an entrepreneurial organization tends to enter into alliances and cooperation with other organizations in order to share and optimize resources. This implies a specifically entrepreneurial organizational structure, namely, "flat hierarchies and multiple informal networks" (Kollmann/Stöckmann 2008: 16). In addition to this, entrepreneurial organizations reward initiative and creativity, tolerate risk, and ac-

---

17 | For the discussion of organizational entrepreneurship see Birkenshaw (2003), Stenenson (1983) Katz/Shepard (2004), and Kollmann/Stöckmann (2008).

cept mistakes. These findings support the claim that new network norms are guiding decision-makers and knowledge workers in the way they go about their daily work and in the goals they pursue. Connectivity, unrestricted flow of information, communication, participation, and flexibility are imperatives in the area of entrepreneurship.

Platforms

Everyone knows the story of how Microsoft took over the PC Market from the innovative pioneer Apple. Apple's products were locked into a proprietary pipeline, a one-sided value-chain in which consumers were offered products from a producer and that was it. Microsoft changed the rules of the market by making their operating system open for all to use as a platform upon which independent producers could offer their own products, whether hardware or software. Within a few years, Microsoft dominated the PC market and Apple was on the brink of bankruptcy. Apple, of course, learned their lesson. When the iPhone came onto the market, Nokia, Motorola, and other major manufacturers of telephones dominated the market. The iPhone, however, was not another telephone, it was a platform that networked app-developers together with consumers in the same way that Microsoft had done with Windows. Google soon followed with Android. Other examples of platforms are Airbnb, eBay, Uber, and Amazon. What these new forms of doing business have in common is that they are *networked markets*. They bring not only a seller together with potential buyers, they bring many sellers together with many buyers in such a way that all participate not only for a profit, but also for growth, innovation, and mutual opportunities. This extraordinary dynamic is called "network effects."[18] Network effects are a way of talking about what happens to markets under the conditions of connectivity, flow, communication, participation and the other network norms. The examples of organizing networks in business discussed above tend to emphasize the digital transformation of bureaucratic hierarchies. Platforms illustrate the digital transformation of markets.

---

18 | See Liebowitz http://wwwpub.utdallas.edu/~liebowit/palgrave/network.html and the discussion and list of literature by Arun Sundararajan on network effects see http://oz.stern.nyu.edu/io/network.html

Economists have documented various kinds of network effects. One of the most important network effects is that increase in usage of a product leads to an increase in the value of the product. The more people who use an iPhone, the more app-developers are interested in creating apps for the iPhone, and the more valuable the iPhone becomes for uses. This is a positive feedback loop. This is called a direct network effect.[19] There are also indirect network effects, whereby increase usage of a product leads to innovation and production of complementary or associated products. Again, Microsoft is a good example insofar as the Windows platform led to the development of many "compatible" products. There are two-sided network effects in which value is gained on both sides, the developer/producer side and the consumer side. For the consumer, the iPhone becomes more valuable, the more value it creates for developers. Uber or Airbnb demonstrate two-sided network effects. Uber is a platform that creates value for both drivers and passengers. It can also be considered a multi-sided platform because it creates opportunities for new services such as delivery of food, doctors' visits, etc.[20]

Parker et al. (2016) have recently summarized the important shifts in organizing and management that platforms bring with them. Platforms organize not a particular production or service, as a typical industrial organization would do, but an entire ecosystem involving many different participants who are connected together in such a way that all gain some kind of value from the free flow of information, open communication, low barriers to participation, transparency, authenticity, and flexibility. There are those who create products, such as apps for iOS, Android, or WindowsPhone. There are users who buy the apps, as well as use them for generating their own value. There are those who provide the connectivity and guarantee the flow of information such as producers of smartphones and operating systems. There are the owners of a platform, for example, Google owns the Play-Store and governs who and how it is to be used. Platforms are organized as networks by focusing on the orchestration of resources and not ownership or control of resources. As already noted above, sharing resources in networks creates value for all participants. What needs to be organized is the sharing transactions. The participants

---

19 | See the classic work by Katz and Shapiro (1985, 1994).

20 | See the many articles on platforms and network economics by Economides http://www.stern.nyu.edu/networks/

contribute their resources themselves. The major resource of the network is the connectivity, flow, and participation of all stakeholders.

In addition to a shift from ownership to the orchestration of sharing, platforms create value by organizing the transactions between participants. This corresponds to the network management framework discussed above. Organizing a platform is an exercise in *facilitating, framing, activating,* and *mobilizing.* Not internal workflows and processes count, but external interactions, collaboration, and cooperation. Furthermore, as noted above when discussing the competitive advantage of networked organizations, it is the performance of the network as a whole and not isolated profits by any participant that count. Not shareholder value, nor customer value, but network value is the decisive indicator of success and the most important goal for platforms. Connectivity, flow, communication, participation, and the other network norms have made platforms into one of the most interesting forms of organizing almost anything, whether it be new businesses such as Uber or Airbnb, open source projects, or new services in the both the profit and non-profit sectors. Quadir (2013) has documented some interesting examples such as Sproxil (sproxil.com), which has created a platform that protects both producers and consumers against fraud. This is important in areas such as global healthcare where fraudulent medications pose a serious problem. "Sproxil provides a scratch-off label with a PIN attached to a product, charging brand owners for the service. A consumer texts the PIN to a phone number and receives a reply text stating whether the product is genuine or counterfeit." (Quadir 2013:9) Another example is bKash in Bangladesh, which allows for cheap money transfers over mobile phones. This makes it possible for poor people and migrant workers who do not have access to normal banking services to transfer money to their homes and to others without risk or high costs. There are unlimited possibilities for platforms in all areas of society. MOOCs in education, which we will discuss below, can be considered as platforms in the area of education. Peer-to-peer based sharing and collaborative consumption platforms are further examples. These can be for either profit as part of an "access economy" or non-profit as part of a "sharing economy." What makes these platforms work are the network norms that have become driving forces in organizing in today's global network society. All these examples show that networked organizing requires management practices that are almost diametrically opposed to the traditional wisdom of management in the industrial age.

This does not mean, however, that traditional organizations cannot, and perhaps must, adopt new management strategies and break with the patterns of traditional management.

Pattern-Breaking Management

The influence of the network norms on organizing can be seen by looking for innovative management practices in organizations that are not obviously networked forms. The strong claim we are making is that networking, staging, sensemaking, and enacted narrative in the global network society follow network norms that foster management practices which are fundamentally different from traditional management. In this regard, the work of Wüthrich et al. (2009) and Kaduk et al. (2015) is interesting because they speak about how managers today are called upon to "break patterns" that have long defined best practices in management. What is interesting about their approach is that they do not attempt to describe networked organizations, but instead, successful management practices, regardless of what kind of organization. The organizations that are cited as examples of "pattern-breaking management" are not at all the typical high-tech and internet companies often cited in discussions of networked management practices. What these examples show is that breaking the traditional patterns of industrial management is an imperative for management in all kinds of organizations, even traditional businesses.

The typical patterns of management in the industrial age were control, standardization, rational decision making, optimizing short-term gains, efficiency, and following the dictates of the economic system. Faced with the growing complexity and unique dynamic of today's global network society, many of these traditional pillars of management wisdom and practice have dissolved into paradoxes and contradictions. Management is no longer able to rely upon strategies for making things simple. Complexity cannot be managed with simplicity, but only with more complexity. However, one must resist the temptation to prescribe management practices and rules that would go to the opposite extreme. Formulated as paradoxes this would imply attempting to steer unsteerability, to mistrust trusted control mechanisms, to standardize diversity, to make decisions emotionally rational, to shortsightedly see into the future, to decelerate acceleration, and to freely choose systemic constraints. The paradoxes of managing organizations in the global network society should be seen rather as occasions to discover appropriate forms of leadership and management strategies, that is, to do sensemaking for new kinds of organizations and new forms of organizing.

Among the lessons learned by observing how leadership and organizations are responding to the new situation, *decentralization* ranks among the most widely accepted. Decentralization is one management strategy that has become a model for managing networked organizations. Large organizations can delegate more autonomy and independence to smaller working units. This fosters trust, enables flexibility, brings decision making closer to the customers, and motivates employees at all levels to take responsibility for the whole organization. The head office becomes more of a support or a coach for the smaller units instead of using budgeting and controlling in order to dictate what they should do. Open communication, trust, transparency, and self-organization emerge as decisive strategies for leadership. Other important pattern-breaking management strategies could be called *self-management, cooperative management, or bottom-up management*. Wüthrich and his colleagues cite the well-known Orpheus Chamber Orchestra that operates without a conductor in that it "rotates musical leadership roles for each work, and strives to perform diverse repertoire through collaboration and open dialogue."[21] The guiding principle of this kind of management is to give those power who do the work, encourage personal responsibility, define roles clearly, distribute decision making, support cooperation, learn to listen as well as speak, look for consensus, and passionately devote oneself to the task at hand. A further example is the Brazilian city of Curitiba, which managed to deal with many of the typical urban problems such as unemployment, health care, education, environmental pollution, transportation, etc. by means of encouraging and enabling citizen participation. We will return to Curitiba below when discussing how networks are being organized in civil society. What is significant about Curitiba is that instead of top down projects, the city government supported the initiative and self-responsibility of its citizens in order to find and implement creative solutions. In this way, planning and decision-making became a social process enacted in non-hierarchical, interorganizational communication.

---

21 | According to Wikipedia https://de.wikipedia.org/wiki/Orpheus_Chamber_ Orchestra.

A further pattern-braking management strategy is *trust-based leadership*. Traditional, hierarchical organizations are characterized by mistrust and rely heavily on bureaucratic rules, rigid systems of control, and discipline. This means that transparency and open communication do not play important roles in managing. Trust-based leadership, on the contrary, enables all co-workers to have access to information about the entire organization. All are encouraged to participate in discovering new ideas and making decisions. These are issues usually discussed under the rubric of organizational culture. Trust, transparency, participation, open communication, information sharing, and similar qualities are values and attitudes not merely processes. They are based on norms and more or less explicit expectations. Norms, however, should not be confused with standards and standardization. Traditionally, management was concerned with setting up standardized processes, job routines, measurement criteria and methods, qualifications, assessments, incentive programs, and other instruments allowing for prediction and control. In many organizations that have come out of the industrial era or are in transition, normalizing and standardizing of employees, processes, and systems is, and continues to be, one of the major preoccupations of management.

Against this tendency, Wüthrich and Kaduk and their colleagues cite management strategies, for example, in human relations and human development, where clearly laid out careers with indicators and milestones are explicitly avoided. Instead, individual preferences, personal interests and abilities, an open horizon of possible paths to take within an organization, all are more important than standard qualifications and assessments. In many areas, it has become almost a commonplace in management theory to emphasize the importance of diversity. Heterogeneous teams, for example, have demonstrated better results in problem solving then groups consisting of people with similar backgrounds, experience, and knowledge. This is a corner stone of Surowiecki's *Wisdom of the Crowds*. Surowiecki showed with many examples how heterogeneous groups are more effective at problem-solving than experts with similar backgrounds. In general, it can be argued that participatory culture fosters diversity, because it normalizes the abnormal and gives equal opportunities of expression to all. In the area of strategic management, Wüthrich and his colleagues plead for a short-sighted far-sightedness. This means flexibility and innovation, with a view to sustainability and resilience. Sustainability is a concept barrowed from environmental science and refers to setting goals with regard to all relevant factors and not merely short-term gains, such as shareholder value. Organizing with a view to many possible connections, the free flow of information, and encouragement of flexibility and innovation is not only to be found in the business world. Organizing networks is something that is going on in novel ways in all areas of society. In the following, we take a look how networks are being organized today in the area of education.

ORGANIZING NETWORKS IN EDUCATION

Citing studies by The World Bank (2003), Collis (2005) lists decisive challenges for education in the global network society. Throughout the world, and not merely in the developed nations, education must create a workforce that is able to "derive local value from information often in creative ways that go beyond expected performances;" that is able "to work in multidisciplinary and distributed teams," that is able to "use information technology (IT) for knowledge management, sharing, and creation," and that is able to meet "the need to 'act autonomously and reflectively; joining and functioning in social heterogeneous groups'" (Collis 2005: 215). A current but by no means complete list of trends in education indicate how these challenges are being met today:[22]

- E-learning
- Knowledge networks and communities of practice
- Open educational resources (OER)
- Learner centered instruction
- Mobile learning

---

22 | There are many trend reports for education. See for example the Horizon Reports http://www.nmc.org/publication-type/horizon-report/, or the OECD Talis Report http://www.oecd.org/edu/school/talis.htm, or the European Schoolnet Briefing Papers http://www.eun.org/observatory/surveyofschools, or the Partnership for 21st Century Learning http://www.p21.org/, or the Education section of the Digital Agenda for Europe http://ec.europa.eu/digital-agenda/en/ict-education, and in the area of learning and development the Cegos Study 2015 https://www. integrata.de/fileadmin/Bilder/Service/Downloads/2015_CEGOS_Research_-_ LD_Globalization.Final_Report.pdf

- Social learning & Learning 2.0
- Work place learning
- MOOCs
- Learning analytics and big data in education
- Personal learning environments (PLE)
- Partnerships
- Flipped classroom
- Connectivism

This list is not exhaustive and perhaps not even representative, since new media in education, or technology assisted education, or whatever word or phrase is being currently used cannot possibly address the entire scope of theories, practices, experiments, pilot projects, strategies, programs, initiatives, etc. that characterize ICTs and education on all levels today. Even before the Internet became the standard for educational technology, there has been a wide range of theories and practices with regard to the use of technology in education or so-called teaching machines.[23] A contemporary and continuously updated German language handbook in the area maps the terrain into areas of services, strategy, pedagogy and didactics, hardware and software for learning, professional learning and learning and development, knowledge management, HRM, and e-business.[24] Another attempt to introduce order into what might at first sight appear to be chaos, distinguishes between what can be called the "digitalization of education" on the one hand, and "networked learning" on the other.[25] The first term is intended to refer to the management, administration, and organization of educational institutions and practices, whether public or private, regardless of level, whereas the second term, "networked learning," has come to refer to teaching and learning with new media, that is, to what educational organizations primarily do and what has traditionally been called e-learning.[26]

The administration of educational organizations has much the same tasks as management in any kind of organization. Organizational

---

23 | For an overview see https://en.wikipedia.org/wiki/Educational_technology.

24 | See Wilbers/Hohenstein (2015).

25 | See Kerres (2016).

26 | For a recent discussion of research and a definition of "networked learning," see Jones (2015).

development, personal management, finances, marketing, quality management and controlling, etc. are similar in most organizations. Specific to education is curriculum development, course administration, assessments, knowledge transfer, and learning evaluation. Much speaks for the distinction between administration and teaching as well as other traditional analyses of the educational system. Nevertheless, education in the network society tends to blur traditional distinctions. Administrators of educational institutions as well as teachers, researchers, and learners are all involved in networking education in today's world. Other traditional attempts to structure the educational system are running into similar difficulties in the global network society. Examples are describing education on the basis of levels, for example, primary to university, or on the basis of sectors, for example, public and private, or on the basis of formal versus informal, or basic versus non-degree career training, etc. Traditional distinctions are becoming increasingly problematic as networked education blurs the boundaries between public and private, formal and informal, and basic and continuing forms of education and training.

Partnerships

Many kinds of networking in education can be ascribed to the normative influence of *connectivity*. Connectivity, as we saw above, can be defined as every form of linking nodes into a network structure or digital infrastructure. In media studies, this phenomenon, which was central for Castells' concept of a global network society, has been discussed under the title of "convergence." Instead of convergence, we wish to use the concept of "connectivity" to analyze the imperative to link up all sources, producers, and users of information both digitally and physically. Connectivity is the norm of networking in all forms. Its principle is that nothing should be excluded from the network. As Weinberger (2012) showed, the Internet is more like a cloud than a pyramid. Connectivity does away with the economy of scarcity in information that was the basis for hierarchical forms of knowledge and communication.

Closely associated with connectivity is of course the norm of *communication*. Links and nodes are useless unless something flows through the network. It should, however, be noted that the network norm of communication refers not primarily to flow as such, but to the *way* in which all participants in the network accept, process, and distribute information. We will discuss these two norms together in order to avoid redundancies. In the following, therefore, whenever we speak of connectivity, communication is also implied. The norm of flow will be discussed with regard to other educational trends.

The best example of connectivity, as well as of communication, is of course the Internet, the network of networks. With regard to educational organizations, including schools from the primary level up to the university, as well as educational and training organizations within both public and private sectors, connectivity can be seen in the fact that all these organizations are becoming digitalized and networked in their administrative as well as pedagogical practices. The most obvious influence of connectivity is the implementation of digital infrastructures for use in all aspects of education. From school servers, to websites, social media sites, learning management systems, laptop classrooms, mobile learning, etc., ICTs are as prevalent in education as in business, media, science, and other areas of society. There is hardly any kind of training or schooling today that does not in some way make use of digital media. This is so well known that we need not attempt to document it again here. Less well known is the example of educational networking in the sense of partnerships.

Educational institutions are benefiting from partnerships and collaborative communities of practice with regard to problems and opportunities in the areas of infrastructure as well as pedagogy. Not only do schools at the same level, for example, primary or secondary schools, or colleges and universities enter into networks, but between levels as well. Schools and other educational institutions enter into network-type communities of practice in order to exchange knowledge and best practices in both administration and teaching, but also to develop better teaching materials, infrastructural solutions, and similar "products." In addition to sharing knowledge and developing products, school networks are involved in transfer projects that spread and implement solutions beyond the participants in the network. Finally, organizational networks also collaborate with businesses, museums, cultural organizations, etc. within communities, cities, and regions in order to coordinate activities with the goal to make an entire community or region more attractive and competitive.[27]

---

27 | For a typology of school networks see Muijs et al. (2011: 37ff.).

In terms of pattern-breaking management practices, in communities of practice and complex networks in which initiative on the part of all participants is encouraged, *trust-based management* plays a decisive role. School administrators are also *decentralizing*, turning more to *self-management, bottom-up management, and collaborative management* in an effort to profit from experiences and resources available beyond the reach of one single school or one group of instructors and teachers.[28] Outcomes of partnerships and networks are often uncertain and cannot be easily incorporated into budgets and quality control processes. Accountability, as important as it is, above all in the public sector, needs to be balanced against innovation and risk-taking for the sake of long-term improvements in teaching, development of learning materials, learning success, assessment, and curricula reform. Those responsible for these processes show how they are influenced by the norms of connectivity and communication by facilitating partnerships and networking in such a way that resources and infrastructures are made accessible to all, so that information is distributed to all participants, and instruments as well processes are set up to transfer knowledge beyond the network.

MOOCs

What in new media studies has been widely discussed under the title of "participatory" culture can in part be attributed to the influence of the network norm of *flow*. The *flow* of information has become a primary value and norm on the basis of the norms of connectivity and communication. Flow refers to the principally unforeseeable, unpredictable, and uncontrollable movement of information (but also people, goods, money, etc.) through global networks. Flow is reciprocal, interactive, and independent of space and time. If every node in the network is generating, modifying, and distributing content, then, as Weinberger (2012) pointed out, it is in principle impossible to enforce hierarchical, exclusive, and restrictive forms of communication. If one looks for an example of flow in educational trends today, then so-called MOOCs come to the fore.[29] A MOOC

---

28 | See for example the discussion on school partnerships in Muijs et al. (2011).

29 | For a discussion of recent research on MOOCs see Jones 2015 as well as the Wikipedia contribution https://en.wikipedia.org/wiki/Massive_open_online_course. See also: Towards a new Pedagogy. *Five Ways MOOCs are Influencing*

(massive open online course) is a form of networked learning which has come to epitomize many of the identifying characteristics of e-learning. As the name suggests, MOOCs are forms of teaching and learning that encourage participation and user generated content. For this reason, one could object that MOOCs are rather an example for the network norm of participation instead of flow. This granted, we propose analyzing MOOCs as embodiments of a "connectivist" theory of learning which emphasizes movement of information in all directions over networks rather than information production. This is admittedly a somewhat arbitrary distinction, but in comparison to a trend such as Open Educational Resources (OER), which emphasize user generated content and participatory information production, MOOCs are a useful illustration of what the norm of flow can mean in education today. With regard to forms of networking in business, MOOCs could also be seen as "platforms," since they orchestrate resources, focus on interaction and sharing, and aim to improve the entire learning community.

Connectivism is a theory of learning that goes beyond the psychological orientation of the traditional learning theories of behaviorism, cognitivism, and constructivism by claiming that knowing is not only a social activity, but is distributed in networks.[30] As Downes puts it, connectivism "is the thesis that knowledge is distributed across a network of connections, and therefore that learning consists of the ability to construct and traverse those

Teaching and Learning: "More people signed up for MOOCs in 2015 than in the previous three years combined. In total, some 35 million registered for a MOOC, with Coursera (https://www.coursera.org/) securing 7 million new registrations in 2015, with this company now occupying some 50 per cent of the MOOC market. FutureLearn (https://www.futurelearn.com/) is now the third largest MOOC provider – they secured growth of 275 per cent in 2015. Around 1,800 new courses were announced in 2015, taking the total number of courses announced since the inception of MOOCs to 4,200. Over 500 universities and colleges around the world, not to mention other organizations, are now offering MOOCs. edX has more than 90 global partners, including the world's leading universities, not for profits and institutions as members (https://www.edx.org/)." (contactnorth.ca 2016, http://teachonline.ca/sites/default/files/tools-trends/downloads/five_ways_moocs_are_influencing_teaching.pdf.)

30 | See Siemens (2005), Downes (2005, 2012), AlDahdouh et al. (2015) for discussions of connectivism.

networks" (2012, 85). In the spirit of ANT, one could say that according to connectivism, it is the network that learns and not the individual, or in other words, learning is a network effect. Siemens (2005) described the principle characteristics of connectivism as the ability to connect diverse nodes or information sources including non-humans. This fosters the capacity to know more than what is currently known. In addition to this, connectivism fosters the ability to see and maintain connections between fields, ideas, and concepts and therefore to continually learn. Decision-making becomes a learning process. For Siemens, connectivism grounds knowledge management because it explains the central importance of information flow in organizations. "Creating, preserving, and utilizing information flow should be a key organizational activity" (2005: 4).

Connectivism has become the pedagogical basis for many new forms of networked learning, among which MOOCs are perhaps the most well known.[31] Downes (2012: 497ff.) bases MOOCs on four types of activities that derive from connectivism; 1) aggregation, 2) remixing, 3) repurposing, and 4) feed forward. Aggregation means that learners are given access to a wide variety of informational sources through different channels, for example, documents, videos, audio files, graphic representations and knowledge visualizations, etc. These information sources are not restricted to a single LMS, learning management system, as is often the case in e-learning, but include blogs, websites, social media sites, twitter, social bookmarking sites, RSS feeds, etc. The learner is challenged to set learning goals, seek relevant information, aggregate this information, as well as the sources, and then move on to the next activity, that is, "remixing." Remixing means keeping track of the information that has been aggregated, storing it in a way that allow not only retrieval, but sharing, and then processing the information in a way that is relevant not only for one's own learning purposes, but for the network as a whole. This is where "re-purposing" becomes important.

Connectivism can only be a theory of learning if participants in the network not merely pass information unchanged on to other participants, but remix the information for new and unforeseen purposes. Making sense of information, indeed, what Karl Weick called sensemaking, is always a creative and constructive process that changes information and gives it new purposes. Re-purposed information is user generated content

---

31 | See the discussion of recent research on MOOCs in Jones (2015: 126ff.).

that flows back into the network. This is what "feed forward" means. Connectivist learning is a continual process of sharing. The basic idea behind MOOCs is flow of information and sharing not only with those who are participating in a network, but beyond the "official" MOOC, after it is completed, with all others who might be interested in the topics that are discussed and reflected upon. This can take the form of transferring knowledge to the Internet via blogs, wikis, websites, repositories, or other means. MOOCs are therefore principally open and unrestricted, even though, as the name also suggests, they are also "courses" that can be integrated into curricula and programs of study for certification within an educational institution.

The MOOC has many different forms. Recently, the original MOOC, as it was conceived by Siemens and Downes and based on social learning, participation, user generated content, and connectivism has been adapted for commercial as well as certification purposes by major universities and consortia of universities throughout the world. Important consortia are Udacity, Coursera, edX, FUN, Iversity, and others. The MOOCs offered by these institutions have come to be called xMOOCs in order to distinguish them from the cMOOCs that are explicity based on interaction, dialogue, and bottom up, learner centered approaches.[32] For our purposes, the original cMOOCs are more interesting from the point of view of educational management, since they are based on the norm of *flow* and therefore demand self-organization, trust-based management, and other pattern-breaking management forms. Much of what has been discussed under the title of "learning 2.0" can also be seen together with MOOCs as involving an educational management based on the open flow of information in networks.[33] Setting up and managing a cMOOC requires skills in network building and social network maintenance. Furthermore, it requires that educational management move away from the traditional forms of information control that in the past have made it possible to design curricula, perform standard assessment, and carry out acknowledged certification. In addition to this, educational management

---

32 | See the discussion in Wikipedia https://en.wikipedia.org/wiki/Massive_open_online_course for the distinction between xMOOCs and cMOOCs, as well as a list of institutions offering MOOCs.

33 | See the contribution in the edutechwiki for a review of literature http://edutechwiki.unige.ch/en/E-learning_2.0

faces financial and infrastructural problems that need to be solved through new forms of school administration.

Open Educational Resources OER

Partnerships, networks, and new forms of teaching such as MOOCs offer significant management challenges. This is also true of Open Educational Resources (OER). If we analyze these challenges in terms of the network norms guiding organizing in the global network society, Open Educational Resources (OER) could be seen as an example of *participation*. New media studies (Jenkins et al. 2005) speak of a participatory culture. Forms of participatory culture, as we saw above, are communities of practice, collaborative problem solving, user generated content, crowdsourcing, social networking, and many similar networked forms of collaborative work. The imperative of participation in education fosters peer-to-peer learning and a changed attitude toward intellectual property such that all participants produce information and information is placed in a commons (often under CC license), free to use by all. Open educational resources are a typical example of what participation in education can mean. Open educational resources are defined as

[...] teaching, learning, and research resources that reside in the public domain or have been released under an intellectual property license that permits their free use and re-purposing by others. Open educational resources include full courses, course materials, modules, textbooks, streaming videos, tests, software, and any other tools, materials, or techniques used to support access to knowledge. (Open Education Resources 2013)[34]

The connection between learners and learning resources is one of the most important tasks of educational management. As Jones (2015) points out, the affordances of ICTs "have the potential to change the relationship between learners and the institutions of learning to their resources," but this potential can only be realized when it is "institutionally enacted" (120). This means that educational institutions "make their materials freely available online for anyone to use" (121). One way to do this is to license texts,

---

34 | See also https://en.wikipedia.org/wiki/Open_educational_resources; and Jones (2015).

images, videos etc. under the Creative Commons license which exists in public domain and does not stand under the usual copyright restrictions. The OECD defines such freely accessible educational materials as

[...] digitised materials offered freely and openly for educators, students, and self-learners to use and reuse for teaching, learning, and research. OER includes learning content, software tools to develop, use, and distribute content, and implementation resources such as open licenses. (OECD 2007: 29)

Jones (2015) correctly points out that OER may be open and accessible to many, but they are not really without costs of some kind. The educational institution allows instructors, researchers, resource administrators such as librarians, and others who create information to place this under Creative Commons and integrate these materials into MOOCs. The institution must have innovative policies and practices that allow it to bear the costs that accrue through this work. Furthermore, even when content is generated by learners, as is often the case in MOOCs, this content must be brought under "organizational and institutional arrangements that can support and sustain open development, curation, and re-use" (Jones 2015: 121). Well-known examples of OER are MIT's Open Courseware initiative and in the UK Open University's Open Learn.[35] The importance of OER can be estimated by referring to the significance and also the "noise level" of the current debates on intellectual property and copyright. There are many vested interests, traditions of doing business, and of organizing education that are at stake when access to learning resources becomes unrestricted and costs are dramatically reduced or transferred to other areas. Instead of attempting to protect obsolete value chains belonging to the industrial age within the network society, management should look for new business models and ways of generating value. This entails major changes in the organization of education. As Selwyn remarks in a critical discussion of OER:

[...] much of the current enthusiasm for openness is (un)consciously yoked to wider ideological motivations of re-engineering and reorientating the social relations of educational technologies and educational institutions. (Selwyn 2014: 75)

---

35 | http://ocw.mit.edu/index.htm; http://www.open.edu/openlearn/

Examples of new ways of generating value on the bases of low cost information access can be found in the so-called "sharing economy."[36] Collaborative use of information and educational materials can become part of the emerging sharing market in which all kinds of goods and services are directly exchanged on a peer-to-peer basis. Managing sharing markets requires turning communication and networking skills into value propositions. This means, as some commentators say, that the focus could shift from open educational resources to *open educational practices* (OEP).[37] Pattern-breaking management practices such as trust-based management and self-organization become effective when it comes to linking up informational resources to learners, teachers, and organizational processes of curriculum design, assessment, and certification. Basing organizational processes on trust, open communication, and knowledge sharing is one of the great challenges, as well as opportunities, with which organizing in the global network society is confronted. As Murphy points out, shifting the focus to open educational practices makes participation a guiding norm for

[...] policies and practices implemented by higher education intuitions that support the development, use and management of OERs, and the formal assessment and accreditation of informal learning undertaken using OERs. (Murphy 2013: 202)

Connectivity, flow, communication, and participation are guiding norms for educational institutions today. Established traditions in educational management do not change easily. What reason do we have to believe that these norms will be followed and that fundamental changes will occur? The possibility of transforming long-established management practices is not illusory and merely the latest hype. The affordances of ICTs that are expressed in the network norms can everywhere be seen and felt. OER and OEP are a case in point. The same may be said of learning analytics.

---

36 | See Benkler (2004).

37 | See Ehlers 2011: "OEP are defined as practices which support the (re) use and production of OER through institutional policies, promote innovative pedagogical models, and respect and empower learners as co-producers on their lifelong learning path. OEP address the whole OER governance community: policy makers, managers/administrators of organisations, educational professionals and learners" (3).

Learning Analytics

One of the most important trends in the use of digital information today in all areas is so-called "big data." Big data refers to the availability of very large data sets (volume) from diverse sources and in many different formats (variety) which can be "analyzed" quickly, if not in real time (velocity), by special analytic software.[38] Analytics aims at discovering trends and correlations in big data. It is only when data becomes big in the above specified sense of volume, variety, and velocity, that correlations and patterns that can otherwise not be found become apparent. This information can be useful for predictions, interventions, and the development of personalized services.[39] A typical statement of the significance of big data for education, which is not limited to the American context, can be found in the Interim Progress Report (2015) to the Presidents Report on Big Data:[40]

Big data has the potential to transform education for the better, creating unprecedented educational opportunities – for instance, by tailoring lessons to a student's learning style, by opening up courses through online platforms, and by making it easier for parents, teachers, and students to identify where an individual student may be struggling and offer targeted instruction. These new technologies hold the potential to vastly improve student performance and to provide researchers with valuable insights about how students learn, which could help improve low-tech educational interventions as well. Beyond educational technology, the mere operation of schools produces vast amounts of data – data that can improve efficiency as well as education. (Interim Progress Report 2015: 5)

This citation shows that at least two major areas in educational management are affected by the affordances of big data, networked learning on the one hand and the digitalization of education administration on the other. Even though most authors speak simply of "learning analytics" to describe all aspects of big data in education, Jones confirms the distinction between

---

38 | See https://en.wikipedia.org/wiki/Big_data for an overview.

39 | See the Presidents Report on Big Data 2014 for a discussion of opportunities as well as dangers in big data, https://www.whitehouse.gov/sites/default/files/docs/big_data_privacy_report_may_1_2014.pdf.

40 | https://www.whitehouse.gov/sites/default/files/docs/20150204_Big_Data_Seizing_Opportunities_ Preserving_Values_Memo.pdf

networked learning and digital administration. Jones (2015) speaks of "learner analytics to identify those aspects of learning analytics that focus on the learner or student as opposed to the institutional or business aspects of analytics" (114). Before the catchword "big data" became widely known and accepted, educational institutions had been collecting student data from learning management systems (LMS). These systems made it possible to register when students logged into a learning platform, for how long, what courses they visited, what functions they used, for example, a forum, or document repository, what their quiz results were, and which communications were sent to teachers and to other students, as well as similar kinds of log-data. This was known as "tracking" and was designed to allow teachers to monitor student learning activities, to pinpoint where students were having problems, and to intervene with personalized support measures. Most learning analytics applications in educational institutions aim to predict and identify which students will need support and allow instructors to intervene in order to optimize learning outcomes.[41]

With the advent of big data, it has become possible to track not only online activities within a LMS, but also to monitor social media usage, search activities on the Internet, emails, and also physical activities such as usage of library, sport, or entertainment facilities on and off campus. This kind of tracking of student activities, as with other big data applications outside the educational context, create a "glass human being" who is completely transparent to those who have access to the data and to analytic applications. Jones (2015) cites the Director of Teaching and Learning at the Open University UK who clearly voiced his concern as follows:

With these possibilities come dangers that the data could be used in ways undesirable to students. These include invading their privacy, exploiting them commercially by selling their data to third parties or targeted marketing of further educational products. (120)

The same danger is there for analytics applications in the area of enterprise resource management or "digitalized education." Analytics allows for a kind of "business intelligence" to be applied to educational institutions. Not only are students being monitored, but teaching staff, non-teaching

---

41 | See the discussion and examples of applications in EduFutures.net http://edfutures.net/Learning_Analytics

employees, and other operations as well. ERP systems monitor not only libraries, laboratories, and suppliers of materials for teaching and learning, but also customer relations, housing, parking, catering, and so on. There are no significant technical barriers to the integration of LMS and ERP systems. This harbors the danger that business imperatives could be applied to teaching and learning. As Jones points out,

> If a broad administrative view of analytics is taken then analytics can be just another management and administrative tool that will shift the balance in institutions away from academic and pedagogic concerns towards market and business concerns with measurable performance and value for money. Measurements of quality, progression and dropout when seen in terms of students as units of resource are quite different from measures of quality understood in terms of human development and citizenship. (Jones 2015: 115)

The challenge to education management coming from big data and learning analytics is to break the patterns of traditional business management and adapt a new *symmetrical transparency* with regard to the information that analytics generates. Analytics should not be implemented as a purely top-down, administrative process. All stakeholders should be involved in decisions about what data will be collected and analyzed for what purpose, and all stakeholders should have equal access to analytics. The results of analytics should be made understandable and useable by all stakeholders, including learners. The pedagogical concern should be given priority over enterprise resource planning. Finally, the unavoidable transparency of all users, whether students or staff, should be compensated by a symmetrical transparency on the side of administration, decision-makers, and governors. Clear guidelines about the use of personal data should apply to all stakeholders as well as clear definitions of misuse of data and corresponding sanctions. Transparency is a norm in the global network society. The norm, however, covers all users and not merely a few. Transparency that is made imperative for students must also be imperative for teachers and administrators.

The norm of transparency can only be followed and implemented as a pattern-breaking managerial practice in combination with the network norms of *participation* and *authenticity*. Stakeholders must not only be given the opportunity to participate in decisions about learning analytics, but also accept the responsibility of supplying veritable information and data such that the results of the analytic processes are indeed useful. Along with volume, variety, and velocity, as the defining characteristics of big data, there should also be veracity, data quality, and data reliability. Transforming top-down transparency into bottom-up transparency can only be successful on the basis of open communication and trust. Authenticity means that participants in a network do not attempt to disguise or misrepresent who they are and what they do. Jones (116) discusses the framework developed by De Laat in which users are themselves responsible for "tagging problems that are part of their learning," "adding people they collaborate with," and "linking themselves with problems others have already described." Within a framework such as this, learning analytics is actively implemented by users such that more and better information is collected which leads to more reliable and more useful results. Instead of being monitored behind their backs, as it were, all participants actively contribute to data aggregation and also consent to uses of the data. Transparency is therefore a double-edged sword. It cuts into the private sphere of individuals and turns users into "glass human beings," but it also puts decision-makers, managers, and leaders into glass houses insuring thereby that they don't start throwing stones. There can be no norm of one-sided transparency, where only some stakeholders are made transparent, while others remain behind informational closed doors. When privacy becomes "publicy," this counts for everyone. Once the imperative of transparency has put everyone in the same informational space and on the same level, there is no acceptable alternative to authenticity. Attempts to erect informational walls and maintain secrets will necessarily appear as disguise or misrepresentation and generate mistrust. This means that open communication and trust are the basis for negotiations on all decisions having to do with implementation and uses of big data and learning analytics.

Personal Learning Environments PLE

The network norm of "flexibility" is directly associated with connectivity, flow, communication, participation, transparency, and authenticity. Flexibility can be described in many ways. One important aspect of flexibility can be seen in the tendency of networks to cross traditional boundaries between institutions and domains. Unlike closed systems with clear boundaries and univocal codes of inclusion and exclusion, networks and their activities cannot easily be delimited. Networks extend beyond closed systems, organizations, and divisions. Flexibility also means that networking is innovative, adaptive, continually reconfiguring and changing in order to accommodate multiple tasks, goals, purposes, and programs. In addition to this, flexibility can be seen in the ability of networks to allow changes and reconfiguration from many different nodes and not from only a one or a few hubs or decision-making centers.[42]

In the area of education, flexibility can be illustrated in what has come to be known as Personal Learning Environments (PLE). The discussion of PLE arose as an alternative to the centrally designed and top-down managed learning management systems (LMS). LMS in one form or another have become standard applications in most educational institutions. The LMS were originally designed as "virtual" classrooms or virtual schools, that is, they carried over into the digital realm the same centralism, top-down administrative procedures, teacher-centered pedagogical practices, and standard curricula and assessment that were typical of traditional schooling.[43] The affordances of digital media, that is, connectivity, flow, communication, participation, transparency, and authenticity all mitigate against traditional ways of organizing education. As a consequence solutions were sought that allowed more learner control, diversity of practices, and communication choices. Learners themselves and not the educational institution should be making decisions about processes, content, and information resources. Behind the idea of a personal learning environment, there also stands the conviction that learning is a lifelong endeavor, extending beyond any one institution, program of studies, or career qualification, and including informal as well formal learning. Lifelong learning is only practicable, when learners themselves take control of educational processes. This means that educational institutions can no longer assume that one-size-fits-all and that standardized instruction and assessment are the way to guarantee equality as well as quality in learning.

Contrary to a proprietary and centralized LMS, a PLE allows individuals access to a wide range of information resources, educational services, peer-communities, aggregators, and publication and distribution tools,

---

42 | For a detailed discussion of flexibility as a network norm see Krieger/Belliger (2014: 181ff.).

43 | For literature see the curated list of publications on PLE by Ilona Buchem https://ibuchem.wordpress.com/ple/

such as blogs and wikis, as well as content management systems such as e-portfolios. The personal learning environment constitutes a kind of hub for learner-centered, lifelong networked learning, both basic and professional, both formal and informal, both public and private. Because of its multipurpose, heterogeneous, integrative, and adaptive character, the PLE is a good example of what the network norm of flexibility means in the area of education. The learning network is no longer bound to a particular organization, institution, or degree program. It is in the control of the learner, open to many different applications, adaptable to different purposes and situations, and principally without limitations coming from external organizational constraints. This has important consequences for educators and decision-makers at all levels of the educational system. Speaking for educational professionals and leaders, Leone writes "The introduction of lifelong learning objectives and policies has poised us on the threshold of major change in education and society" (Leone 2010: 30). This means that there is a "need for greater emphasis to be put upon flexibility, transferability, individualization, modularization, and mobility in education" (31) and, we might add, it is the task of educational leaders to change the system.

On the level of policy, already in 1999 the UNESCO put lifelong learning on the agenda for all nations: "Lifelong learning is a cultural term denoting a new paradigm. It is a shift away from the notion of provider-driven 'education' toward individualized learning." The European Commission (2002) made this concrete when it stated that lifelong learning means "learning activity undertaken throughout life, with the aim of improving knowledge, skills and competencies within a personal, civic, social and/or employment-related perspective." In the meantime, lifelong learning has become an explicit concern in the educational and training policies of most European member nations and beyond the EU. For educational institutions, these policies imply new roles and new opportunities. After having gone to great efforts to bring e-learning into schools, universities, and training programs, governments must now develop, or at least participate in the development of personalized learning environments that include links to resources, programs, cooperative learning processes and much more that is not directly under their control or within their administrative competence. There is a consensus among experts that a PLE should use the entire Internet as a platform and not merely a proprietary LMS. Furthermore, learning materials are often user generated and under commons license and open to use by all. A personal learning environment links up to open educational resources, to MOOCs, to social networking sites and much more. Learning takes place not in particular places at set times, but is a continual flow in much the same way as work and life are constantly changing flows of activities. The learner must be able to manage these flows and processes and be able to use all materials and resources for easily moving between schooling, training, and work situations no matter where they take place. Leone sums up recent discussions on PLEs as follows, "A Personal Learning Environment is an open system, interconnected with other PLEs and with other external services; it is an activity-based learning environment, user-managed and learner centered" (37).

One approach by educational decision-makers has been to attempt to develop PLE applications and install them within traditional institutions in much the same way that LMS were set up as a solution to the demands of e-learning. However, as Conole (2010), citing Attwell, points out "a PLE is not an application, but more of a new approach to using technologies for learning...it is comprised of all the different tools we use in our everyday life for learning" (7). Nonetheless, great efforts have been made to develop software solutions for PLEs modelled after learning management systems. Schneider (2014) discusses various attempts to design software specifications and applications that can serve as PLEs. Among the applications Schneider discusses are the Jafari model for lifelong learning, the Chatti framework for the integration of communities and services, the Personal Learning Environment Framework of the University of Aachen, the PLEX project or Personal Learning Toolkit, the ELGG aggregation portal, and the ROLE project supported by the European Commission under the 7th Framework Program.[44] Summarizing the requirements for PLEs, which can be seen in most of these applications, Chatti (2007) says that what is needed is "a learner-controlled unique integrated environment bringing together multiple services into one place."[45]

Others argue that the role of educational institutions should not be to develop and install universal applications, but to assist learners in setting up their own PLE with those tools that they themselves choose.

---

44 | See http://edutechwiki.unige.ch/en/Personal_learning_environment for Schneider's description of these applications with links to all sources.

45 | See Chatti's blog post http://mohamedaminechatti.blogspot.ch/2007/01/towards-personal-learning-environment.html

Martin, for example offers her own personal learning environment as an example.[46] Martin divides the functionality of the PLE into tools for gathering information, for processing information, and for various learning activities. These tools are to be chosen by the learner, used as the learner wishes, freely supplemented or exchanged with other tools, and configured together according to the learning preferences and needs of the individual. The role of the educational institution and the teaching staff then becomes one of coaching, providing access to learning materials, helping learners to link various activities together, advising learners on opportunities for associating formal with informal learning, and assisting learners to achieve their goals beyond enrollment in any particular program or institution. This will certainly involve new forms of cooperation, counseling, assessment, and certification that must be actively pursued and implemented by educational managers on all levels both within the public and the private sectors.

Conclusion

The affordances of ICTs in the global network society are making demands on educational decision-makers to break out of the patterns that have guided education for a hundred years or more. Decentralization and the practices of self-management, trust-based management, and bottom-up management are among the pattern-breaking practices that can be found in innovative, successful organizations today. We have argued that these practices can be seen as deriving from the network norms of connectivity, flow, communication, participation, transparency, authenticity, and flexibility. These norms guide networking, sensemaking, and organizing in the global network society. Applied to education, we have seen that trends such as communities of practice and partnerships, MOOCs, social and mobile learning, open educational resources, learning analytics, personal learning environments, to name only a few, illustrate how the network norms influence the ways in which education and training is being organized today. Organizations should be understood as practices of organizing. These practices are best understood as networking, whereby both human and non-human actors play important roles. This is what

46 | See blog post http://michelemartin.typepad.com/thebambooprojectblog/2007/04/my_personal_lea.html

Karl Weick called "sensemaking." Sensemaking is an enacted narrative that changes not only what is said, but also changes – and is changed by – the technologies we use to say it. Understanding organizing and organizations in this way gives managers and decision-makers a basis for reorientation and cooperative transformation of institutions not only in educational, but also in other areas of the global network society.

ORGANIZING NETWORKS IN HEALTHCARE

Quantified Self

One of the most interesting recent developments in the area of networked healthcare, e-health, or connected health is the so-called "quantified self" (QS) movement.[47] Quantified self designates a broad range of devices, software applications, services, user practices, and values that all aim at collecting, aggregating, evaluating, sharing, and also commercializing personal health and wellness-related data. Other terms for quantified self are life-logging, body tracking, self tracking, auto analytics, body hacking, and self-surveillance. It is important to emphasize that this trend is not limited to healthcare. Similar technologies and practices can be found in other areas. We have already looked at applications of this kind in the area of education in terms of personal learning environments or learning analytics. The concept "personal informatics" has become a general term describing many different kinds of digital self-monitoring, not only with regard to the body, health, and wellness, but also other areas of life such as work, hobbies, and education. The official Personal Informatics website defines the term as follows:

Personal informatics is a class of tools that help people collect personally relevant information for the purpose of self-reflection and self-monitoring. These tools help people gain self-knowledge about one's behaviors, habits, and thoughts. (www.personalinformatics.org)

---

47 | See https://en.wikipedia.org/wiki/Quantified_Self as well as the official website http://quantifiedself.com/

Personal informatics includes not only body-related information, but also the monitoring of psychological states, such as feelings, stress, happiness, sleep, and relaxation. In addition to this, many different technologies and services can be classified as personal informatics, such as monitoring productivity at work, tracking consumer behavior, registering learning processes (as discussed above under personal learning environments or learning analytics), tracking financial activities, hobbies, etc. Personal informatics is therefore a general term that stands for any kind of digital monitoring of personal activities by individuals themselves. In this broad understanding of self-monitoring, there are many different kinds of networks and organizations involved. Data from personal informatics, as all data, do not remain in silos, but enter into networks. Individuals are networked to providers, developers, employers, social and professional communities, educational institutions, businesses, government, health-care organizations, and patient communities.

In these networks, individuals are not merely nodes, but also hubs, insofar as they take more and more control of their data. Personal informatics therefore also refers to the many new opportunities, dangers, and challenges for decision-makers in organizations that are using this data in different ways. It should be kept in mind that personal informatics is also linked to developments such as the Internet of Things, Ambient Assisted Living, smart buildings, smart neighborhoods, and smart cities. Making cities smart is not merely a matter of building networked infrastructures, but of making organizations smart, of linking government, education, healthcare, and civil society to each other in new ways.[48] There are no smart cities without smart governments, smart education, smart businesses, etc. Moreover, these classic domains of society are not smart unless they connect up to each other and form new kinds of networks. These many interfaces show that organizing in the network society crosses boundaries and links activities that were traditionally isolated in different domains, departments, jurisdictions, and social systems. Land development, city planning, architecture, workspace design, transportation, energy, education, and healthcare suddenly find themselves being influenced by the forces of connectivity, flow, participation, transparency, and flexibility. This is why the quantified self movement is an interesting illustration

---

48 | We will see an example of this in the discussion of the Brazilian City of Curitiba below.

of the many new challenges that managers and decision-makers in healthcare are confronted with. Quantified self has many similarities to what was discussed above under personal learning environments and learning analytics in the area of education. In education as well as in healthcare, information and communication networks form around individuals, but they cross institutional boundaries and branch out into many different organizational fields. For this reason, QS can serve as a good illustration for the influence of the different network norms in the area of healthcare.[49]

The devices, the hardware of quantified self, are smart phones, smart watches, armbands, smart scales, wearables, smart clothes, implants also referred to as "insideables" including injected or swallowed microchips, and similar technologies. These devices are equipped with sensors that measure chemical, magnetic, mechanical, visual, acoustic, and thermal changes in the body or near environment. The data is registered and transmitted, usually via wireless or NFC technologies, to a smartphone or computer, which then evaluates it and or sends it into the Internet, to service providers, portals, community websites, etc. In this process, specially designed software, or apps for mobile devices, play an important role. There are hundreds of thousands of health-related apps available in the major app-stores maintained by Google, Apple, and Microsoft.[50] These devices and apps are able to continually monitor vital functions such as blood pressure, heart rate, calorie consumption, sleep quality, movement, glucose levels, stress, emotional states, posture, as well as environmental influences such as UV radiation, air quality, etc. For the evaluation, presentation, and interpretation of this data there are many different services available. Services are often integrally connected with devices and apps. Typical services are aggregation of data, data visualization, evaluation, comparison, sharing, recommendations and tips, health-related advice, e-consultling, and referral to consultation by medical

---

49 | The digitalization of health care goes, of course, beyond QS and includes tele-health, telemedicine, medical e-learning, electronic patient records, hospital and clinical information systems, health data analytics, e-patient communities, shared decision making, and much more. For an overview see Belliger/Krieger (2014b).

50 | Lutpon (2014a: 608) found over 100,000 health and medical apps mid 2014 in the Apple App Store and Google Play.

professionals and by peers in patient communities, as well as personalized advertising by sellers of health products.

In many cases, self-tracking can become part of diagnosis, therapy, and rehabilitation processes. In this case, not only are hardware producers and software developers involved, but also doctors, clinics, hospitals, laboratories, health insurance companies, and regulatory agencies.[51] In the area of fitness, wellbeing, and prevention, self-tracking is important not only for concerned individuals, but also for health insurers, public health programs, and organizations of all kinds that are interested in having healthy and productive employees. Quantified self is more than a technology; it can be understood as a new kind of network involving individuals across all demographic distinctions and many different kinds of organizations both within and without the traditional healthcare sector. Quantified self is reconfiguring healthcare not only by blurring the distinction between the primary and secondary health markets, that is, therapy and prevention, but also by empowering patients, giving them access to their medical data, changing medical and clinical research, enabling citizen science, and disrupting the traditional healthcare system. From this perspective, it offers challenges to healthcare management and organization both in the private and the public sectors.

How are individuals and organizations being networked by QS? On the side of organizations there are medical and health service providers such as doctors, hospitals, laboratories, insurers, pharmaceutical companies, and medical technology companies. In the area of prevention, there are drugstores and pharmacies, telecommunications and IT companies, as well as large retailers who are interested in linking health data generated by self-tracking apps to products and services. Many devices, apps, and tracking practices are being integrated into diagnosis, therapy, and rehabilitation. They are increasingly being certified by government health agencies, such as the FDA in the USA or the NHS in the UK. Increasingly, apps and devices are being prescribed by doctors. A recent study in Germany showed that about one half of the new start-ups in the digital health sector are developing products for doctors, insurers, clinics, pharmaceutical companies, and medical technology producers.[52] In addition to this, self-tracking data can be easily aggregated into data on

---

51 | See Lupton (2014c) for a discussion of medical apps and usage practices.

52 | http://epatient-rsd.com/epatient-survey/

entire populations and thus become a valuable resource for governments, public health programs, and policy makers. Not only device producers, app developers, and service providers, but also governments are important stakeholders in the quantified self movement. It is therefore necessary to understand QS not merely as a social movement among fitness enthusiasts, but as a disruptive network in healthcare and beyond.

Despite the many institutional and organizational links, quantified self, as the name suggests, is centered on individuals. The primary "users" of QS technologies and networks are persons who are concerned with fitness, health, and wellbeing. The majority of developers and providers of QS products and services consider the individual health consumer to be the primary user group, and most studies indicate that this is the sector of society that will be affected most by QS. Research has classified individual QS users into at least five different groups.[53]

The first group of QS users can be described as those individuals who monitor their vital states and behavior out of curiosity and out of a concern to experiment with themselves. They seek for correlations between the data that self-tracking yields and different behavior patterns, such as diet, exercise, life-style, etc. with the goal of improving health, wellbeing, and productivity. The major motivation of this group lies in self-knowledge and self-optimization. This is entirely in accord with the proclaimed goal of the QS movement as "self knowledge through numbers."[54]

The second identifiable group of QS users are persons, who do not keep their data to themselves only for personal use, but freely communicate, share, compare, and donate their health data in online communities, health portals, patient platforms, and by means of other channels such as blogs or wikis, as well as at conferences and quantified self "meetups." These people are concerned to gain insight through discussion with other QS users and to share information about technologies, data interpretation tools and methods, and related topics. They are also willing to contribute or donate their data to third parties for medical research. Their motivation is primarily oriented toward the community and toward achieving common goals. Among this group are to be found the many patient communities oriented around specific illnesses, or groups with common health related issues, such as weight watchers. They often seek advice and support not

---

53 | See Lupton (2014b) for a typology of self-trackers.

54 | http://quantifiedself.com

only from each other, but also from concerned health professionals who participate in their communities.

A third group is made up of all those who in one way or another do not do self-tracking voluntarily. People in this group practice forms of self-tracking within the parameters of programs for fitness and health that are organized by employers, health insurance companies, or other organizations in which they are members. Such programs are often officially declared voluntary and non-compulsive, but people may feel that they are under more or less explicit pressure to participate because of peer-pressure, or incentive systems, such as reduced health insurance premiums. It is obviously in the interest of many organizations that their members are healthy and productive. It is therefore to be expected that organizationally sponsored or encouraged forms of self-tracking will increase in the future.

The fourth group consists of persons who use self-tracking in one form or another as part of diagnosis, therapy, or rehabilitation. Doctors or therapists have "prescribed" these people self-tracking much as a course of medication is prescribed. For this group it can be said that self-tracking is not voluntary but compulsive and therefore QS becomes a matter of compliance. Indeed, self-tracking technologies are a major step toward insuring compliance and optimizing health outcomes.

Finally, there is a group of QS users that consists of persons from all of the previously listed groups who have in common that the data that is collected by devices and apps are more or less automatically sent to the developers and providers of devices, apps, and services. QS data are often sent directly to the servers of the developers and providers. The data is then aggregated, evaluated, and possibly sold to third parties such as advertising agencies or health product companies in order to target individuals or groups with specific products. User profiling, personalized marketing, research, and other uses of health data are major sources of value in the global digital economy. Health related data, as can be said for all personal data, are the oil of the 21st Century. Health data and other personal data are not only of value for medical science and business, but also for governments and public health agencies. In this context, one can speak of the "exploitation" of health data, since it occurs often without the knowledge or explicit consent of the individuals whose data is being gathered, evaluated, and sold.

E-Patient Movement

The digital transformation of healthcare has many names, health 2.0,[55] digital health, or internet medicine. Self-tracking is an important trend, but not the only one in the broader process of digitalizing healthcare. As in other areas of society, such as education, which we discussed above, digitalization, brings many changes not only in how individuals appropriate and use health data, but also in how businesses and healthcare service providers adapt to the new networked environments. Digital healthcare changes not only personal behavior and expectations, but also traditional and well-established health delivery processes.[56] It changes the way in which value is generated by doctors, hospitals, insurers, laboratories, pharmaceutical companies, medical research centers, care-givers, and public health agencies. As noted above, the driving force behind these changes remains the empowerment of individuals with regard to accessing, understanding, and acting upon health-related data and information. Paternalistic medicine in which doctors are "gods in white" and patients have nothing to say and do but obey is becoming increasingly dysfunctional.

What QS shows is that connectivity, flow, communication, and par-ticipation have enabled normal people to access, understand, and use health-related information in new and unforeseen ways. This changes expec-tations that patients have toward healthcare professionals and institutions, as well as the possibilities that these established players have in dealing with their customers and clientele. Patients and care-givers now can easily obtain information on all aspects of their health concerns, communicate and get advice and support from others in similar situations as well as from healthcare professionals. Patients can participate constructively in diagnosis, therapy, and rehabilitation. As in other areas of society, healthcare is becoming a part of the "sharing economy." Challenges for healthcare decision-makers lie in managing the networks that are emerging in order to lower costs by better use of information, to increase the effectiveness of prevention, to improve compliance and patient monitoring, to personalize

---

55 | See Belliger (2014) for a good German language summary of "connected health" trends that can all be subsumed under the 2.0 title that is derived from Web 2.0.

56 | See Chayko (2016) for a summary of "superconnected" healthcare.

medicine, create transparency and trust instead of attempting to maintain top-down, intransparent communication. In short, the democratization of healthcare is an effect of networking. Perhaps nowhere is this new awareness of healthcare more appropriately expressed as in the slogans of the e-patient movement, "Give me my damn data" and "Let patients help."[57]

The *e-patient movement* is formally organized around the non-profit Society for Participatory Medicine.[58] The e-patient movement defines itself as "a movement in which networked patients shift from being mere passengers to responsible drivers of their health."[59] In contrast to the quantified self movement, which operates mostly in the secondary healthcare sector of fitness and prevention, the e-patient movement operates within the primary healthcare sector of diagnosis, therapy, and rehabilitation. Networked healthcare in the primary sector is characterized by a new role for patients and new relationships between patients and healthcare providers such as doctors, clinics, hospitals, insurers, regulative agencies, pharmaceutical companies, and the medical technology industry. The driving force in this new constellation of roles and relationships are the patients themselves, who increasingly demand to play a more participatory role in healthcare. The explicit goals of the Society for Participatory Medicine are: 1) "to guide patients and caregivers to be actively engaged in their health and health care experiences;" 2) "to guide health professional practices where patient experience and contribution is an integral goal of excellence;" and 3) "to encourage mutual collaboration among patients, health professionals, caregivers and others allowing them to partner in determining care."[60]

Examples of how the network norms of connectivity, flow, communication, participation, transparency, and authenticity influence the e-patient movement are online communities such as Patients Like Me,[61] Cure-

---

57 | See *Let Patients Help* by e-Patient Dave deBronkart http://www.epatientdave. com/let-patients-help/. On the e-patient movement in general see Belliger (2014) and https://en.wikipedia.org/wiki/E-patient.
58 | http://participatorymedicine.org/
59 | http://participatorymedicine.org/about/
60 | http://participatorymedicine.org/about/
61 | https://www.patientslikeme.com/

Together,[62] and Acor[63] where patients are connected to peers, to information throughout the Web, and to medical professionals. Not only are patients connected to each other and to healthcare professionals, the flow of information throughout the Internet makes it possible that patients are sometimes better informed about their specific problems than doctors are. With regard to transparency, patients can rate the performance of medical service provides. The website CureTogether.com for example, offers access to millions of ratings not only of doctors and hospitals, but also treatments and medications.[64] With regard to participation, e-patients can donate their data to medical research via portals and communities, whereas doctors share their data in the "Open Notes" movement.[65] An important example of data donation supported by the US government is the Blue Button Movement that encourages and enables providers to allow patients to access their medical records.[66] 23andMe, a web-based personal genome service, not only allows individuals to get information about their genetic disposition for certain diseases, but also to donate this data to research.[67] Echoing the explicit goal of the Society for Participatory Medicine in the USA, the EU Action Plan 2012-2020 for the use of digital solutions in the healthcare system proclaims: "Putting patients in the driving seat: A digital future for healthcare."

"Putting patients in the driver's seat" and "letting patients help" means that patients stand in the foreground and that they responsibly and systematically use their "health literacy" and networked technologies in a way deemed appropriate to deal with their health and disease-related issues.[68] A simple example of participatory medicine is the German website "Was hab ich.de" [What do I have]. Since 2011, a volunteer team of medical students and physicians have translated more than 25,000

---

62 | http://curetogether.com/

63 | http://www.acor.org/

64 | http://curetogether.com/

65 | http://www.opennotes.org/

66 | https://www.healthit.gov/patients-families/join-blue-button-movement

67 | https://www.23andme.com/en-int/

68 | "Health literacy is the ability to obtain, read, understand and use healthcare information to make appropriate health decisions and follow instructions for treatment." https://en.wikipedia.org/wiki/Health_literacy. See Bessiere et al. (2010) for a discussion of the positive effects of networked health.

medical findings into understandable language for non-experts at no cost. The project delivers crucial momentum for healthcare in two directions: First, the service provides better educated and professionally well-informed patients. Second, the medical students who clarify the findings become better prepared for their future careers and for patient-friendly communication. Participatory medicine arises from the fundamental principle of "shared decision-making," a specific form of interaction between medical staff and patients, which is based on shared information and equal decision-making rights with respect to issues such as diagnosis and treatment. In the area of health and disease, this illustrates the network norms of authenticity and transparency. Formal titles are becoming increasingly irrelevant, while proven skills are taking a leading role instead.

By gaining access to information, medical records, peer-communities, and other resources available on the Internet, e-patients are empowered to constructively contribute to diagnosis and therapy. They can provide information and support to other patients by means of online patient communities. In addition to this, e-patients can contribute to medical research not only by donating health related data, but also by collaborating with scientists on agenda-setting for clinical studies and research programs. They form a healthcare-related civil society in which patient advocacy organizations engage in promoting better health services by working with government agencies, healthcare providers, and health related industries such as pharmaceutical companies. In all these areas, whether it be healthcare, education, or business, networking and organizing tend to disregard traditional divisions, institutional boundaries, and organizational domains. Networking in one way or another always has to do with civil society.

ORGANIZING NETWORKS IN CIVIL SOCIETY

Networks have often been theoretically positioned as a third form of organizing distinct from markets and hierarchies.[69] This places networks on a par with definitions of *civil society*. The concept of civil society is controversial as well as ambiguous. Its primary organizational inhabitants are usually defined by negation, that is, as either "non-profit" or "non-

---

69 | See Powell (1990), Thorelli (1986), and Podolny/Page (1998).

governmental" organizations.[70] However different definitions of civil society may be, there seems to be a consensus that whatever civil society is, it is "not" politics, "not" business, that is, it is "not" any of the functional subsystems of society.[71] If civil society is neither government, nor market, what is it then? Civil society stands for a "public sphere." The public sphere is somehow outside of the official political system, as well as outside of business or any other social domain. This position outside the tasks of the functional subsystems lends it at least three unique characteristics. First, civil society serves as a place of *free association*, second, it is a *community* based on solidarity and common values, and third, it is a *forum* for debate and deliberation on all matters concerning the common good.[72] As a place of free association, civil society consists of families, hobby and interest groups, clubs and associations from football clubs to Rotary International. Civil society is the place of voluntary association, from the parent-teachers association to international NGOs and NPOs such as Green Peace, the World Wild Life Fund, Amnesty International, etc. Second, as a community, civil society is based on solidarity and common values. Solidarity can be both local and global. It can be based on local religious, moral or cultural traditions and on the global level, civil society is often based on universal values such as the Declaration of Human Rights. Third, as a forum for debate and democratic deliberation, civil society is what Habermas has called the "public sphere."[73] For Habermas, the public

---

70 | The World Bank defines civil society as "the wide array of non-governmental and not-for-profit organizations that have a presence in public life, expressing the interests and values of their members or others, based on ethical, cultural, political, scientific, religious or philanthropic considerations." http://web.world bank.org/WBSITE/EXTERNAL/TOPICS/CSO/0,,contentMDK:20101499~menu PK:244752~pagePK:220503~piPK:220476~theSitePK:228717,00.html. For an overview, see the discussion in Setianto (2007).

71 | Setainto (2007) summarizes "civil society lies between the state and the market, where state interests and market interests are contested. Civil society thus stands in opposition to the market as well as to the state [...]" (117).

72 | See Edwards (2013) for a discussion of the history and structure of civil society.

73 | See Krieger/Belliger (2014: 151-161) for a discussion of the theory of the public sphere and how the affordances of ICTs are changing traditional conceptions of democratic deliberation.

sphere is the place within democratic societies in which citizens can come together and not only discuss their private interests and business opportunities, but also criticize government power and policies and build consensus motivating political action. The public sphere does not need common values or even a shared world-view. It explicitly accepts religious and moral pluralism. According to Habermas, civil society is based on unrestricted and undistorted communication in which every citizen can form their own opinion and express it without fear of sanctions. It is the place where "private people came together as a public" (Habermas 1989: 27) and where the nonviolent force of the better argument creates consensus and makes cooperative action possible. Civil society in this sense can therefore serve as a measure of general accountability against organizations operating within the systemic boundaries of government, business, education, healthcare, etc. Civil society is the society to which, if anything at all, corporations and government are accountable.

The view of civil society as the realm of free association, common values, and public deliberation based on unrestricted communication has been criticized as an ideal that does not describe social reality, not even in the democratic nations of the developed world.[74] On the contrary, even in the first world governmental and corporate power have, as Habermas puts it "colonized" civil society.[75] Open, free, and undistorted communication is structurally impeded, not only by governmental privileges or corporate power, but also by the very system of representation that is supposed to guarantee democracy. The channeling of political processes into bureaucratic parties and hierarchical governmental agencies seems unavoidable. After all, what alternative do we have? The question is legitimate because it would seem that representation in one form or another is the only way to organize democratic political processes. Representation has long been understood to be the inevitable outcome of the transformation of communication from egalitarian, face-to-face communication in small groups into hierarchical, one-to-many

---

74 | Castells (2009) has extensively documented the crisis of representation and legitimation in today's world.

75 | The concept of "colonization" of civil society locates the structural problem of the public sphere in the dominance of instrumental action and functional reason and not in the covert transformation of face-to-face into one-to-many communication and a system of representation as we do.

communication in large groups. The ideal of egalitarian face-to-face communication in which everyone has their say on an equal footing and the best argument carries the day can only be realized, if at all, in small groups. Whenever large groups attempt to coordinate action, other methods of communication take over. There is simply not enough time and space for everyone to speak to everyone and reach a consensus. Habermas (1987: 181) admits that attempts to coordinate action among large numbers of people "'overburden' the communicative resources of the population and so some form of 'relief mechanism' must be found." Given the limitations of time and space that condition communication in large assemblies of people, it is simply impossible for large groups of people to discuss complex issues openly and effectively, reach a consensus, and coordinate action.

In the modern period, the mechanisms that "relieved" one-to-one communication of the burden of the many in the public sphere took the form of corporate owned mass media communication and the development of a system of representation in politics. These "relief mechanisms" have created a crisis of legitimation and a structural distortion of communication within civil society. Neither mass media, nor political representation, nor a free market could bridge the gap between unrestricted face-to-face communication among free citizens and hierarchical one-to-many communication that inevitably takes over when very large groups must communicate and coordinate their actions. If it is at all legitimate to speak of a digital media revolution, then it is because ICTs have radically changed this age-old situation. According to Castells, the digital communication revolution has transformed the structural limitations on communication and for the first time in history made many-to-many communication possible. Not only has this structural transformation led to a global network society, but it has also revealed and sharpened the legitimation crisis of traditional institutions and of hierarchies in general. The digital media revolution has not only deepened the crisis of the state, it has also created its own solutions in the form of networked social movements. For Castells, networks are not only forms of power, but also forms of liberation and empowerment. Castells grounds these new opportunities for social and political change in the rise of what he calls "mass self-communication:"

In recent years, the fundamental change in the realm of communication has been the rise of what I have called mass self-communication – the use of the Internet and wireless networks as platforms of digital communication. It is mass communication because it processes messages from many to many, with the potential of reaching a multiplicity of receivers, and of connecting to endless networks that transmit digitized information around the neighborhood or around the world. It is self-communication because the production of the message is autonomously decided by the sender, the designation of the receiver is self-directed and the retrieval of messages from the networks of communication is self-selected. Mass self-communication is based on horizontal networks of interactive communication that, by and large, are difficult to control by governments or corporations. Furthermore, digital communication is multimodal and allows constant reference to a global hypertext of information whose components can be remixed by the communicative actor according to specific projects of communication. Mass self-communication provides the technological platform for the construction of the autonomy of the social actor, be it individual or collective, vis-à-vis the institutions of society. (Castells 2015: 6-7)

To speak of organizing networks in civil society implies that civil society is no longer a clear defined area somehow "outside" the functional sub-systems of business, government, education, etc. Networks in civil society are not "in" civil society alone. They extend beyond the boundaries of what has traditionally been thought of as civil society. They are independent of, but nonetheless integrally related to politics, business, science, religion, as well as other social subsystems. Furthermore, to speak of non-governmental, non-profit, non-denominational, etc. organizations as networks ultimately derives from the fact that networks are the major structural characteristic of today's world. Just as organizations within the functional subsystems of society such as government and business are being organized as networks, so are free associations, communities, and forums of deliberation also becoming networked. This changes the structural relationship between civil society and the functional subsystems of society. If organizing civil society in the past was necessarily characterized by negation, that is, by being "non" government, "non" business, etc., the networks that characterize today's world have done away with clear boundaries, not only between functional subsystems such as business, education, government, and so on, but also between these and civil society.

The global network society is not divided up into distinct institutional domains. We live in a situation in which sharp boundaries and a strict division of labor no longer define social order. Networks move seamlessly from politics to business to science, education, healthcare, and also into civil society. Networks are not easily definable as either business, or government, or education, or any other functional subsystem. They are a complex mixture of all.[76] It is becoming increasingly fruitless to define networked social movements and organizations as if they were not part of the subsystems to which their activities relate. Moreover, it has become theoretically unfruitful to conceptualize politics, business, healthcare, education and so on as if they were not distributed throughout society and also across national boundaries. New strategies of localizing and globalizing are emerging. Consumers have become "prosumers" and citizens have become networked participants in both local and global political processes. Social activism for the promotion of equality, justice, human rights, environmental sustainability, open education, affordable healthcare, and peace need not take place outside of or against political or economic institutions, nor are they restricted to citizen communities within national boundaries. The network society is permeated with the civil in all areas, and civil society has become networked into government, business, education, healthcare, and all other domains.

In the area of government, for example, Hajer and Wagenaar (2003) point to the new discourse of "governance." "What the rise of the vocabulary of governance makes clear is that we experience a shift in language from institutions to networks" (5). Networked governance includes "collaborative policymaking" and "governance through dialogue." As Hajer and Wegenaar put it

Many pressing problems no longer comport with established systems of politics, adminsitration and society. [...] Organizations themselves have become aware of how much more fluid their boundaries are. The demands of business highlight interdependencies and realtionships among tasks and prompt the development of inter-organizational networks. Governments also see the tie between interaction, ccoperation and results. The consequences of these new inter-organizational activities do not stop with how politics is conducted. They reshpae what politics and policymaking are about. (Hajer/Wagenaar 2003: 2)

---

76 | See Krieger/Belliger (2014: 157ff.) for a discussion of this mixed form of social reality under the title of the "socio-sphere."

It is precisely the inclusiveness and flexibility of networks that make new forms of social protest, participatory policymaking, accountability, and community activism within a global civil society possible. These new networked forms of civil engagement bridge traditional gaps and link up actors from all areas and across institutional boundaries. In the following we will sketch out some of the ways in which organizing networks in civil society is being done today. For the sake of analysis, we distinguish between bottom-up, self-organizing protest movements on the one hand, and governance oriented, cooperative networks such as global public policy networks, national as well as international forms of participatory democracy, and social entrepreneurship on the other hand.

Networked Social Movements of Protest and Change

The global statistical report *We Are Social* 2016 shows that 31 per cent of the world's population uses online social networks.[77] Guilló (2015) comments that "the irruption of social networks has led Internet users to become part of global networks connected through virtual environments that allow them to integrate into large online communities," and that "this new social reality appears as a perfect scenario for civic renewal, increasing citizens' active role in social life through a boost to civic engagement supported by the enormous potential offered by social networking sites" (44). Castells has consistently emphasized the significance of new networked social movements. In the forefront of the discussion are such well known examples as the Arab Spring, Icelandic revolution, Occupy Wall Street, the 11-M movement, and many others. As Castells points out,

In all cases the movements ignored political parties, distrusted the media, did not recognize any leadership and rejected all formal organization, relying on the Internet and local assemblies for collective debate and decision-making. (Castells 2015: 4)

These examples of networked social activism are at once local and global, physical and virtual, diverse and sharing common values. The role that ICTs, in particular the Internet and social networking sites have

---

77 | http://de.slideshare.net/wearesocialsg/digital-in-2016-executive-summary-57533062

played in these recent social movements is controversial (cf. Park/Perry 2008; Livingstone et al. 2007). Sabatini and Sarracino (2004), however, show that "the online networking revolution is allowing the Internet to support – rather than destroy – sociability and fact-to-face interactions" (35). This view is confirmed by the detailed studies of many of these new movements.[78] On the basis of empirical studies of many of these networked social movements, Castells has found not less than eleven common characteristics of networked social movements:[79]

1) Networked social movements are characterized by connectivity. They are networked in many different ways. They are based on social networks both online and offline, both already existing and newly formed. They are connected up with other movements around the world, with media, and with the larger society. They connect local, physical spaces with the virtual "space of flows" in the Internet. They have no identifiable command and control centers, nor do they have formal leadership. They are heterogeneous, open and tolerant of many different viewpoints, thus increasing and supporting wide participation. They are difficult to suppress, since they cannot be easily targeted for repression or sanctions. Despite diversity and pluralism, they enjoy a solidarity based on common goals and shared values.

2) Networked social movements do not exist only in cyberspace. As the various "occupy" movements show, they claim real space, usually in urban settings and at symbolically significant places and buildings. Networked social movements have their own kind of "space," which Castells (2015: 250) calls "the space of autonomy." This is a hybrid space, or a mixed reality consisting of both physical and virtual places.

3) Networked social movements are at once global and local. They may originate in specific cities or nations, but soon link up with supporters throughout the world. Events transpiring in real time at physical places are globally documented via social media and other internet services. As both global and local, they encourage communication and participation

---

78 | See Castells (2009, 2011, 2015).

79 | See Castells (2015: 249-256) for the following description of the common traits of networked social movements.

thus uniting communities beyond national boundaries and creating a form of global citizenship.

4) Just as the new social movements have their own specific space, so do they have their own characteristic temporality. This is the "timeless time" of global immediacy and transparency made possible by the Internet.

5) Although they are usually spontaneously triggered by local events, they quickly spread into global communities, coordinated events, demonstrations, associated actions, and similar programs in other areas around the world.

6) They are conditioned by the effects of viral communication such that they can reinforce each other and inspire each other. An event that usually would go unnoticed and undocumented by the established media can be posted to a social media site and within hours become known to hundreds of thousands of people all over the world.

7) What may have begun as an expression of outrage turns into political and social hope on the basis of communication, participation, and deliberation leading to coordinated action both locally and globally. This hope is nourished by a common distrust of established political processes and systems of representation.

8) Networked social movements are typically a "work in progress" (253) empowered by the goal of community building. "The horizontality of networks supports cooperation and solidarity while undermining the need for formal leadership" (253). Transparency and authenticity replace authority and hierarchy.

9) These movements are "highly self-reflective" and are constantly placing themselves in question, flexibly renegotiating their values and goals. This discussion is both local and global and is strongly supported by the Internet.

10) Another important characteristic of the new social movements is expressed goal of non-violence. Despite the often witnessed degeneration of conflicts into violent confrontations, the general tenor of protests within

these movements is to attempt to avoid violence and any association with what could be seen as terrorism.

11) Castells finds that the networked social movements are rarely programmatic. In contrast to political parties, labor unions, NGOs, and other traditional forms of civil society, the new networked social movements tend not to formalize goals, programs, or leadership. This is both a strength with regard to wide support and flexibility, but it is also a weakness, when it comes to implementing concrete policies and changes in cooperation with government, business, and established NGOs. This means that networked social movements are primarily directed to changing the way people think, the values of society as whole and not particular political or economic policies and institutions.

What these new networked social movements show is that despite their origins in protest against established institutions, they adopt much the same principles of networking and follow the same network norms as do their opponents. Networking is simply the way organizing is done in the global network society, whether it be on the side of the establishment or the side of protest. This fact of today's world has implications for how governments, international agencies, NGOs and citizen groups work together in non-rejectionist modes to attempt to solve the problems we are facing today.

Networked Governance

The social movements that Castells has described are above all movements of protest based on the rejection of established political and business institutions. Networking, however, is not the prerogative of protest movements. Government, business, education, and healthcare can use the same networking strategies that Castells finds in protest movements in order to initiate cooperation between stakeholders in all areas. Brandtzaeg et al. (2012) do not focus on protest movements. They understand networked social activism as "action in response to societal needs, in the form of supportive, deliberative, and collaborative practices in social media" (67), regardless of whether the initiative comes from civil society or from established institutions. Websites, social media, and other internet services support social change and cooperation among citizens, interest groups, government, and the business community by various means. One important form of networking is simply making information available to all concerned. Information can be distributed via websites, online petitions, Facebook, Twitter, visual content platforms such as Tumblr, Instagram, and Pinterest, and other channels. Transparency on the part of government and business, and open access to information of all kinds can change how people think and feel and motivate support for social change as well as help in finding viable and innovative solutions to societal problems. It is on the basis of shared information that processes of deliberation and collaborative action can be successful.

Once information sharing has been implemented, *deliberative* platforms allow discussion, debate, the expression of differing opinions, and thus consensus building and motivation for cooperative action. Examples are the global youth think tank Challenge Future (www.challengefuture.org), the Forum for the Future on issues of sustainability (www.forumforthefuture.org), the Open Ideo platform (www.openideo.com) for crowdsourcing solutions to global problems, and the United Dreams of Europe for developing common visions on the future of the European Union (www.uniteddreamsofeurope.eu). Deliberation, however, can be taken a step further into networked forms of *collaboration*. Among collaborative platforms, the most well known example is perhaps Wikipedia, whose purpose, as its founder proclaimed, is to create a world "in which every single person on the planet is given free access to the sum of all human knowledge."[80] Wikipedia can be considered collaborative instead of merely aggregating and distributing information, because articles are community products.

Many different open source projects as well as crowdsourcing and crowdfunding platforms allow networks to do more than merely spread information and share ideas. Examples that have been studied are the CALFED, a collaborative group in California consisting of government representatives, business leaders, social groups, and other stakeholders concerned with managing the precarious water supply situation in California.[81] Citizen forums of different kinds are allowing for wide participation in policy development in government as well as product development in the business sector. Citizen participation goes beyond

80 | https://en.wikipedia.org/wiki/User:Jimbo_Wales/Statement_of_principles
81 | Booher/Innes (2010).

mere suggestions about improvements in policy, products, or services and plays an important role in quality assessment and accountability. Open government programs and open data are forming networks with civil society and the business community in order not only to make government more transparent and more responsive to social needs both within national borders and internationally, but also to create economic opportunities and new business models. For Guilló

The discussion on how the Internet and social media could affect civic engagement requires conceptualizing participation in a multidimensional way, and this requires taking into account not only different types of communities focused on different topics (politics, economics, culture, etc.), but also different frameworks of reference (local, regional, national, supranational), both in physical and virtual environments. (Guilló 2015: 45)

Much research into new forms of interaction between government, the business world, and civil society has been done under the title of "network governance."[82] Many governments are establishing networked forms of interaction not only with other governments on the international level, and not only between traditionally distinct agencies within individual nations, but also with stakeholders and citizens both within and without their national borders.[83] For van Dijk and Winters-van Beek (2009), "the prospect of E-government is the technological drive behind the rise of networks as a steering or governance principle for the government as a whole" (235). They propose a developmental model of e-government beginning with traditional hierarchies that are currently evolving toward governance by network. A first stage is the linking up of heretofore separate governmental agencies ("joined-up" government), followed by more outsourcing of services and public-private partnerships ("government by

---

82 | See Bogason/Zølner (2007) for an overview of topics and methods as well as a definition: "Rather than envisioning policymaking as a top-down process fully controlled by the government, network governance approaches it as the result of negotiated interaction between a plurality of public and private actors, and that takes place within relatively stable frameworks in particular policy fields [...] Network governance is neither market nor government nor civil society, it is a hybrid organizational form" (5).

83 | For an overview see Reinicke/Deng (2000) and Goldsmith/Eggers (2004).

network"), and culminating in "digital democracy" wherein "networks, the Internet in particular are used as a medium of political participation" (240). Typical examples are global public policy networks such as the World Commission in Dams, the International Competition Network, and the Global Water Partnership. What these examples show is that such networks are not only state entities; they are not necessarily legally incorporated, nor do they necessarily have the status of NGOs. They are composed of various actors including governmental agencies, businesses, as well as NGOs, and other interest groups. They pursue many different activities including making policy proposals, agenda setting, facilitating negotiations, coordinating activities, implementation of programs, and evaluation and accountability.[84] In addition to this kind of networked cooperation between governments, business, and global civil society, there are many forms of networked cooperation and network governance within nations, such as the CALFED network in California mentioned above. Sørensen and Torfing characterize governance networks on all levels in terms of five aspects. They consist of:

1) a relatively stable horizontal articulation of interdependent, but operationally autonomous actors; 2) who interact through negotiations; 3) which take place within a common regulative, normative, cognitive and imaginary framework; 4) that is self-regulating within limits set by external agencies; and 5) which contributes to the production of public purpose. (Sørensen/Torfing 2007: 9)

What this means concretely is spelled out by Goldsmith and Eggers (2004: 19) in their analysis of "governing by network." There is a high level of public-private collaboration, combined with the network management capabilities illustrated by closely linked intergovernmental agencies, assisted by ICTs, and guided by the goal of empowering citizens to shape policy and services. Managing by network is no easy task, as is shown by the many examples that Goldsmith and Eggers discuss. The first among the principles they suggest for governing by network is that government agencies should focus less on program and more on public value. This amounts to fundamental changes in the relation of government to civil society and the in the role of administrators:

---

84 | See Stone (2013) and https://en.wikipedia.org/wiki/Global_public_policy _networks

A greater focus on public value also will gradually change the way government is conceptualized; the idea of government based on programs and agencies will give way to government based on goals and networks. Instead of seeing their jobs mostly as managing public employees, public executives will view their role as working out how to add maximum public value by deploying and orchestrating a network of assets. (Goldsmith/Eggers 2004: 181).

Social Entrepreneurship and Social Enterprises

Another important development in networked forms of cooperation across organizational and social boundaries, this time at the interface of civil society and business is what has come to known as "social entrepreneurship" and "social enterprises." According to the traditional view, economic actors seeking profit produce value and distribute it through the market. The market is concerned with buying and selling, but indifferent to social welfare, ecological sustainability, and issues of justice, equality, and the common good, which are supposed to be taken care of by the famous "invisible hand." This is where the state comes in to rectify and compensate the unbalances created by the free market. Where the market fails to create social order, state hierarchies step in. Not only does the state regulate markets in order to guarantee fair play, but it also compensates the social (and natural) damages that seem an inevitable corollary of profit seeking. The increasing complexity of society, the apparent structural distortions of the market, the well-documented inefficiency of administrative bureaucracies, as well as the general crisis of representation have called this centuries old market-state model into question. One promising answer to this question is "social enterprises" or "social entrepreneurship."[85] There are many definitions of social enterprises and social entrepreneurship. Mair et al. offer a broad definition:

The concept of social entrepreneurship (SE) is, in practice, recognized as encompassing a wide range of activities: enterprising individuals devoted to

---

85 | Despite their novelty, the literature on social enterprises and social entre-preneurship is vast. See for example Leadbeater (1997, 2006), Becchettti/Borza-ga (2010), Nicholls (2006), Mair et al. (2006), Borzaga/Defourny (2001), Nyssens (2006), Hackenber/Empter (2011), and Foyolle/Matlay (2010).

making a difference; social purpose business ventures dedicated to adding for-profit motivations to the nonprofit sector; new types of philanthropists supporting venture capital-like 'investment' portfolios; and nonprofit organizations that are reinventing themselves by drawing on lessons learned from the business world. (Mair et al. 2006: 1)

So important have social enterprises become that Forbes in 2011, for the first time in their 94-year history, assembled the "Impact 30," a list of the world's top thirty social entrepreneurs.[86] Well-known examples of social enterprises are the Grameen Bank, Acumen Fund, and other micro-financing initiatives. The Skoll Foundation, Ashoka, and the Schwab Foundation support social entrepreneurship. Many forms of fair-trade co-operatives, work integration programs, and innovative products and services have proven successful both as businesses and as instruments for social improvement. Although the exact nature of a social enterprise is vague, at least one thing seems common to the many different forms such endeavors have taken; namely, they are an integral part of civil society, while at the same time being integrated into the business world and into government.[87] Social enterprises are neither against or outside of business, nor are they against or outside of government. They are therefore not to be located in a "third sector" somehow equivalent to civil society. In other words, they represent a form of social order that bridges the gap between markets and hierarchies, integrating both, while not limiting themselves to a domain that could be seen as civil society. This makes them interesting as examples of networked forms of social order.

In an important article, *The Socially Entrepreneurial City*, Leadbeater (2006) has emphasized the specifically networked character of social enterprises and social entrepreneurship. The Brazilian city of Curitiba, which we encountered already above as an example of "pattern-breaking" management, is for Leadbeater an important example of what social entrepreneurship is all about. Curitiba is a city of more than 2 million people about 1000 km south of Rio de Janeiro. It has been challenged by all the typical problems of urbanization such as mass unemployment,

---

86 | http://www.forbes.com/impact-30/list.html9. See also Wikipedia's list https://en.wikipedia.org/wiki/List_of_social_entrepreneurs

87 | See Martin/Osberg (2007) for a detailed and well-founded definition of social entrepreneurship.

transportation congestion, and lack of basic services in areas of healthcare and education, as well as the uncontrolled growth of slums. Nonetheless, Curitiba was awarded the Global Sustainable City Award in 2010 for innovative solutions to these problems. What Leadbeater emphasizes is that these solutions illustrate networked principles of governance that connect up government, business, and civil society such that each sector is supported by the others in doing what it does best. Social entrepreneurship does not happen in a vacuum, but depends on support and cooperation from all areas of society. This is what the example of Curitiba shows and why it is important for understanding what organizing networks in civil society means.

Leadbeater (2006) points out that the Curitiba city council itself acted as a social entrepreneur in that is adopted " a highly networked form of civil organization, working to achieve its goals through a distributed network of players" (233). An example of such a network is the way the city dealt with its waste problem. The city has a waste disposal system organized in such a way that many different actors, not only government, are involved. The garbage is separated into organic and non-organic. Citizens put their waste in front of their houses two times a day. Unemployed people and people from the slums are encouraged to pick up the non-organic waste before city trucks come by and trade this in for money, fruit, and vegetables. This "green exchange" serves various purposes, the separating of recyclable waste, giving jobs to the unemployed, keeping the city clean, lowering costs to the city for waste disposal, since fewer trucks are needed and by removing waste from areas difficult to access with trucks. People from the slums can become micro-entrepreneurs, which raises self-esteem and encourages civil engagement among those usually disenfranchised and condemned to unemployment and poverty. The recyclable waste is sorted out and reenters the economy via a factory that severs as a work integration program, creating jobs for reformed alcoholics, drug addicts, and slum-dwellers. The cooperative efforts of business, government, and citizens allow Curitiba to recycle more than 60 per cent of its waste with the benefit of creating jobs, reducing landfill, generating revenue and income and even creating a library of recycled books available to schoolchildren. According to Leadbeater, "the system as a whole is a prime example of mass social innovation" (234). He speaks of "structured self-organization," which "provides public leadership to encourage people to devise self-organizing solutions; top-down rules, incentives, and tools to allow massive bottom-up innovation" (235). Curitiba found similar solutions for problems of transportation and housing. The driving elements of this specifically networked form of social entrepreneurship are new forms of governance, shared platforms, distributed resources, and collaborative civic engagement, whereby people actively participate in the solutions to the cities problems rather than simply be passive recipients of top-down services. The city council of Curitiba operated by "orchestrating a network rather than just running an autocratic organization" (236). Summarizing the lessons learned from Curitiba, Leadbeater writes:

The Curitiba example suggests a very different model of social entrepreneurship and how it can scale: networked social entrepreneurship. In networked social entrepreneurship, the aim is not to grow a single organization but to achieve greater impact through a network of collaborators and partners. An organization – like the council in Curitiba – might be at the core of the network, but most of the impact comes from the reach of the network of partners. That increases the range of resources that can be brought to bear on an issue and multiplies the number of experiments and innovations, allowing solutions to be tailored to particular circumstances. Curitiba council's network mobilize resources beyond the council, resources that lie in households, civil society, and the private sector. (Leadbeater 2006: 240)

CONCLUSION

Organizing networks in business, education, healthcare, and civil society display similar traits and are influenced by similar guiding norms or principles of governance. Whether we are looking at global projects, interorganizational networks, personal learning environments, protest movements, or social entrepreneurship, what comes to the fore is how networking, that is, processes of localizing and globalizing, are being guided by what we have called network norms. The imperatives of connectivity, the free flow of information, a culture of open communication and participation, demands for transparency and authenticity, and an astonishing flexibility in addressing complex problems are everywhere visible. Regardless of scale, social sector, control of resources, and other factors, networks in all areas are transforming the ways in which social order is created, sustained, and transformed. We propose speaking of the new domain in which networking is transforming social order as the "socio-sphere."[88] The socio-sphere is the place of networking. It arises from the affordances of ICTs and on the basis of the network norms. Wherever connectivity, flow, communication, participation, transparency, authenticity, and flexibility condition narrative performance, sensemaking, and therefore the communicative constitution of organizations, this is the socio-sphere. It is not a functional subsystem of society, such as politics, business, education, science, or the media. It is also not some kind of civil society defined by not being a functional subsystem. Traditional ways of dividing up and partitioning the social realm are perhaps no longer useful. The socio-sphere emerges as the stage upon which social processes and the constitution of organizations take place in today's world. The basic units within the socio-sphere are neither governmental agencies nor corporations, nor are they non-governmental or non-profit organizations, but actor-networks. In one form or another, whether in business, education, government, or healthcare, what we have are actor-networks involved in localizing and globalizing in new and innovative ways.

The conflicts characterizing the global network society are being carried out on the terrain of the socio-sphere and with the weapons of networking, that is, translation, enrollment, and mobilization under the

---

88 | See Krieger/Belliger (2014: 157ff.) for a discussion of the concept of the socio-sphere.

conditions of network norms. The socio-sphere is neither market nor hierarchy, neither private nor public. It is based upon the new possibilities of many-to-many communication arising from the affordances of ICTs. Networking today is influenced by connectivity, flow, communication, participation, transparency, authenticity, and flexibility. The digital transformation has, at least in principle, done away with traditional forms of private and public organizing. What takes their place is the space of networks. It is in the socio-sphere as a space of networks that business is reforming itself in close association to what before was a different realm of common concerns in civil society, education, healthcare and government. These domains no longer exist apart from one another with their own codes of inclusion/exclusion and their own ways of organizing. What the examples above show, is that a network society is everywhere connected, that information flows in unpredictable ways between all nodes, and that open, authentic, and transparent communication enable flexible solutions to complex problems. From the point of view of organization theory, it would seem that what is needed in the global network society is a theory of networks and of networking. This is what we have attempted to sketch out in this book. In the concluding section, we will review the road we have taken to reach this goal.

6. Conclusion

The story we set out to tell was a story about organizations, about what they are, how they come to be, how they are maintained, and how they are transformed. Our goal was to show how organizations can theoretically be defined as processes of networking and empirically described as networked organizations. In order to define what networks are and how networking is done we turned to actor-network theory (ANT). ANT implies the following assumptions: Organizations do not emerge from the interests and decisions of individual human actors, much as the "invisible hand" is supposed to bring order into the chaos of markets. Nor do organizations somehow precede individuals in the form of overarching macro-social structures. Organizations are not wholes that are always somehow more than the sum of their parts. They are therefore not containers into which individuals are "socialized." They do not exist on some higher level from which they influence individuals, as it were, behind their backs. This means that we no longer need to describe organizations as social "entities" or "structures." Organizations are not some kind of social substance, nor do they make up an "ecosystem" of their own in which they must adapt to environmental or "institutional" pressures in order to establish viability and legitimation.

Networks as we have described them on the basis of ANT are scalable actors, and actors are always made up of many heterogeneous associations. The social actor *is* the network. Networks are processes of organizing in which heterogeneous actors, both human and non-human, are constantly negotiating and re-negotiating programs of action. All actors are constantly attempting to constrain, that is, in the language of ANT, to "translate" and "enroll" other actors into "programs of action." We are well aware that it would probably be more appropriate not to speak of networks at all, but only of *networking*. Nonetheless, language usage also has its constraints and it is almost impossible not to speak of networks as well as networking. We have attempted to constantly remind the reader that when we use the word "network," we always understand this term to imply the activity of networking as it is defined by ANT. This means that social order in general and organizations specifically are constituted by both human and non-human actors who influence each other, enter into associations, and build actor-networks. We therefore understand the title *Organizing Networks* in the sense of networks that are always in the process of organizing, that is, networks are doing the organizing as well as being organized. Networking does not necessarily stop at clear boundaries, nor does it privilege human actors. It does not limit itself to standard procedures, nor conform to goals and strategies of an encompassing system. It is neither an effect of markets nor hierarchies nor a mixture of the two.

Our story began with the question of what makes human social organization different from the behavior of apes. We argued that the usual answer to this question, the specifically human use of symbols, signs, and language, does not explain how social bonds become durable, lasting, and repeatable. Contrary to traditional views that assume that meaningful action is the prerogative of conscious, intentional speakers who can account for what they are doing, we argued that meaningful action, as opposed to instinctual behavior, is dependent on relations to things. For our social relations, our "significant others" are not merely other humans, but things, artifacts, or technologies. ANT is interesting for social and organizational theory because it proposes a non-linguistic concept of communication. Not words, but things make the difference. What makes human social relations different from apes is that humans can "do words with things." Latour speaks of "technical mediation" to describe how things take on agency and become "actors" with "programs of action," or "affordances" of their own. Non-humans need not be restricted to playing the role of commodities in trade relations, or of gifts in community building. Humans build their social relations together with things, which lend stability and repeatability to human relations. For ANT, technical mediation is what networking is all about. This view has recently received support from the new non-Cartesian cognitive science which interprets mind as embodied, embedded, enacted, and extended. Meaningful action is not limited to – nor does it even originate – in cognitive processes inside of brains, but is "distributed" among heterogeneous actors and extended beyond the brain, and even beyond the body into the environment. Of course, the use of sings, symbols, and language are part of this. For ANT, however, things can come to have a "voice" of their own. They are not passive recipients of intentional, meaning giving acts, but participate as actors in making the associations that create information and build social order.

After explaining what networking means by describing the role of artifacts as social actors via the concept of technical mediation, the second episode of our story dealt with the role of communication in the constitution of organizations and in organizational studies. What role does communication play in understanding organizations and what difference does it make for organizational practice? Ever since the linguistic turn in philosophy and social sciences, this question has motivated much theoretical and empirical research in the area of management and organization science. We discussed the important work being done under the title of "communicative constitution of organizations" by such thinkers as McPhee and Zaug, Taylor, and Cooren. For these thinkers, the traditional view of organizations as social entities, institutions, and macro-structures has yielded to a process view based on communication. The CCO movement follows Weick in explicitly understanding organizations as the process of sensemaking.

The processes that CCO focuses on seem to be primarily linguistic forms of communication. It would seem that all that is needed for organizations to come into existence is "talking heads." With regard to the role that ANT ascribes to non-humans in creating social order, the various theories and models of society that are associated with CCO raise many questions. A careful examination of how social interaction actually takes place emphasizes things, artifacts, spatial constructions, and many non-linguistic props. This is what Goffman's dramaturgical theory of interaction shows. Non-humans play important roles in making interaction possible. Furthermore, we showed that Weick's notion of "sensemaking" should not be reduced to linguistic communication. The communicative processes that constitute organizations turn out to involve many non-linguistic and non-human participants. The question becomes, "Who is doing the communicating?" How is communication constitutive of organizations? Can non-humans as well as humans be considered as social actors? If so, what roles do they play?

We argued that Weick's seminal concept of sensemaking is best understood as networking, provided that sensemaking includes Goffman's dramaturgical staging of social interaction as well as a theory of narrative informed by non-Cartesian cognitive science. Weick, and many others, pointed out that sensemaking is actually storytelling. Narrative has something to do with that unique kind of communication that is able to constitute organizations. In narrative, as the founding myths and rituals of every society illustrate, all kinds of beings "speak" and "do" things. To speak of the communicative constitution of organizations, therefore, is to understand communication not merely as verbal utterances, but also as *performance*, whereby performance means that "sensemaking" (Weick) is embodied, enacted, embedded, and extended in the environment. Cognition is distributed in actor-networks. The network is the actor. This is where the new non-Cartesian cognitive science comes in and explains how social order is not the prerogative of heads with big brains, even if they also play important parts. Narrative, from the perspective of non-Cartesian cognitive science, can be understood as embodied, enacted, embedded, and extended and thus distributed among non-humans as well as humans. From this perspective, narrative can be aligned with networking understood as technical mediation as well as with Goffman's staging. Networking holds the key to understanding how many different entities, both human and non-human, and their many different activities can be "coordinated" and thus brought into a kind of order that "makes sense" in the specific organizational meaning that Weick gives this term. We conclude: *Making sense via enacted narrative is the kind of communication that constitutes organizations.* Networking, sensemaking, staging, and narrative all refer to the same process by which organizations are constructed, maintained, deconstructed, and transformed.

The point of this story is that we no longer need to think of society as consisting of small interactions on one side and large organizations on the other. The small and the large do not constitute distinct ontological levels, but exist on a continuum. This continuum consists of "localizing" and "globalizing" narratives. Every event and every story takes place not only within a concrete local context, but also at the same time within larger frames. Stories can include other stories, just as frames can be within frames, starting for example from a classroom and going all the way up to the global network society. These frames, however, are not encompassing structures like matryoshka dolls, one within the other. Talking about, that is, "performing" instruction in the classroom, the school system, the city, the economy, legal regulations, political processes, norms, international relations, cultures, etc. simply adds more links, more actors, and more events to the same story. No matter how small or large the network and no matter how complex and long the story, it is the same world. If it were not, we would have a serious organizational problem. The local and the global build a continuum. Once we get beyond the classroom, we do not have a higher ontological level of macro-structures, institutions, norms, nations, or cultures. What we have is a much longer and much more complicated story to be told.

Doing away with structure does not mean that there are no norms or constraints on what will be accepted as a socially binding and organizationally constitutive story. Networking, sensemaking, staging, and narrative performance move seamlessly from individual to collective actors. This is not a scale of freedom and constraint. At every point along the way, there is both freedom and constraint. No actor is completely free or completely constrained. This is what the principle of "irreduction," at the basis of ANT's relational ontology means. The concepts of localizing and globalizing are useful for understanding how small interactions are linked to larger, collective interactions and for explaining how networks are scalable. Insisting upon the role of non-humans in narrative performance, however, raises the question of how those artifacts and technologies that are our most significant non-human others in today's world influence the communicative constitution of organizations.

Communication is not merely a human mental and linguistic process. It is distributed, embodied, embedded, and extended into the environment. The very idea of networking implies that non-humans, that is, artifacts and technologies change what the communicative constitution of organizations means and how it takes place. If networking, sensemaking, and narrative performance is a distributed form of communication involving not only humans, but also non-humans, the affordances that dominant technologies have on the kinds of stories that can be told and consequently on the kinds of organizations that can successfully be set up is of decisive importance. What makes sense? What makes a narrative performance powerful and convincing? What kind of narrative performance can constitute an organization in today's global network society? What do these organizations look like? These questions address not only issues raised by CCO thinkers, but also by new institutionalism's concern for the influence of cultural and historical "norms" and "values" on the creation of organizations. Not any story that can be told will "make sense" and successfully construct an actor-network and thus be able to constitute social order. What makes certain stories constitutive of organizations and others not?

We argued that there are indeed norms influencing or conditioning what stories and what kinds of sensemaking constitute social order and thus organizations. These norms arise from the conditions of successful networking. The conditions of successful networking depend on the technologies that we use to communicate and coordinate our activities. We refer to these conditions, which depend on the affordances of the technologies that we are linked up to, as *network norms*. The main actor in this episode of our story was ICTs, or new media. The affordances of digital information and communication technologies are considered by many to be nothing short of revolutionary. Just as the printing press created new forms of life, labor, and organizing in all areas, so too new digital media are transforming every aspect of society. Networked organizations are more and more taking the place of traditional organizations. Networks no longer appear as a more or less interesting exception to markets and hierarchies. The global network society is characterized by a "structural transformation," as Castells put it, in which technology does not determine society, it *is* society. The new media revolution puts us in the position to appreciate the potential of network models of organizing, both theoretically and heuristically. Our claim is that networking, sensemaking, and narrative performance are constitutive of organizations in today's world when informed by the affordances of new media. The affordances of new media translate and enroll communicative action into new network norms.

We argued that the network norms guiding communication in today's global network society can be said to be connectivity, flow, communication, participation, transparency, authenticity, and flexibility. After the new media revolution, *organizing appears explicitly as networking*. Networks do not respect the traditional division of society into domains, functional subsystems, areas, etc. Networking moves easily between business, politics, civil society, education, healthcare, and other areas of social activity and creates new forms of association, cooperation, and cooperative action in which organizations in all areas participate. We refer to this new commons in which organizations find themselves as the "socio-sphere." Organizing networks within the socio-sphere makes it increasingly difficult to maintain even the appearance of markets, hierarchies, macro-structures, institutions, and closed systems. Furthermore, it makes traditional organizations based mostly on bureaucratic hierarchies increasingly inefficient, since the connectivity of all nodes in the network and the flow of information can no longer be easily controlled. Organizing according to network norms results in forms of social order that can not be governed well by the principles that had proven so useful in the industrial age. The various new theories of organization that are associated with titles such as "chaotic," "fractal," "holocratic," "adhocracy," "organization 2.0," and "networked" support this claim. The communicative constitution of organizations influenced by the affordances of new media favor organizations that are decentralized, non-hierarchical, self-organized, flexible, innovative, transparent, connected, and collaborative. Organizing in this way demands "pattern breaking" management practices.

In order to make this theoretical view of networked organizing plausible, we turned to concrete examples of what organizing networks can mean for management and decision-makers in business, education, healthcare, and civil society. Where once organizations in all these areas were modeled as closed systems with clear boundaries, functional roles, and standard processes, we are more and more seeing open, flexible, non-hierarchical networks. Networks in all these areas take on many forms and involve many different kinds of actors. Interorganizational businesses, global projects, corporate entrepreneurship, and other new forms of doing business show that networking is becoming one of the most important ways to do business. In education, for example, personal learning environments seamlessly link up formal schooling with informal workplace learning, learning on demand, social learning, and life-long learning. In healthcare, e-patients, self-trackers, health 2.0, and connected healthcare are changing the very meaning of healthcare by empowering patients and contributing to public health and medical research in new ways. New social movements and a networked, global civil society are challenging political as well as economic organizations. These changes confront managers and decision-makers with new questions. What are the great narratives of education, healthcare, business, citizenship, etc. in a global network society? How is networked organizing changing society? Can organizing in today's global network society best be described by a theory such as ANT, which emphasizes the partnership of humans and non-humans in constructing networks?

We attempted to tell the story of how traditional bureaucratic, hierarchical institutions are more and more being transformed into smart networks. This is known as the "digital transformation." The moral of the story is that what is driving the digital transformation is pattern-breaking management practices that follow the network norms of connectivity, flow, communication, participation, transparency, authenticity, and flexibility. It is our hope that the theoretical perspective we attempt to sketch out here has sufficient heuristic value to inspire empirical research and lead to surprising and useful answers to the problems of today's world.

Literature

Aakhus, M./Ballard, D./Flanagin, A. J./Kuhn, T./Leonardi, P./Mease, J./ Miller, K. (2011): "Communication and materiality: A conversation from the CM Café," in: Communication Monographs 78(4), 557-568.

Abbott, H. P. (2002): The Cambridge Introduction to Narrative. Cambridge: Cambridge University Press.

AlDahdouh, A. A./Osorio, A. J./Caires, S. (2015): "Understanding Knowledge Network Learning and Connectivism." in: International Journal of Instruction Technology and Distance Learning, Oct. Vol. 12. No. 10, 3-46.

Ainamo. A. (2008): "Global Projects as New Organizational Form," in: Wankel 2008, Vol. 1, 482-489.

Appadurai, A. (1986): The Social Life of Things: Commodities in Cultural Perspective. UK: Cambridge University Press.

Anderson, Ch. (2006): The Long Tail: Why the Future of Business is Selling Less of More. New York: Hyperion.

Apel, K.-O. (1988): Understanding and Explanation. A Transcendental-Pragmatic Perspective. G. Warnke (trans), Boston: MIT Press.

Arsenault, A. (2011): "Networks: The Technological and the Social," in: Dealnty, G./Turner, S. P. (eds.) Routledge International Handbook of Contemporary Social and Political Theory, 259-269. UK: Routledge.

Asbhy W. R. (1956): An Introduction to Cybernetics. London: Chapman & Hall.

Austin, J. L. (1962): How to do Things with Words: The William James Lectures delivered at Harvard University in 1955, Urmson, J. O./Sbisà, M. (eds.). Oxford: Clarendon Press.

Autio, T./Ropo, E. (2005): "Networking as a Strategy for Restructuring Basic and Further Teacher Education," in: Wiel, V./O'Hair, M. J. (eds.)

Network Learning for Educational Change. UK: Open University Press.

Bal, M. (1997): Narratology: An Introduction to the Theory of Narrative. Toronto: University of Toronto Press.

Barney, J. (1991): "Firm Resources and Sustained Competitive Advantage," Journal of Management, 17(1), 99-117.

Bateson, G. (1972): Steps to an Ecology of Mind. New York: Ballantine.

Becchetti, C./Borzaga, C. (eds.) (2010): The Economics of Social Responsibility. The World of Social Enterprises. New York: Routledge.

Belliger, A. (2008): "Wissensmanagement – ein Instrument auf dem Weg zur Lernenden Organisation," in: Schweizerische Zeitschrift für Heilpädgogik 9.

Belliger, A. (2010a): "Enterprise Social Networking. Kollaboration im Unternehmen 2.0: Organisation oder Netzwerk?," in: Wissensmanagement. Zeitschrift für Führungskräfte, 5/2010.

Belliger, A. (2010b): "Human Resource Management in Zeiten von Facebook, Twitter, iPhone & Co. Von Unternehmen als Netzwerken, Kontextsteuerung und Grenzmanagement," in: Risikofaktor Personal. Wie viel Kontrolle ist nötig. Management von Unsicherheit. Zeitschrift HR Today.

Belliger, A. (2010c): "eLearning und Wissensmanagement: Chancen und Herausforderungen von elektronischen Lern-Hilfsmitteln für Nutzer und Anbieter; wie eLearning effizient eingesetzt und genutzt werden kann," in: Organisator. Das Magazin für KMU, 7-8/2010.

Belliger, A. (2010d): "Die Akteur-Netzwerk-Theorie – oder: Wie sozial sind soziale Netzwerke?" in: Wissensmanagement. Zeitschrift für Führungskräfte, 6/2010

Belliger, A. (2011a): "Lernen und Lehren mit Technologien aus der Sicht der Akteur-Netzwerk-Theorie," in: Lehrbuch für Lernen und Lehren mit Technologien (L3T), TU Graz.

Belliger, A. (2011b): Social Media und Wissensnetzwerke in der Personalentwicklung, in: Jahrbuch Personalentwicklung 2012, Luchterhand.

Belliger, A. (2013a): "Werte und Normen vernetzter Organisationen oder Digitale Geschäftsprozesse sind nur der Anfang," in: Wirtschaftsmagazin 1/2013.

Belliger, A. (2013b): "Social Media und Wissensnetzwerke in der Personalentwicklung, in: Handbuch eLearning," Wolters Kluwer Verlag (gemeinsam mit D. Krieger), 6.25, 1-10.

Belliger, A. (2014): "Vernetzte Gesundheit," in: Belliger, A./Krieger, D. J. (eds.) Gesundheit 2.0. Das ePatienten-Handbuch. Bielefeld: transcript, 97-135.

Belliger, A./Krieger, D. J. (2006): ANThology. Ein Einführendes Handbuch zur Akteur-Netzwerk-Theorie. Bielefeld: transcript Verlag.

Belliger, A./Krieger, D. J. (2008): "Netzwerk," in: Lexikon Soziologie und Sozialtheorie. Hundert Grundbegriffe, Stuttgart: Reclam.

Belliger, A./Krieger, D. J. (2009a): "ANT: Nichts Neues? Nichts Nützliches? Eine Replik zu Gesa Lindemann," in: Zeitschrift für Kulturwissenschaften.

Belliger, A./Krieger, D. J. (2009b): „Virtuelle Grenzen und Räume in Organisationen," in: G. Thomann, G./Bucher, Th/Hagmann, Th./Kuhn, R. (eds.) Grenzmanagement, Resonanz Bd. 1, 71-84, Bern: hep-verlag.

Belliger, A./Krieger, D. J. (2014a): "Netzwerke der Dinge (aus der Sicht der Akteur-Netzwerk-Theorie)," in: Samida, M. K. H./Eggert, H. P/ Hahn, S. (eds.) Handbuch Materielle Kultur. Bedeutungen, Konzepte, Disziplinen, J.B. Metzler.

Belliger, A./Krieger, D. J. (2014b): Gesundheit 2.0. Das ePatienten-Handbuch, Bielefeld: transcript Verlag.

Belliger, A./Krieger, D. J. (2016a): "The End of Media. Reconstructing Media Studies on the Basis of Actor-Network Theory," in: Ochsner, B./ Spöhrer, M. (eds.) Applying Actor-Network Theory in Media Studies. IGI-Global.

Belliger, A./Krieger, D. J. (2016b): "From Quantified to Qualified Self: A Fictional Dialogue at the Mall," in: Abend, P./Fuchs, M./Reichert, R./Richterich, A./Wenz, K. (eds.) Digital Culture & Society. Vol. 2, Issue 1/2016 – Quantified Selves and Statistical Bodies, 25-41.

Benkler, Y. (2004): "Sharing Nicely: On Shareable goods and the emergence of sharing as a modality of economic production," in: The Yale Law Journal 114.

Benkler, Y. (2006): The Wealth of Networks: How Social Production Transforms Markets and Freedom, New Haven, CT: Yale University Press.

Berger, P. L./Luckmann, T. (1966): The Social Construction of Reality: A Treatise in the Sociology of Knowledge. Garden City, NY: Anchor Books.

Bessiere, K./Pressman, S./Kiesler, S./Kraut, R. (2010): "Effects of internet use on health and depression: A longitudinal study," in: Journal of Medical Internet Research, 12(1).

Bijker, W. E. (1995): Of Bicycles, Bakelites and Bulbs. Toward a Theory of Sociotechnical Change. Cambridge, MA: MIT Press.

Bijker, W. E./Hughes, Th. P./Pinch, T. (eds.) (1987): The Social Construction of Technological Systems: New Directions in the Sociology and History of Technology. Cambridge, MA: MIT Press.

Birkenshaw, J. (2003): "The Paradox of Corporate Entrepreneurship," in: Strategy+Business. http://www.strategy-business.com/article/8276?gko=8c782

Blaschke, S./Schoeneborn, D./Seidl, D. (2012): "Organizations as networks of communication episodes: Turning the network perspective inside out," in: Organization Studies, 33(8).

Bogason, P./Zolner, M. (eds.) (2007): Methods in Democratic Network Governmance. New York: Palgrave/Macmillan.

Boje, D. M. (2011): "Introduction to Agential Antenarratives That Shape the Future of Organizations," in: Boje, D. M. (ed.) Storytelling and the Future of Organizations. An Antenarrative Handbook, London: Routledge.

Booher, D. E./Innes, J. E. (2010): "Governance for Resilience: CALFED as a Complex Adaptive Network for Resource Management," in: Ecology and Society, 15(3), 35.

Borzaga, C./Defourney, J. (eds.) (2001): The Emergence of Social Enterprises. London: Routledge.

Brandtzeag, P. B.,/Folstad, A./Mainsah, H. (2012): "Designing for Youth Civic Engagement in Social Media," in: Proceedings of the IADIS International Conference of Web Based Communities and Social Media. Lisbon. 65-73.

Brooks, P. (1984): Reading for the Plot: Design and Intention in Narrative. Cambridge, MA: Harvard University Press.

Brown, A. D./Colville, I./Pye, A. (2015): "Making Sense of Sensemaking in Organization Studies," in: Organization Studies. Vol. 36(2), 265-277.

Brown, J. S./Duguid, P. (2000): The Social Life of Information. Cambridge, MA: Harvard Business School Press.

Brummans, B. (2006): "The Montréal School and the question of agency," in: Cooren, F./ Taylor,J. R./Van Every, E. J. (eds.) Communication as organizing: Empirical and theoretical explorations in the dynamic of text and conversation, 197-211, Mahwah, NJ: Lawrence-Erlbaum.

Brummans, B./Cooren, F./Robichaud, D./Taylor, J. (2014): "Approaches in Research on the Communicative Constitution of Organizations," in: Putnam, L.L./Mumby, D. K. (eds.) Sage Handbook of Organizational Communication. 3rd ed. London: Sage Publications.

Bruner, J. (1986): Actual Minds, Possible Worlds. Cambridge, MA: Harvard University Press.

Buber, M. (1937): I and Thou. Reprint Continuum International Publishing Group, 2004.

Buckingham Shum, S. (2012): Learning Analytics. UNESCO Policy Brief. Nov. 2012. http://iite.unesco.org/pics/publications/en/files/3214711.pdf

Callon, M. (1987): "Society in the Making: The Study of Technology as a Tool For Sociological Analysis," in: Bijker, W./Hughes, T./Pinch, T. (eds.) The Social Construction of Technological Systems. Cambridge: MIT Press.

Callon, M. (1991): "Techno-Economic Networks and Irreversibility," in: Law, J. (ed.) A Sociology of Monsters: Essays on Power, Technology and Domination. London: Routledge.

Castells, M. (1996): The Rise of the Network Society. The Information Age: Economy, Society and Culture Vol. I, 2nd ed. 2000. Oxford: Blackwell.

Castells, M (1997a): The Power of Identity. The Information Age: Economy, Society and Culture Vol. II, 2nd ed. 2004. Oxford: Blackwell.

Castells, M. (1997b): "An Introduction to the Information Age," in: City 7, 6-16.

Castells, M (1998): End of Millennium. The Information Age: Economy, Society and Culture Vol. III. 2nd ed. 2000. Oxford: Blackwell.

Castells, M. (2000): "Materials for an Exploratory Theory of the Network Society," in: British Journal of Sociology, Vol. 51 Issue 1 (January/March 2000) pp. 5-24.

Castells, M. (2001): The Internet Galaxy. Oxford: Oxford University Press.

Castells, M. (2004): "Informationalism, Networks, and the Network Society: A Theoretical Blueprint," in: Castells, M. (ed.): The Network Society. A Cross-cultural Perspective. UK: Edward Elgar, 3-45.

Castells, M. (2005): "The Network Society: From Knowledge to Policy," in: Castells, M./Cardoso, G. (eds.) The Network Society from Knowledge to Policy. Washington, DC: Center for Transatlantic Relations.

Castells, M. (2009): Communication Power. New York: Oxford University Press.

Castells, M. (2011): "A Network Theory of Power," in: International Journal of Communication 5, 773-787.

Castells, M. (2015): Networks of Outrage and Hope, 2nd ed. Cambridge, UK: Polity Press.

Castells, M./Cardoso, G. (eds.) (2005): The Network Society from Knowledge to Policy. Washington, DC: Center for Transatlantic Relations.

Chaffee, S. H./Metzger, M. J. (2001): "The End of Mass Communication?," Mass Communication and Society, 4, 365-379.

Chayko, M. (2016): Superconnected. The Internet, Digital Media, and Techno-Social Life. UK: Sage.

Chrislip, D. D./Larson, C. E. (1994): Collaborative Leadership how Citizens and Civic Leaders can Make a Difference. San Francisco: Jossey-Bass.

Clemens, J./Nash, A. (2015): "Being and Media: Digital Ontology after the Event of the End of Media," in: Fibreculture Journal, 173, 6-32.

Clark, A. (2008): Supersizing the Mind: Embodiment, Action, and Cognitive Extension. Oxford: Oxford University Press.

Clark, A./D. Chalmers (1998): "The extended Mind," in: Analysis 58:7-19. Reprinted in Menary 2010.

Collis, B. (2005): "E-Learning and the Transformation of Education for a Knowledge Economy," in: Castells, M./Cordosa G. 2005, 215-223.

Conole, G. (2010): "Personalization through Technology-Enhanced Learning," in: O'Donoghue, J. (ed.) Technology-Supported Environments for Personalized Learning. IGI Global.

Cooren, F. (2000): The Organizing Property of Communication. Philadelphia, PA: Benjamins Publishing Company.

Cooren, F. (2004): "Textual agency: How texts do things in organizational settings," in: Organization, 11(3), 373-393.

Cooren, F. (2010): Action and Agency in Dialogue: Passion, incarnation, and Ventriloquism. Amsterdam: John Benjamins.

Cooren, F./Fairhurst, G. T. (2009): "Dislocation and stabilization: How to scale up from interactions to organization," in: Putnam, L. L./Nicotera, A. M. (eds.) Building theories of organization: The constitutive role of communication, 117-15, New York: Routledge.

Cooren, F./Taylor, J. R. (1997): "Organization as an effect of mediation: Redefining the link between organization and communication," in: Communication Theory, 7(3), 219-260.

Cooren, T./Taylor,J. R./Van Every, E. J. (eds.) (2006): Communication as Organizing: Empirical and Theoretical Explorations in the Dynamic of Text and Conversation, Mahwah, NJ: Lawrence Erlbaum.

Cooren, F./Kuhn, T./Cornelissen,J. P./Clark, T. (2011): Communication, organizing and organization: An overview and introduction to the special issue," in: Organization Studies, 32(9), 1149-1170.

Cubitt, S. (2013): "Media Studies and New Media Studies," in: J. Hartley/J. Burgess/A. Bruns (eds.) A Companion to New Media Dynamics. Blackwell, 15-32.

Cyert, R. M./March, J. G. (1963): A Behavioral Theory of the Firm. Englewood Cliffs, NJ: Prentice-Hall.

Czarniawska, B. (1997): Narrating the Organization: Dramas of Institutional Identity. Chicago: University of Chicago Press.

Czarniawska, B. (1998): Narrative approach in organization studies. UK: Sage.

Czarniawska, B. (2004): Narratives in Social Science Research. UK: Sage.

Czarniawska, B. (2008): A Theory of Organizing. London. UK: Edward Elgar.

Czarniawska, B./Hernes, T. (eds.) (2005): Actor-Network Theory and Organizing. Liber.

Dawkins, R. (1976): The selfish gene. Oxford, UK: Oxford University Press.

De Jaegher, H./Di Paolo, E. (2007): "Participatory sense-making: An enactive approach to social cognition," in: Phenomenology and Cognitive Sciences 6, 485-507.

Dess, G. G./Lumpkin, G. T. (2005): "The Role of Entrepreneurial Orientation in Stimulating Effective Corporate Entrepreneurship," in: Academy of Management Executive, 19(1), 147-156.

Dewey, J. (1916/1944): Democracy and education. New York: The Free Press.

DiMaggio, P. J./Powell, W. (1983): "The Iron Cage Revisited: Institutional Isomorphism and Collective Rationality," in: Organizational Fields, American Sociological Review 48, 147-160.

DiMaggio, P. J./Powell, W. (eds.) (1991): The New Institutionalism in Organization Analysis. Chicago: University of Chicago Press.

Donald, M. (1991): Origins of the Modern Mind: Three Stages in the Evolution of Culture and Cognition. Cambridge, MA: Harvard University Press.

Downes, S. (2007): "An Introduction to Connective Knowledge," in: Hug, T. (ed.) Media, Knowledge & Education – Exploring new Spaces, Relations and Dynamics in Digital Media Ecologies. Proceedings of the International Conference held on June 25-26, 2007. Referenced from http://www.downes.ca/post/33034

Downes, S. (2012): Connectivism and Connective Knowledge. Essays on Meaning and Learning Networks. CCL. Version 1.0, May, 2012.

Dreyfus, H. (1992): Being-in-the-World. Cambridge, MA: MIT Press.

Drucker, P. F. (1999): Management Challenges for the 21st Century. New York: Haprer.

Dubreuil, B. (2010): Human Evolution and the Origins of Hierarchies. The State of Nature. Cambridge UK: Cambridge University Press.

Easterby-Smith, M./Lyles,M. A. (eds.) (2011): Handbook of Organizational Learning and Knowledge Management, 2nd ed. UK: Wiley.

Edelman, L. F. (2008): Organizational Emergence. Business Start-Up Issues, in: Wankel 2008, 2-10.

Edwards, M. (2004): Civil Society. Cambridge, UK: Polity Press.

Ehlers, U. D. (2011): "From open educational resources to open educational practices," in: Elearning Papers, 23, 1-8. http://openeducationeuropa. eu/en/paper/open-educationchanging-educational-practices

European Commission. (2002): European Report on Quality Indicators of Lifelong Learning. Brussels: European Commission

Fadiga, L./Fogassi, L./Pavesi, G./Gallese, V. (1995): "Motor facilitation during action observation: a magnetic stimulation study," in: Journal of Neurophysiology, 73, 2608-2611.

Fairhurst, G. T./Cooren, F (2009): "Charismatic leadership and the hybrid production of presence(s)," in: Leadership, 5(4), 1-22.

Fairhurst, G. T./Putnam, L. L. (1999): "Reflections on the communication-organization equivalence question: The contributions of James Taylor and his colleagues," in: The Communication Review, 3(1-2), 1-19.

Fairhurst, G. T./Putnam, L. L. (2004): "Organizations as discursive constructions," in: Communication Theory, 14(1), 5-26.

Fayolle, A./Matlay, H. (ed.) (2010): Handbook of Research on Social Entrepreneurship. UK: Edward Elgar.

Feldman, T. (1997): Introduction to Digital Media. London: Routledge.

Fiske, A.P. (1991): Structures of Social Life: The Four Elementary Forms of Human Relations. New York: The Free Press.

Floridi, L. (2004): "Open Problems in the Philosophy of Information," in: Metaphilosophy. Vol 5, No. 4, July 2004, 554-582. Oxford: Blackwell.

Floridi, L. (2014): The Fourth Revolution. Oxford: Blackwell.

Fogel, A. (1993): Developing Through Relationships. New York: Harvester Wheatsheaf.

Fukuyama, F. (2011): The Origins of Political Order: From Prehuman Times to the French Revolution. New York: Farrar, Straus and Giroux.

Gamble, C./Poor, M. (eds.) (2005): The Hominid Individual in Context. Archeological Investigations of Lowe and Middle Paleolithic Landscape, Locales and Artefacts.

Garfinkel, H. (1967): Studies in Ethnomethodology. Englewood Cliffs, NJ: Prentice Hall.

Garfinkel, H. (1992): "Two incommensurable, asymmetrically alternate technologies of social analysis," in: Watson, G./Seller, R. M. (eds.) Text in context: Contributions to ethnomethodology, 175-206. London, UK: Sage.

Gephart, R. P. (1993): "The textual approach: Risk and blame in disaster sensemaking," in: Academy of Management Journal, 36(6), 1465-1514.

Genett, G. (1982): Figures of Literary Discourse. Translated by Marie-Rose Logan. New York: Columbia University Press.

Gibson, J. (1977): "The Theory of Affordances," in: Shaw, R./Bransford, J. (eds.) Perceiving, Acting, and Knowing: Toward an Ecological Psychology. New York: Wiley.

Gibson, J. (1979): The Ecological Approach to Visual Perception. Boston: Houghton Mifflin.

Gibson, C. B./Birkinshaw, J. (2004): "The Antecedents, Consequences, and Mediating Role of Organizational Ambidexterity," in: Academy of Management Journal, 47(2), 209-226.

Giddens, A. (1984): The Constitution of Society: Outline of the Theory of Structuration. Berkeley, CA: University of California Press.

Goffman, E. (1959): The presentation of self in everyday life. Garden City, NY: Doubleday.

Goffman, E. (1961a): Asylums. Garden City: Anchor.

Goffman, E. (1961b): Encounters. Indianapolis: Bobbs-Merrill.

Goffman, E. (1963): Stigma. Englewood-Cliffs: Prentice Hall.

Goffman, E. (1967): Interaction Ritual. Chicago: Aldine.

Goffman, E. (1969): Strategic Interaction. Philadelphia: University of Pennsylvania Press.

Goffman, E. (1971): Relations in Public, New York: Basic.

Goffman, E. (1974): Frame analysis: An essay on the organization of experience. Boston, MA: Northeastern University Press.

Goffman, E. (1976): Gender Advertisements. New York: Harper.

Goffman, E. (1981): Forms of Talk. Philadelphia: University of Pennsylvania Press.

Goffman, E. (1983): "Felicity's Condition," in: American Journal of Sociology 89 (1): 1-53.

Goldsmith, S./Eggers, W. D. (eds.) (2004): Governing by Network: The New Shape of the Public Sector. Washington: The Brookings Institution.

Greimas, A. J. (1983): Structural Semantics: An Attempt at a Method. McDowell, D./Schleifer, R./Velie, A. (trans). Nebraska: University of Nebraska Press.

Greimas, A. J. (1987): On Meaning. Collins, F./Perron, P. (trans). Minneapolis: University of Minnesota Press.

Guilló, M. (2015): "Futures of Participation and Civic Engagement within Virtual Environments," in: Winter/Ono (eds.) The Future Internet. Alternative Visions. Switzerland: Springer.

Gundry, L. (2008): "Managing Crativit and Innovation in the 21st Centruy," in: Wankel 2008, 450-460.

Habermas, J. (1976): Legitimation Crisis, T. McCarthy (trans), Cambridge: Politiy Press.

Habermas, J. (1981): Theory of Communicative Action. 2 Volumes. McCarthy, Th. (trans). Boston, MA: Beacon Press

Habermas, J. (1989): The Structural Transformation of the Public Sphere: An Inquiry into a Category of Bourgeois Society, Cambridge: Polity Press.

Hackenberg, H./Empter, S. (eds.) (2011): Social Entrepreneurship – Social Business: Für die Gesellschaft unternehmen. Wiesbaden: VS Verlag.

Haddon, L./Mante-Meijer, E./Loos, E. (2008): "Introduction," in: Loos, E/ Haddon, L./Mante-Meijer, E. (eds.) The Social Dynamics of Information and Communication Technology. UK: Ashgate Publishing.

Hajar, M. A./Wagenaar, H. (eds.) (2003): Deliberative Policy Analysis. Understanding Governmance in the Network Society. Cambridge UK: Cambridge University Press.

Hartley, J./Burgess, J./Bruns, A. (2013): A Companion to New Media Dynamics. Oxford: Blackwell.

Haugeland, J. (1995): "The mind embodied and embedded," in: Having Thought: Essays in the Metaphysics of Mind. Cambridge, MA: Harvard University Press.

Heidegger, M. [1927] (1962): Being and Time. Macquarie, J. (trans). Oxford: Blackwell.

Hesse, B. W./Nelson, D. E./Kreps, G. L./Croyle, R. T./Arora, N. K./Rimer, B. K./Viswanath, K. (2005): Trust and sources of health information: The impact of the internet and its implications for health care providers: Findings from the first health information national trends survey. Archives of Internal Medicine, 165(22), 2618-2624.

Herman, D. (ed.) (2007): The Cambridge Companion to Narrative. Cambridge, UK: The Cambridge University Press.

Herman, D. (2009): Basic Elements of Narrative. Oxford, UK: Wiley-Blackwell.

Herman, D. (2013): Storytelling and the Sciences of the Mind. Cambridge, MA: MIT Press.

Hernes, T. (2008): Understanding Organization as Process: Theory for a tangled World. New York: Routledge.

Hill, R. C./Levenhagen, M. (1995): "Metaphors and mental models: Sensemaking and sensegiving in innovative and entrepreneurial activities," in: Journal of Management 21(6), 1057-1074.

Hjorth, D. (ed.) (2012): Handbook on Organisational Entrepreneurship. Northhampton, MA: Edward Elgar.

Howe, J. (2008): Crowdsourcing. Why the Power of the Crowd is Driving the Future of Business. New York: Crown Business Publishing.

Hutchins, E. (1995): Cognition in the Wild. Cambridge, MA: MIT Press.

Huxham, C./Vangen, S. (2000): "Leadership in the shaping and implementation of collaboration agendas: how things happen in a (not quite) joined-up world," in: Academy of Management Journal, 43(4), 1159-1176.

Iacoboni, M. (2005): "Grasping the Intentions of Others with One's Own Mirror Neuron System," in: PLOS Biology 3, e79.

Jarrillo, J. C. (1993): Strategic Networks: The Borderless Organisation. Oxford: Butterworth-Heinemann.

Jenkins, H. (2006): Convergence Culture. New York: New York University Press.

Jenkins, H. et al. (2005): Confronting the Challenges of Participatory Culture: Media Education for the 21st Century, http://www.newmedia

literacies.org/wp-content/uploads/pdfs/NMLWhitePaper.pdf (accessed January 2016).

Jones, Ch. (2015): Networked Learning: An Educational Paradigm for the Age of Digital Networks. Switzerland: Springer.

Kaduk, S./Osmetz, D./Wüthrich, H. A./Hammer, D. (2015): Musterbrecher. Die Kunst, das Spiel zu drehen. Hamburg: Murmann.

Katz, J./Gartner, W. B. (1988): "Properties of Emerging Organizations," in: Academy of Management Review, 13(3), 429-441.

Katz, J. A./Shepherd, D. A. (2004): Corporate Entrepreneurship. New York: Elsevier.

Katz M. L./Shapiro C. (1985): „Network externalities, competition, and compatibility," in: American Economic Review 75: 424-440.

Katz, M. L./Shapiro, C. (1994): „Systems competition and network effects," in: Journal of Economic Perspectives 8: 93-115.

Kerres, M. (2016): "E-Learning versus Digitalisierung der Bildung? Neues Label oder neues Paradigma?," in: Hohenstein, A./Wilbers, K. (eds.) Handbuch E-Learning. Köln: Fachverlag Deutscher Wirtschaftsdienst. 61. Ergänzungslieferung, 22.2.

Kickert, W./Klijn, E.-H./Koopenjan, J. (1997): Managing Complex Networks. London: Sage.

King, B. (2004) The Dynamic Dance. Cambridge: Harvard University Press.

King, W. R. (2009). "Knowledge Management and Organizational Learning," in: Annals of Information Systems 4, 3-13.

Kittler, F. (1999): Gramophone, Film, Typewriter. Stanford CA: Stanford University Press.

Kollmann, T./Stöckmann, Ch. (2008): "Corporate Entrepreneurship," in: Wankel 2008, 11-21.

Koppenjan, J. F. M./Klijn, E.-H. (2004): Managing Uncertainties in Networks. A Network Approach to Problem Solving and Decision Making. London: Routledge.

Krieger, D. J./Belliger, A. (2014): Interpreting Networks: Hermeneutics, Actor-Network Theory, and New Media. Bielefeld: transcript.

Kuhn, T. (2008): "A communicative theory of the firm: Developing an alternative perspective on intra-organizational power and stakeholder relationships," in: Organization Studies, 29(8&9), 1227-1254.

Latour, B. (1987): Science in action: How to follow scientists and engineers through society. Cambridge, MA: Harvard University Press.

Latour, B. (1993y): Pasteurization of France. Cambridge, MA: Harvard U. Press.

Latour, B. (1993b): We Have Never Been Modern. Cambridge, MA: Harvard University Press.

Latour, B. (1994): "On Technical Mediation," in: Common Knowledge Vol.3, n2, 29-64.

Latour, B. (1996a): "On Interobjectivity," in: Mind, Culture, and Activity. Vol. 3, No. 4, 228-245.

Latour, B. (1996b): Review of Ed Hutchins' Cognition in the Wild. In: Mind, Culture, and Activity. Vol. 3, No. 1, pp. 54-63.

Latour, B. (1999): Pandora's Hope: Essays on the Reality of Science Studies, Cambridge MA: Harvard University Press.

Latour, B. (2005): Reassembling the social: An introduction to Actor-Network Theory. Oxford, UK: Oxford University Press.

Latour, B. (2010): On the Modern Cult of the Factish Gods. Durham NC: Duke University Press.

Latour, B. (2012): "The Whole is Always Smaller Than Its Parts. A Digital Test of Gabriel Tarde's Monads," in: British Journal of Sociology 63(4) 591-615.

Latour, B. (2013a): "What's the story? Organizing as a Mode of Existence," in: Robichaud, D./Cooren, F. (eds.) Organization and Organizing: Materiality, Agency, and Discourse. New York: Routledge.

Latour, B. (2013b): An Enquiry into Modes of Existence. An Anthropology of the Moderns, Cambridge, MA: Harvard University Press.

Lavie, D. (2008): "The Competitive Advantage of Interconnected Firms," in: Wankel (2008), Vol 1, 324-333.

Law, J. (1992): "Notes on the Theory of the Actor-Network: Ordering, Strategy and Heterogeneity," in: Systems Practice 5, 379-393.

Law, J. (2008): "Actor Network Theory and Material Semiotics," in: Turner, B. S. (ed.) The New Blackwell Companion to Social Theory, 3rd Edition. Oxford: Blackwell, 141-158.

Leadbeater, C. (1997): The Rise of the Social Entrepreneur. London: Demos.

Leadbeater, C. (2006): "The Socially Entrepreneurial City," in: Nichols, A. (ed.). Social Entrepreneurship. New Models of Sustainable Social Change. UK: Oxford University Press.

Leonardi, P. M./Barley, W. C. (2011): "Materiality as Organizational Communication: Technology, Intention, and Delegation in the Production of Meaning," in: Kuhn, T. (ed.) Matters of Communication: Political, Cultural, and Technological Challenges to Communication Theorizing, 101-122. Cresskill, NJ: Hampton Press.

Leone, S. (2010): PLE: A Brick in the Construction of a Lifelong Learning Society. In: O'Donoghue, J. (ed.) Technology-Supported Environments for Personalized Learning. IGI Global.

Livingstone, S./Couldry, N./Markham, T. (2007): "Youthful Steps Towards Civic Participaton: Does the Internet Help?" in: Loader B. D. (ed.) Young Citizens in the Digital Age: Political Engagement, Young People and New Media. London: Routledge. 21-33.

Lorino, P./Tricard, B. (2012): "The Bakhtinian Theory of Chronotope (Time-Space Frame) Applied to the Organizing Process," in: Schultz, M./Maguire, S./Langley, A./Tsoukas, H. (eds.) Constructing Identity in and Around Organizations. UK: Oxford University Press.

Luhmann, N. (1992): "What is Communication?," in: Communication Theory, 2(3), 251-259.

Luhmann, N. (1995): Social systems. Stanford, CA: Stanford University Press.

Luhmann, N. (2000): Organisation und Entscheidung. Opladen, Germany: Westdeutscher Verlag.

Luhmann, N. (2003): „Organization," in: Bakken, T./Hernes, T. (eds.) Autopoietic Organization Theory: Drawing on Niklas Luhmann's Social Systems Perspective, 31-52. Oslo, Norway: Copenhagen Business School Press.

Luhmann, N. (2005): "The paradox of decision making," in: Seidl, D./ Becker, K.H. (eds.) Niklas Luhmann and Organization Studies. Copenhagen, Denmark: Copenhagen Business School Press.

Lumpkin, G. T./Dess, G. G. (1996). « Clarifying the Entrepreneurial Orientation Construct and Linking it to Performance," in: Academy of Management Review, 21(1), 135-172.

Lupton, D. (2014a): "Self-tracking Cultures: Towards a Sociology of Personal Informatics." Paper delivered at the OzHCI Conference 2014. (https://simplysociology.files.wordpress.com/2014/09/self-tracking-cultures-ozchi-conference-paper.pdf)

Lupton, D. (2014b): Self-Tracking Modes: Reflexive Self-Monitoring and Data Practices (August 19, 2014). Available at SSRN: http://ssrn.com/abstract=2483549 or http://dx.doi.org/10.2139/ssrn.2483549.

Lupton, D. (2014c): Apps as Artefacts: Towards a Critical Perspective on Mobile Health and Medical Apps. Societies 4, 606-622.

Mackay, D. (1967): "Ways of looking at perception," in: Watthen-Dunn, D. (ed.) Models for the Perception of Speech and Visual Form. Cambridge, MA: MIT Press.

Mackenzie, C./Akins, K. (eds.) (2008): Practical Identity and Narrative Agency. New York: Routledge.

Mair, J./Robinson, J./Hockerts, K. (eds.) (2006): Social Entrepreneurship. New York: Palgrave Macmillan.

Maitlis, S./Christianson, M. (2014): "Sensemaking in Organizations: Taking Stock and Moving Forward.," in: The Academy of Management Annals, Vol. 8, No. 1, 57-125.

Manovich, L. (2001): The Language of New Media. Cambridge MA: MIT Press.

Manovich, L. (2013): Software Takes Command. New York: Bloomsbury Academic.

Marcus, G. E. (1995): "Ethnography in/of the World System: The Emergence of Multi-sited Ethnography," in: Annual Review of Anthropology, 24, 95-117.

March, J. G. (1991): "Exploration and exploitation in organizational learning," in: Organization Science, 2: 71-87.

March, J. G./Simon, H. A. (1958): Organizations. New York, NY: John Wiley.

Martin, R. L./Osberg, S. (2007): Social Entrepreneurship: The Case for a Definition. Stanford Social Innovation Review. Stanford, CA: Stanford University Press.

Maturana, H. R./Varela, F. (1980): Autopoiesis and Cognition. Dordrecht: Reidel.

Maturana, H. R./Varela, F. (1987): The Tree of Knowledge: The biological roots of human understanding. Boston, MA: Shambhala.

McLuhan, M. (1964): Understanding Media: The Extensions of Man; 1st Ed. McGraw Hill, NY; reissued by MIT Press, 1994, with introduction by Lewis H. Lapham; reissued by Gingko Press, 2003.

McAfee, A. P. (2006): "Enterprise 2.0: The dawn of emergent collaboration," in: MIT Sloan Management Review, Vol. 47, no. 3, 21-28.

McFarlane, C. (2013): "Relational Sociology, Theoretical Inhumanism, and the Problem of the Nonhuman," in: Power, Ch./Dépelteau, F. (eds.)

Conceptualizing Relational Sociology. Ontological and Theoretical Issues. New York: Palgrave Macmillan.

McPhee, R. D. (2004): "Text, agency, and organization in the light of structuration theory," in: Organization, 11(3), 355-371.

McPhee, R. D./Zaug, P. (2009): "The Communicative Constitution of Organizations: A Framework for Explanation," in: Putnam, L. L./Nicotera, A M. (eds.) Building Theories of Communication: The Constitutive Role of Communication, 21-47. New York: Routledge.

Menary, R., ed. (2010): The Extended Mind. Cambridge, MA: MIT Press.

Meyer, J. W./Rowan, B. (1997): "Institutionalized Organizations: Formal Structure as Myth and Ceremony," in: American Journal of Sociology 83: 340-363.

Miller, D. (1983): "The Correlates of Entrepreneurship in Three Types of Firms," in: Management Science, 29(7), 770-791.

Mingers, J./Willcocks, L. (eds.) (2004): Social Theory and Philosophy for Information Systems. UK: Wiley & Sons, Ltd.

Mintzberg, H. (1992): Structure in Fives: Designing Effective Organizations. Upper Saddle River, NJ: Prentice Hall.

Mintzberg, H. (2009): Tracking strategies: Toward a General Theory of Strategy Formation. New York, NY: Oxford University Press.

Mitchell, S. D. (2003): Biological complexity and integrative pluralism. Cambridge, UK: Cambridge University Press.

Monge, P. R./Contractor, N. S. (2003): Theories of Communication Networks. UK: Oxford University Press.

Mujis, D./Ainscow, M./Chapman, C./West, M. (2011): Collaboration and Networking in Education. Dordrecht: Springer.

Murphy, A. (2013): "Open Educational Practices in Higher Education: Institutional Adoption and Challenges," in: Distance Education, 34 (2), 201-217.

Negroponte, N. (1995): Being Digital. New York: Knopf.

Nicholls, A. (ed.) (2006): Social Entrepreneurship. New Models of Sustainable Social Change. Oxford: Oxford University Press.

Nicolini, D. (2009): "Zooming in and out: Studying practices by switching theoretical lenses and trailing connections," in: Organization Studies, 30(12), 1391-1418.

Noë, A. (2004): Action in Perception. Cambridge, MA: MIT Press.

Nyssens, J. (2006): Social Enterprise. At the Crossroads of Market, Public Policies and Civil Society. London: Routledge.

OECD (2007): Giving Knowledge for Free: The Emergence of Open Educational Resources. Center for Educational Research and Innovation. http://www.oecd.org/edu/ceri/38654317.pdf

Onega, S./Landa, J. A. G. (1996): "Introduction., in: Onega, S./Landa, J. A. G. (eds.) Narratology: An Introduction. London: Longman.

Ong, W. J. (1982): Orality and Literacy: The Technologizing of the Word. New York: Methuen.

Open Educational Resources (2013): The William and Flora Hewlett Foundation. http://www.hewlett.org/programs/education/open-educational-resources

Oudshoorn, N./Pinch, T. (2003): How Users Matter: The Co-Construction of Users and Technologies. Cambridge, MA: MIT Press.

Park, H. M.,/Perry, J. L. (2008): "Does Internet Use Really Facilitate Civic Engagement?" in: Yang, J./Bergrud, E. (eds.) Civic Engagement in a Network Society. Scottsdale: Information Age Publishing. 237-269.

Parker, G./Choudary, S. P,/Van Alstyne, M.W. (2016): Platform Revolution: How Networked Markets are Transforming the Economy – And How to Make them Work For You. New York: Norton.

Pinch, T./Bijker, W. E. (1984): "The Social Construction of Facts and Artefacts: Or How the Sociology of Science and the Sociology of Technology Might Benefit Each Other," in: Social Studies of Science 14 (August 1984): 399-441.

Podolny, J. M./Page, K. L. (1998): "Network Forms of Organization," in: Annual Review of Sociology, 24: 57-76.

Polkinghorne, D. E. (1987): Narrative Knowing and the Human Sciences, Albany, NY State of New York University Press.

Poster, M. (1995): The Second Media Age. Cambridge: Polity Press.

Powell, W. W. (1990). Neither Market nor Hierarchy: Network Forms of Organization. Research in Organizational Behavior, 12, 295-336.

Powell, W./Colyvas, J. (2008): "New institutionalism," in: Clegg, S./Bailey, J. (eds.) International Encyclopedia of Organization Studies, 976-980. Thousand Oaks, CA: SAGE Publications.

Preda, A. (1999): "The Turn to Things: Arguments for a Sociological Theory of Things," in: The Sociological Quarterly Vol. 40, No. 2 (Spring, 1999), pp. 347-366.

Putnam, L. L./Nicotera, A. M. (eds.) (2009): Building Theories of Organization: The Constitutive Role of Communication. New York: Routledge.

Putnam, L. L./Nicotera, A. M. (2010): "Communicative constitution of organization is a question: Critical issues for addressing it," in: Management Communication Quarterly, 24(1), 158-165.

Prince, G. (2003): Dictionary of Narratology, 2nd edition. Lincoln: University of Nebraska Press.

Prince, G. (1982): Narratology: The Form and Functioning of Narrative. Berlin: Mouton.

Quadir, I. (2013): "Form, Transform, Platform: How the Ubiquity of Mobile Phones is Unleashing an Entrepreneurial Revolution," in: Innovations, Volume 7, Number 4, 3-12.

Quinn, R. W./Dutton, J. E. (2005): "Coordination as Energy-Conversation," in: Academy of Management Review, 30(1), 36-57.

Reed, M. (2010): "Is communication constitutive of organization?," in: Management Communication Quarterly, 24(1), 151-157.

Reinicke, W. H./Deng, F. (2000): Critical Choices. The United Nations, Networks, and the Future of Global Governance. International Development Research Center.

Rheingold, H. (2000): The Virtual Community: Homesteading on the Electronic Frontier.

Ricoeur, P. (1981a): Hermeneutics and the Human Sciences. Thompson, J. (ed & trans). Cambridge, UK: Cambridge University Press.

Ricoeur, P. (1981b): "Narrative Time," in: Mitchell, W. J. T. (ed.) On Narrative. Chicago: University of Chicago Press.

Ricoeur, P. (1984-1988): Time and Narrative, Volumes 1-3, Blamey,K./Pellauer, D. (trans). Chicago: University of Chicago Press.

Rizzolatti, G. (2005): "The Mirror Neuron System and its Function in Humans," in: Anatomical Embryology, 210, 419-421.

Rowlands, M. (2010): The New Science of the Mind. From Extended to Embodied Phenomenology. Cambridge, MA: MIT Press.

Sabatini, F./Sarracino, F. (2004): "Will Facebook Save or Destroy Social Capital. An Empirical Investigation ito the Effect of Online Interactions on Trust and Networks," in: Economics and Econometrics Research Institute (EERI). Brussels.

Saussure, F. D. (1959): Course in General Linguistics. Baskin, W. (tans), Bally, C./Sechehaye, A, (eds.). New York: Philosophical Library.

Saz-Carranza, A./Ospina, S./Vernis, A. (2008): Leadership in Interorganizational Networks," in: Wankel (2008), Vol. 2, 291-300.

Shapiro, L. (2004): The Mind Incarnate. Cambridge, MA: MIT Press.

Schoeneborn, D. (2011): "Organization as Communication: A Luhmannian Perspective," in: Management Communication Quarterly, 25(4), 663-689.

Schoeneborn, D./Steffen Blaschke (2014): "The Three Schools of CCO Thinking: Interactive Dialogue and Systematic Comparison," in: Management Communication Quarterly 28 (2), 285-316

Schneider, D. (2014): Personal Learning Environment. Edutech Wiki http://edutechwiki.unige.ch/en/Personal_learning_environment (retrieved Jan. 2016)

Scoble, R./Israel, S. (2006): Naked Conversations: How Blogs are Changing the Way Businesses Talk with Customers. New York: Wiley.

Scott, R. W. (2001): Institutions and Organizations, 2nd ed. Thousand Oaks: Sage Publications.

Seely Brown, J./Denning, S./Groh, K./Prusak, L. (2005): Storytelling in Organizations: Why Storytelling is Transforming 21st Century Organizations and Management. UK: Elsevier.

Seidl, D. (2005): "Organization and Interaction," in: Seidl, D./Becker, K. H. (eds.) Niklas Luhmann and Organization Studies, 145-170. Oslo, Norway: Copenhagen Business School Press.

Seidl, D./Becker, K. H. (2006): "Organizations as distinction generating and processing systems: Niklas Luhmann's contribution to organization studies," in: Organization, 13(1), 9-35.

Selwyn, N. (2014): Distrusting Educational Technology: Critical Questions for Changing Times. London: Routledge.

Setianto, B. D. (2007): "Somewhere in Between: Conceptualizing Civil Society," in: The International Journal of Not-for-Profit Law. Vol 10, 1, December, 109-118.

Shirky, C. (2008): Here Comes Everybody. How Change Happens When People Come Together. New York: Penguin Press.

Siemens, G. (2005): "Connectivism: A Learning Theory for the Digital Age," in: International Journal of Instructional Technology and Distance Learning. Vol. 12. No. 1 Jan.

Simon, H.A. (1996): The Sciences of the Artificial, Cambridge, MA: MIT Press.

Smith, W. (2001): "Chaos Theory and Postmodern Organization," in: International Journal of Organizational Theory and Behavior. Vol. 4, pp. 159-286.

Sørensen, E./Torfing, J. (eds.) (2007): Theories of Network Governance. New York: Palgrave/Mcamillan.

Spencer Brown, G. (1969): Laws of Form. London, UK: Allen and Unwin

Stevenson, H. H. (1983): A perspective on entrepreneurship (Working paper 9-384-131). Boston: Harvard Business School Press.

Stone, D. (2013): Knowledge Actors and Transnational Governance: The Private-Public Policy Nexus in the Global Agora. Palgrave Macmillan.

Strum, S. S./Latour, B. (1987): "Redefining the social link: From baboons to humans," in: Social Science Information, 26(4), 783-802.

Surowiecki, J. (2004): The Wisdom of Crowds: Why the Many Are Smarter Than the Few and How Collective Wisdom Shapes Business, Economies, Societies and Nations. New York: Randomhouse.

Tapscott, D. (1997): Growing Up Digital. New York: McGraw-Hill.

Tapscott, D. (2009): Grown Up Digital: How the Net Generation is Changing Your World. New York: McGraw-Hill.

Tapscott, D./Ticoll, D. (2003): The Naked Corporation: How the Age of Transparency Will Revolutionize Business. New York: Free Press.

Tapscott, D./Williams, A. D. (2006): Wikinomics: How Mass Collaboration Changes Everything. New York: Penguin USA.

Taylor, J. R. (1999): "What is "organizational communication"?: Communication as a dialogic of text and conversation," in: The Communication Review, 3(1-2), 21-63.

Taylor, J. R. (2000): "What is an organization?," in: Electronic Journal of Communication/ La Revue Électronique de Communication, 10.

Taylor, J. R. (2001a): "The rational organization re-evaluated," in: Communication Theory, 11(2), 137-177.

Taylor, J. R. (2001b): "Toward a theory of imbrication and organizational communication.," in: American Journal of Semiotics, 17(2), 1-29.

Taylor, J. R. (2009): "Organizing from the bottom up? Reflections on the constitution of Organization in Communication," in: Putnam, L. L./ Nicotera, A. M. (eds.) Building Theories of Organization: The constitutive Role of Communication, 153-186. New York: Routledge.

Taylor, J. R. (2011): "Organization as an (imbricated) configuring of transactions," in: Organization Studies, 32(9), 1273-1294.

Taylor, J. R./Cooren, F. (1997): "What makes communication 'organizational'? How the many voices of the organization become the one voice of an organization," in: Journal of Pragmatics, 27(4), 409-438.

Taylor, J. R./Van Every, E. J. (2000): The emergent organization: Communication as its site and surface. Mahwah, NJ: Lawrence Erlbaum.

Taylor, J. R./Van Every, E. J. (2011): The Situated Organization: Case Studies in the Pragmatics of Communication Research. New York: Routledge.

Taylor, J. R./Cooren, F./Giroux, N./Robichaud, D. (1996): "The communi-
cational basis of organization: Between the conversation and the text,"
in: Communication Theory, 6(1), 1-39.

The World Bank Group, (2003): Lifelong learning in the Global Knowledge Economy. Washington, DC: The World Bank.

Thompson, E. (2007): Mind in Life: Biology, Phenomenology, and the
Sciences of Mind. Cambridge, MA: Harvard University Press.

Thorelli, H. B. (1986): "Networks: Between Markets and Hierarchies," in:
Strategic Management Journal, V. 7, 1 (Jan.-Feb.), 37-51.

Tönnesen, Ch./Molloy, E./Jacobs, C. D. (no date): Lost in Translation?
Actor-Network Theory and Organizational Studies. https://www.
researchgate.net/publication/36381601_Lost_in_translation_Actor_
network_theory_in_organization_studies

Tomasello, M. (1999): The Cultural Origins of Human Cognition. Cambridge, MA: Harvard University Press.

Tomasello, M. (2014): A Natural History of Human Thinking. Cambridge,
MA: Harvard University Press.

UNESCO Institute for Education. (1999): Glossary of Adult Learning in
Europe. Hamburg, Germany: UNESCO.

Van Dijk, J. A. G. M. (2006): The Network Society. Social Aspects of New
Media. London: Sage.

Van Dijk, J./Winters-van Beek, A. (2009): "The Perspective of Network
Government. The Struggle Between Hierarchies, Markets and Net-
works as Modes of Governance in Contemporary Government," in:
Meijer et al. (eds.), ICTs, Citizens & Governance: After the Hype!, IOS
Press., 235-255.

Vogotsky, L. (1978): Mind in Society: The Development of Higher Psychological Processes. Boston, MA: Harvard University Press.

Volti, R. (2014): Society and Technological Change. 7th ed. New York:
Worth Publishers.

Walsh, I. P./Ungson, G. R. (l99l): Organizational memory. Academy of
Management Review, 16, 57 -91.

Wankel, C. (ed.) (2008): 21st Century Management: A Reference Handbook. 2 Vols. UK: Sage Publications.

Warnecke, H. J. (1992): Die Fraktale Fabrik: Revolution der Unternehmenskultur. Berlin Heidelberg: Springer Verlag.

Watzlawick, P./Beavin, J./Jackson, D. (1967): The pragmatics of communication. New York: W. W. Norton.

Weick, K. E. (1979): The Social Psychology of Organizing (2nd ed.). New York: McGraw-Hill.

Weick, K. E. (1995): Sensemaking in Organizations. Foundations for Organizational Science. London: Sage Publications.

Weick, K. E./Sutcliffe, K. M./Obstfeld, D. (2005): "Organizing and the process of sensemaking," in: Organization Science, 16(4), 409-421.

Wheeler, M. (2005): Reconstructing the Cognitive World: The Next Step. Cambridge, Mass.: MIT Press.

Wheeler, M. (2008): "Minds, things, and materiality," in: The Cognitive Life of Things. Renfrew, C./Malafouris (eds.). UK: Cambridge University Press.

Wheeler, M. (2010): "In defense of extended functionalism," in: The Extended Mind.

Wiel, V./O'Hair, M. J. (eds.) (2005): Network Learning for Educational Change. UK: Open University Press.

Wilbers, K./Hohenstein, A. (eds.) (2015): Handbuch E-Learning. Köln: Fachverlag Deutscher Wirtschaftsdienst. 61.

Winograd, T./Flores, F. (1986): Understanding Computers and Cognition: A new Foundation for Design. Norwood, NJ: Ablex.

Winter, J./Ono. R. (2015): "Introduction to the Future Internet: Alternative Visions," in: The Future Internet. Alternative Visions. Winter/Ono (eds.). Switzerland: Springer.

Wüthrich, H. A./Osmetz, D./Kaduk, S. (2009): Musterbrecher – Führung neu leben. Wiesbaden: Gabler.

GPSR Authorized Representative: Easy Access System Europe, Mustamäe tee
50, 10621 Tallinn, Estonia, gpsr.requests@easproject.com